The Idea of the West

Also by Alastair Bonnett

White Identities: Historical and International Perspectives (2000)
Anti-racism (2000)
How to Argue: A Students' Guide (2001)

The Idea of the West

Culture, Politics and History

ALASTAIR BONNETT

First published 2004 by
PALGRAVE MACMILLAN
Houndmills, Basingstoke, Hampshire RG21 6XS and
175 Fifth Avenue, New York, N.Y. 10010
Companies and representatives throughout the world

PALGRAVE MACMILLAN is the global academic imprint of the Palgrave
Macmillan division of St. Martin's Press, LLC and of Palgrave Macmillan Ltd.
Macmillan® is a registered trademark in the United States, United Kingdom
and other countries. Palgrave is a registered trademark in the European
Union and other countries.

ISBN 1–4039–0034–5 hardback
ISBN 1–4039–0035–3 paperback

This book is printed on paper suitable for recycling and made from fully
managed and sustained forest sources.

A catalogue record for this book is available from the British Library.

A catalog record for this book is available from the Library of Congress.

10   9   8   7   6   5   4   3   2   1
13 12 11 10 09 08 07 06 05 04

Printed in China

To my father and mother, with love

Raymond Bonnett
Shirley Bonnett

Contents

Acknowledgements

Thanks to Kate Wallis, Catherine Gray, and Beverley Tarquini at Palgrave for their patience and support for this project. Also to Rachel Holland and the members of the Social and International Development Studies group at the University of Newcastle upon Tyne go my thanks for their assistance and encouragement.

Chapter 1 is a substantially revised version of 'From white to Western: "racial decline" and the idea of the West in Britain, 1890–1930', *Journal of Historical Sociology* (2003), 16, 3. Chapter 2 is a revised version of 'Communists like us: ethnicized modernity and the idea of "the West" in the Soviet Union', *Ethnicities* (2002), 2, 4. Chapter 3 is a revised version of 'Makers of the West: national identity and occidentalism in the work of Fukuzawa Yukichi and Ziya Gökalp', *Scottish Geographical Journal* (2002), 118, 3. Chapter 4 draws on material published as 'Occidentalism and plural modernities: or how Fukuzawa and Tagore invented the West', *Environment and Planning D: Society and Space* (2004), 22.

I am grateful to the University of California Press for permission to reprint 'Seven Versions of the "West"', from Martin Lewis and Karen Wigen (1997) *The Myth of Continents: A Critique of Metageography* (Berkeley, University of California Press).

Introduction

we have always been watching the West

(Al-e Ahmad, 1982, p. 11)

This book is about Western and non-Western ideas of the West. It argues that the West is not merely a Western creation but something that many people around the world have long been imagining and stereotyping, employing and deploying.

'The West' is a phrase in constant use. It trips off the tongue so very easily. Often this casual articulation is made in the company of the assumption that the West is important and dominant. Within historical and political debate it has become traditional to emphasise the way the West *acts* and the non-West *reacts*. An orthodox model of global relations has been established, a model shaped by a fascination with Western power and creativity.

The intellectual lineage of this attitude is impressive. From Toynbee's (1923) *The Western Question in Greece and Turkey* to Said's (1978) *Orientalism*, we can find significant insights into the West's ability to invent itself and mould the identities of others. Yet there is something unsatisfying, something partial, about accounts of Western pre-eminence. Perhaps a root cause of my own unease is that, if I am honest and at the risk of sounding contrary, *being Western* has never meant much to me. Born and living in England, and being white to boot, I am unmistakably a Westerner. But what a strange and ungainly label. A Westerner: I think of John Wayne, of weather vanes. I do not think of me. I cannot recall a single incident in which I have actively identified myself as Western. Yet the daily news is full of talk of the West. Moreover, in my academic life, I seem to be surrounded by weighty books concerning the West: Western philosophy, Western history, Western Marxism...I have also come across volumes on Western architecture, literature, costume, science, art, birds and flower arrangement. For the most part, these are

1

fat tomes; mighty slabs, places of certainty and epic sweep. So it feels like a guilty secret, a confession, when I say that I am not sure where this constantly talked about 'West' actually is, or whose in it, whose out, and why.

There are, of course, places where 'Westerner' is a popular self-definition. Amongst European heritage ex-patriots living outside the West, the term is common currency. However, what is far more striking is the importance of representations of the West amongst those who are *non-Western*. A few years ago, whilst dissecting Asian images of Asia, the Chinese social scientist Sun Ge (2000a, p. 336) noted in passing that:

> In the narratives of the Asian intellectuals, the West – an idealistic category with almost no significance to intellectuals of the West – is already there. Historically speaking, this idealistic category functions as the medium that pushes Asians into forming self-recognition.

Sun's remark was the starting point for this book. For her insistence on the West as something put to work in Asia and by Asians stimulated me to begin thinking about the West in ways I had not done before. As I began to search round the topic, it soon became apparent that the scale and range of non-Western debate on the West is vast. Moreover, far from being merely a response to Western images of 'self' and 'other', it has often exhibited novel and influential ways of defining the West. Indeed, it appears that non-Western ideas about the West, in many cases, precede Western ones; that it was the non-West that invented the West.

Today, in the first years of the twenty-first century, the need to develop a wider and more truthful vision of the West is stark. The West appears triumphal and brazen in its power. A muscular self-confidence has taken hold of the Anglo-American media. This self-confidence has led to a distinctly partial way of judging non-Western representations of the West. Open contempt for 'their' atavistic refusal to acknowledge 'our' superiority is widespread. The terrorist attacks of September 11, 2001 on the USA consolidated this trend. Thus Victor Davis Hanson, who completed his book *Why the West has Won* in 2000, was embellishing an established narrative when, in 2002, he wrote his article, 'Occidentalism: the false West', for *The National Review*. In this piece Hanson (2002) argues that 'the East continues to stereotype the West, with not a clue about its intrinsic nature'. He mockingly portrays non-Westerners as baffled by a 'mysterious Western paradigm – the freedom to speak freely'. Turning up the rhetorical heat to full blast, Hanson tells us that the most unaware and ignorant American knows more about 'what his own culture is and is not, about; what the Arab world stands, and does not stand, for' than the 'most sophisticated' intellectual of Middle Eastern origin.

In January of the same year another article titled 'Occidentalism' appeared making a similar point. For Margalit and Buruma (2002), writing in *The New York Times Review of Books*, occidentalism 'is a cluster of images and ideas of the West in the minds of its haters'. They add that what is really hated about the West, by those who only know it from afar, is its secularity and rationalism: 'Occidentalists extol soul or spirit but despise intellectuals and intellectual life.'

Non-Western myths of the West are part of the empirical focus of this book. It is a focus incompatible with *defending* the non-West, even less with claiming it to be superior to the West. However, the kind of belligerence exhibited by Hanson, Margalit and Buruma does suggest that a Western arrogance is abroad that needs to be confronted with certain realities of history and geography. Hanson's notion that non-Westerners do not know about the 'real West' needs to be set against the fact that non-Westerners have been on the sharp end of Western influence and power for several generations. Indeed, despite Hanson's claims to the contrary, Westerners are often ignorant of and indifferent to the most basic details of Western influence on non-Western societies. If they were not, it would be harder for Margalit and Buruma to get away with the idea that non-Westerners who hold negative stereotypes of the West are atavistic 'haters' of the West. Margalit and Buruma's more specific association, of the West with secularity, should also not pass without comment. For it illustrates how strategic and mobile definitions of the West can be. After all, it was only a couple of decades ago that Christianity was constantly appealed to as something that helped define the West against the atheistic menace of communism. What has changed since the collapse of Soviet communism is not the secularity of the West (the USA remains, relative to many East Asian societies, a notably religious country) but the rise of a new, religiously defined, opponent in Islam.

In sum, at the start of the twenty-first century, it is salutary to be reminded of the continuing salience of Arnold Toynbee's evaluation, written in 1922, of 'Western sentiment' about the East. It is, he said,

> for the most part ill-informed, violently expressed and dangerously influential. It is an irresponsible revolutionary force – a signal instance of that fatal conjunction of unconsciousness and power which characterises the modern Western attitude towards the rest of mankind. (Toynbee, 1923, p. 327)

In this kind of climate it becomes understandable that scholars have sometimes avoided examining non-Western images of the West. They do not want to supply ammunition to those who have the non-West in their sights. I have a specific example in mind. Having read Mohamad Tavakoli-Targhi's article on Iranian stereotypes of Western women, which appeared in 1990, I was looking forward to his book-length study of the topic. Yet whilst *Refashioning Iran*, which finally appeared in 2001, is a subtle and useful work, it is not the book promised. Tavakoli-Targhi explains in his preface that, because he had become 'concerned with the use-value of this [earlier] project in scapegoating Muslims and Iranians in the United States, I hesitantly abandoned it in mid-course' (p. xiii). It would be presumptuous to find fault with this decision. Nevertheless, controversy is inevitable for those who wish to study the West. There remains a need for explorations of the West that neither celebrate nor defame it but are unsentimental and wide-ranging. In this way we can begin to understand how the idea of the West has been put to use for diverse political and social ends in different societies around the world.

The West: ancient and modern

The word 'west' is as old as the English language. The earliest references to the term recorded in the Oxford English Dictionary date back to the ninth and tenth centuries and pertain simply to geographical direction. (In this book I shall be using the term 'west' with lower case 'w' to denote mere directionality, and 'West' with the upper case 'W' for political and cultural usages.) However, this is a word and an idea whose origins may be traced back much further, to the first rudimentary practical and symbolic geographies of pre-history. Unsurprisingly, it is in China, the country with both the longest recorded history and (along with Korea) the largest amount of contiguous land to its west, that we find the oldest heritage of discovering and interpreting these far horizons. Accounts of 'Traditions Regarding Western Countries' became a regular part of dynastic histories from the fifth-century CE. From early accounts of explorations as far west as Syria (Hirth, 1966), through to depictions of the modern West (Teng and Fairbank, 1979), one can identify a continuous tradition of Chinese commentary on the exotic lands of the setting sun.

That the west is the place where the sun goes down ensured its most ancient and enduring connotation: the west is the place of death. The west has been seen as a site of life's ending, of finality but also of mystery and mature completion. The notion that ideas arise in the east and move westwards reflects this chain of association. In the late fourth-century CE the Christian theologian, Bishop Severian of Gabala in Syria, explained why God had placed the Garden of Eden in the east:

> in order to cause [man] to understand that, just as the light of heaven moves towards the West, so the human race hastens towards death. (cited by Glacken, 1976, p. 277)

For Baritz (1961) this symbolic combination may be traced from Egyptian deities of death and the west, through to notions of the west as a site of imperial culmination and rebirth in sixteenth-century England. However, the connection between death and the west has numerous lines of ascent, many of which have led towards feelings of suspicion and dread of the west. Thus, for example, the fact that white is the traditional colour of death in some East Asian and African societies, when conjoined with the spectacle of white conquerors coming from the west, the direction of death, produced a fearful connotative concoction.

Such venerable lineages can be as deceptive as they are intriguing. The west is an old word. But is also a modern idea. The assumption that being Western means being law-governed and socially and technologically advanced is relatively recent. It was only in the late nineteenth and early twentieth century that the idea of the West acquired the role and range of meanings *in the West* that are familiar to Westerners today. Moreover, the West's West has been changing ever since. The association between the West and capitalism is illustrative of this fluidity. Today, it is a link taken for granted. Yet it would have shocked many socialists one hundred years ago, who saw red revolution as the acme of Western civilisation. The erasure of this version of the West, and the consequent narrowing of the political range of what it means to be Western, are addressed in Chapter 6.

Another indication of the mobility of the idea of the West was the emergence of the USA as the central and defining Western power in the early twentieth century. This was an important development for, until then, the West meant Europe, particularly Western Europe. The USA was understood to be Western only in so far as it was a product of Europe. An equally important twentieth-century transition has been towards the inclusion of non-European heritage societies within the West, most notably Japan. As this latter development suggests, unlike racial labels, such as 'white', 'the West' is a highly expandable category. The notion that the entire world can become Westernised results from this elasticity.

Such is the flexibility, but also the appeal and power, of the idea of the West that it appears to thrive on contradictory usage. There is no better example than the way the West is simultaneously pronounced to be all-conquering and defeated, both of the future and the past. From its first, recognisably contemporary deployment in the West, the West has been claimed to be in decline. It has been gasping its last breath from *The Doom of Western Civilization* (Little, 1907) to *The Death of the West* (Buchanan, 2003). Over roughly the same period and with equal conviction the West has been hailed as triumphant. From Benjamin Kidd's *Principles of Western Civilisation*, published 1902, to Victor Hanson's *Why the West has Won*, published 2001, the West has been seen as, not merely healthy, but unstoppable. So, for the past one hundred years, the West has been in decline and on the ascendant, it has been dying but also being born.

What are we to make of this unlikely story? What we have here is evidence of an idea with extraordinary appeal; an idea that can be used to narrate diverse fears and desires. People use 'the West' to articulate and structure their thoughts. It is a category, an intellectual resource, that helps map out the big picture; that gives coherence and statue to what, otherwise, can appear eclectic and tendentious opinion. The fact that contradictory things are said about the West does not imply its redundancy but its extraordinary intellectual and political *utility*.

Knowing the West

We are familiar with the West. Yet, the fact that we are familiar with it does not mean that we know much about it. Much of the material in this book will be new to most readers. This book is not designed to service an existing familiarity with the topic but provide knowledge of it.

Deconstructing 'the concept, the authority, and the assumed primacy of the category of "the West"', Young (1990, p. 19) tells us, is the central project of contemporary social theory. *Has the West really been such an object of scrutiny?* Or is what Young is referring to really the critique of attitudes and practices merely *assumed* to be Western? For although critical social theory in Europe and North America has challenged the West in many ways it has been largely uninterested in how the West is imagined, either in the West or around the world. Sadly, the rise of 'post-colonial studies' has, so far, failed to subvert this tendency. I say this with a tottering pile of 'post-colonial' Handbooks, Readers, and Anthologies at my side. Far from examining the idea of the West, these volumes offer general and generalising meditations that take its form and nature as pre-given and beyond dispute. In fact, the nature and role of both Western and non-Western narratives of the West have been almost invisible within the social sciences and humanities. This is why the literature on occidentalism that has emerged over the past decade is so exciting. Though it is a disparate body of work, there is a basic division between those who define occidentalism as a Western project of self-invention and those who ally it with the examination of images of the West from across the globe. The first endeavour may be seen as a natural extension of Said's (1978) studies of orientalism (GoGwilt, 1995; Nadel-Klein, 1995; Venn, 2000). Thus, for Coronil (1996, p. 57):

> [c]hallenging Orientalism . . . requires that Occidentalism be unsettled as a style of representation that produces polarised and hierarchical conceptions of the West and its Others.

This aim may also be furthered by the second, broader, approach to the topic. Yet this latter perspective also insists on the importance of studying non-Western representations of the West in their own right, as both intrinsically important and as possessing a degree of autonomy from Western global hegemony. This book is firmly within this second camp. As such it contributes to a debate that is emerging, in large part, from outside the West. Within the English language, such work has included studies of occidentalism in China (Chen, 1995; Ning, 1997; Song, 2000), Sri Lanka (Spencer, 1995), Egypt (Al-Ali, 2000), Japan (Creighton, 1995; Hutchinson, 2001), and Iran (Tavakoli-Targhi, 2001). All these contributions are typified by their combination of empirical detail and theoretical insight. They build on a large, yet scattered and specialised literature of how the West has been viewed around the world (for example, Siddiqi, 1956; Keene, 1969; Chang, 1970; Hay, 1970; Teng and Fairbank, 1979; Aizawa, 1986). Although individual contributions from this earlier body of work, such as Stephen Hay's (1970) study of Tagore's visions of East and West, remain unsurpassed, the critical focus of the emerging field of occidental studies is distinctive. More specifically, a concern with the political and social *uses* and *deployment* of occidentalism in the context of non-Western forms of modernity, as well as its emphasis on the mutually constitutive nature of Western and non-Western identities, make the new school of occidental studies a significant development.

Geography and the world

One might imagine that if any academic field would be receptive to international research on the West it would be human geography. This, after all, should be the most anti-parochial of disciplines. However, the tendency in contemporary academic geography has been to shy away from such ambitions (see Bonnett, 2003). Seemingly paralysed by memories of how geography emerged as a colonial tool to acquire knowledge of distant lands, many geographers have come to favour more local and policy driven agendas. Yet insularity is not a sustainable option, for it makes it impossible to understand even the immediate, local, world around us. Some geographers are now beginning to re-establish geography's claim to be the world discipline. A good example is Lewis and Wigen's (1997) *The Myth of Continents*. Indeed, Lewis and Wigen's graphic portrayal of 'seven versions of the west' (Figure 1), along with its explanatory legend, provides a useful starting point for our own enquiries.

As we shall see, even these seven versions offer a partial portrait and one, moreover, drawn largely from the perspective of the West. Thus, for example, the equation – common outside Europe and North America – of the West with industrial, white-dominated countries, whether communist or capitalist, is not presented to us. However, these little maps clearly show both the changeable boundaries of the West and its historical expansion. Maps one to seven represent a chronology: a West that was once insignificant is seen looping a thick black line across the globe; outward, westward, southward, until it disappears, becoming co-terminus with the circumference of the world. It is this last map that is most striking. As Lewis and Wigen point out, 'the world as Western' was a prophesy of Arnold Toynbee. However, Toynbee was a more subtle sayer than this charted miniature suggests. For it was not simply Western dominance he predicted, but also a kind of multicultural unification of the globe:

> Our non-Western contemporaries have grasped the fact that, in consequence of the recent unification of the world, *our* past history has become a vital part of *theirs*...we mentally still-slumbering Westerners have now to realise...our neighbours' past is going to become a vital part of our own Western future. (1948, p. 89)

We have become familiar with an encompassing, all-inclusive notion of Western power. With a West that erases itself by virtue of its own success. Does this, then, explain my difficulty in recognising myself as Western? It would be a neat conclusion. Yet if we cast our enquires wider, raising our sights from what the West has done to itself and others, it becomes plain that the West is not simply or merely a thing of the West, but something far more diverse and with many points of creation. This implies a transposition within Roberts easy cliché that 'the

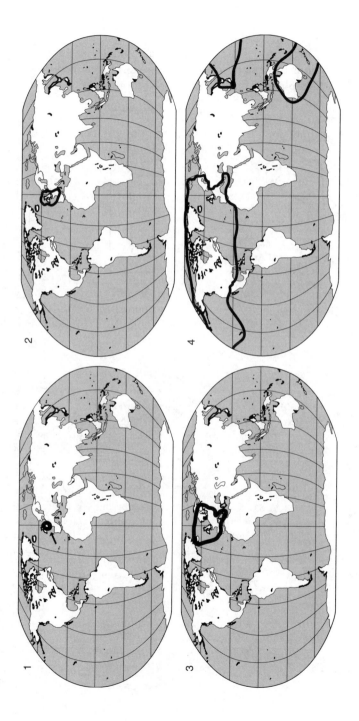

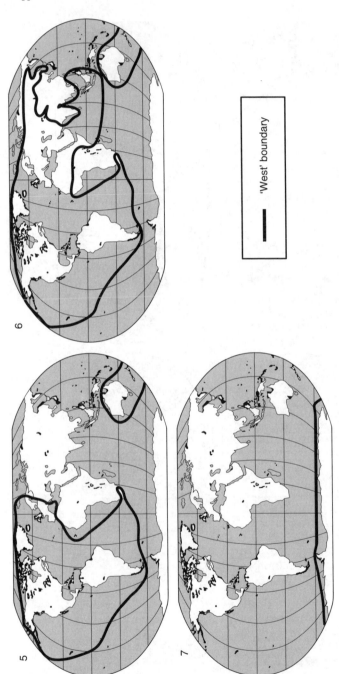

Figure 1 Lewis and Wigen's 'Seven Versions of the West': (1) One extreme incarnation, where the West includes only England ... (2) The standard minimal West, which is essentially Britain, France, the Low Countries, and Switzerland ... (3) The historical West of medieval Christendom, circa 1250. (4) The West of the Cold War Atlantic alliance, or Europe and its 'settler colonies' (with Japan often included as well). (5) The greater 'cultural' West ... (6) The maximum West of the eco-radical and New Age spiritual imagination. In this formulation, all areas of Christian and Islamic heritage are included. (7) The global (future?) West of modernization.
Source: Lewis and Wigen. 1997. p. 51.

story of western civilisation is now the story of mankind' (1985, p. 431). For it is more accurate to say that the West has been one of the stories of 'mankind'.

The West in context: chapters in a global history

This book is not a comprehensive survey of the idea of the West. Indeed, I hope it leaves readers with an appreciation of how little is yet known about the history of this commonplace category. What is presented are episodes in a contemporary global history. Each of these windows onto the West sustains my general argument that the West is not simply a Western invention and that it has been deployed around the world in relationship to the key ethnic and political categories of our era. Thus, and as the outlines below make clear, *each chapter looks at the West in a relational fashion, assessing it in the context of some other identity or identities.*

Throughout I use influential intellectuals as my prime sources. I employ them to give expression both to more general processes as well as to their own particular contribution to the idea of the West. The parade of 'great men' that marches across the book does, I admit, provide a myopic methodology. It is the West as imagined from the top, rather than the bottom of society and the West as seen by men but not, so often, by women. My focus on individuals does, however, have the benefit of pulling us back from unwarranted claims of national representiveness. It is not 'Japan's west' I introduce but Fukuzawa's, not India's but Tagore's.

The first four chapters concern the late nineteenth and early twentieth centuries. Chapter 5, 6 and 7 move us to the present day, drawing largely on material from the mid-late twentieth century.

Chapter 1 offers a British case study on the relationship between narratives of racial whiteness and the West. It allows us to see how the West, in the West, emerged in the context of the inadequacies and contradictions of a more racially explicit discourse. I identify a literature of 'white crisis' between 1890 and 1930, a literature that exposed both the shortcomings of notions of white solidarity and the utility of the idea of the West.

In Chapter 2 my focus is upon how the idea of the West was employed and deployed by Soviet politicians in order to define the meaning of communism. The West was originally associated by the Bolsheviks with socialist modernity. It was then re-cast as the polar opposite of the Soviet state. This transition can also be used to elucidate the distinctive colonial politics of the USSR. It is argued that the central figure in Soviet modernity, the proletarian worker, had an ethnocentric as well as a political character.

Chapter 3 begins a sequence of three chapters on the relationship between Asia and the West. In this, the first of them, I explore the position of Westernisers in the late nineteenth and early twentieth centuries. I address the work of two key intellectuals, one Japanese (Fukuzawa Yukichi) and one Turkish (Ziya Gökalp). Both men asserted a unique place for their own nations as superior to Asia and open to the West. This process of cultural severance and attachment demanded a negative stereotype of Asia, alongside a 'Western-style' nationalist agenda. For both Fukuzawa and Gökalp, Westernisation was seen as providing the tools (intellectual, military, economic) that could sustain independence. Thus Westernisation was not simply about joining the West but, more fundamentally, about having an autonomous national future.

Chapter 4 assesses notions of Western materialism and Asian spirituality through the work of Rabindranath Tagore. I seek to demonstrate the creative and original nature of the Bengali poet's activities as a missionary for a spiritual vision of Asia. This emphasis is used to challenge the assumption that stereotypes of Eastern spirit and Western industry are Western concoctions, or that 'Asianess' is a mere inversion or inflection of a pre-existing Western identity.

The contrast between the West and Asia is also central to Chapter 5. However, in moving from the early to the late twentieth century, we encounter a very different set of stereotypes. Where once the West was portrayed as a monotonous landscape of industrialism and rationalism now it is painted as a scene of social anarchy and idleness. For those who espouse 'Asian values', Asia is the home of efficiency and selfless duty. Yet, this dismissal of the West remains vulnerable both to the power of a Western-dominated neo-liberal global model and to nostalgia for a less instrumental definition of the value of Asia.

My focus in Chapter 6 is upon the narrowing of the idea of the West. It is a process that has tied the West to a particular and prescriptive vision of economic and politics, namely neo-liberal democracy. After tracing the eclipse of social democracy, I look at how neo-liberalism has become a Western blueprint for the rest of the world. Emphasising the idealised nature of neo-liberal thought, I suggest that it bears the hallmarks of utopian thinking. Thus I use the charge of utopianism to criticise the mythic structure of neo-liberal ideology.

In Chapter 7, we encounter dystopian images of the West developed within both radical Islamism and some of its putative forbears.

My account focuses upon the work of two very different thinkers, the leftist cultural critic, Jalal Al-e Ahmad and the Islamist Maryam Jameelah. I demonstrate how Al-e Ahmad's pluralist anti-Westernism has been absorbed by radical Islamism. It is a process reliant upon dystopian visions of the West and utopian visions of Islam, perspectives which are exemplified by Jameelah's book, *Western Civilization Condemned By Itself*.

Chapter 1

From White to Western: 'Racial Decline' and the Rise of the Idea of the West in Britain, 1890–1930

Introduction

The idea of the West cannot be understood in isolation from other ways of dividing up humanity. Drawing on British examples, this chapter explores the rise of the West in relation to the fall of whiteness. Thus it offers an account that distinguishes and analyses two ubiquitous ideas that are often confused and conflated. More specifically, I will show that what happened to whiteness tells us a great deal about why the West became such a popular and influential idea.

Today 'Western civilisation' is a commonplace expression. One only has to look back some hundred years or so to find that something called 'white civilisation' was once also taken for granted. Yet, at the start of the twenty-first century, this is a phrase that sets alarm bells ringing. It sounds not only racist but somewhat ridiculous. In contemporary Britain, as in other Western societies, the explicit affirmation of whiteness is taboo within public debate. Such a position appears to have become, perhaps irredeemably, associated with racism and a reactionary and ignorant populism. In stark contrast, an advocacy of the West, of Western values and Western democracy, seems to be expected of public figures. How can we understand this transition? And what is the difference between being white and being Western?

Drawing largely on British works of imperial and social commentary, this chapter shows how between 1890 and 1930[1] there emerged a literature of white crisis, a literature that, whilst claiming to celebrate white identity, in fact exposed the *limits of whiteness* as a form of social solidarity.

By identifying whiteness as inherently vulnerable to attack and, moreover, as based upon an allegiance between the masses and the elite that neither side was willing to support, this literature of white crisis unwittingly exposed the unsustainable logic of white racism. The idea of the West, developing alongside, within and in the wake of this crisis literature, provided a less racially reductive but not necessarily less socially exclusive vision of community.

Thus I shall be describing a varied arena of transformation in which whiteness gradually came to seem inappropriate, whilst the idea of the West became increasingly attractive and useful. However, whilst the temptation to claim that 'the West' became popular merely because it acted as a euphemism for 'white' is strong, it should be resisted. The 'West' and 'white' were rarely entirely synonymous, either in terms of their meaning or usage. The idea of the West did far more than simply erase the embarrassment of race. More specifically, it could evoke a set of political principles and values that could be both cosmopolitan and subtly ethnocentric, potentially open to all but rooted in the experiences and expectations of a narrow social strata.

White decay

The period when 'the white race' was represented as undergoing a grave crisis was, in Britain, also the period when white supremacism was most fully and boldly incorporated within public debate.[2] This relationship is unsurprising, for the one is the flip-side of the other. One of the core attributes of white identity were the extraordinary claims of superiority made on its behalf, claims that led to a profound sense of vulnerability. The threat of miscegenation and the struggle to maintain white racial purity provide one expression of this vulnerability. However, although such concerns are central to some of the works we will be considering here (for example, Gregory, 1925), they do not provide a predominant motif within the literature of white crisis. The sense of racial threat this literature explores is not discrete and particular. It is sprawling and expanding: it mirrors the vast reach and extraordinary boasts of whiteness.

The dialectical momentum that makes whiteness fragile precisely because of its ascendancy is a familiar one. It is neatly summarised in the title of Chamberlain and Gilman's (1985) study of fears of decay, *Degeneration: The Dark Side of Progress*. However, recent cultural historians err when they encourage us to view the theme of racial decline as an illustration of a specifically *fin de siècle* concern with degeneration (see also Greenslade, 1992; Ledger and Luckhurst, 2000). The romantic melancholia of Max Nordau's (1993, first published 1892) *Degeneration* has a central place in this contemporary narrative. In a typically languorous passage Nordau depicts his time as the '[d]usk of nations, in which all suns and all stars are gradually waning, and mankind with all its institutions and creations is persisting in a dying world' (p. 1). Yet, Nordau provides neither a paradigmatic text for the style nor a substance of the literature of white crisis. The resolutely unromantic racial pessimism of Charles Pearson's *National Life and Character: A Forecast* (1894) provides a far more convincing founding text.[3]

Basing his predictions on economic and demographic patterns, Pearson states that the 'lower races' will inevitably gain markets and territories from white societies that are becoming reliant on the comforts and security of the state.[4] There is nothing dewy eyed about his forecast: 'when we are swamped in certain parts of the world by the black and yellow races, we shall know that it has been inevitable' (p. 32). The economic ascendancy of those who Inge, following Pearson, was later to term 'the cheaper races' (Inge, 1922, p. 227), meant that the white 'will be driven from every neutral market and forced to confine himself within his own' (Pearson, 1894, p. 137).

Pearson's role as '[c]hief among these prophets' of racial pessimism (Giddings, 1898, p. 570) established his defeatist reputation both within and outside the literature of white crisis. 'Although ... the White Race be nearing the twilight', counselled Curle (1926, p. 142), 'let us not lose our bearings'. Certainly, the evidence that white power was in decline was far from impressive. The crisis of whiteness pre-dates the receding tide of empire. White control over the world's peoples increased throughout the period being considered in this chapter. The Dean of St Paul's Cathedral, William Inge noted in 1922 that, 'No important non-European governments remain, except in China and Japan' (p. 214). Yet, just one paragraph later, the famously 'gloomy dean' joins the chorus of racial panic, telling us that by 1901 'the tide had really begun to turn' against the white world. The significance of this year is not explained by Dean Inge, although he does alight upon the 1897 Diamond Jubilee celebrations as the 'culmination of white ascendancy'. Much of the uncertainty of Inge's portrait reflects the propensity, found throughout this genre, to find the seeds of racial disaster everywhere. Indeed, for Inge, the 'magnificent pageant' of the Jubilee also sounded a death-knell for white power, for:

> the spectators ... could observe the contrast between the splendid physique of the coloured troops and the stunted and unhealthy appearance of the crowds who lined the streets (p. 214).

White self-doubt appeared to be substantiated by a stunning military defeat. The rout of Italian forces by the Ethiopians at Adowa in 1896 had been greeted with consternation in some quarters (Lyall, 1910). However, in Britain it was the outcome of the Russo–Japanese war that produced the real shock. In 1904 it was generally expected that the Russo–Japanese war, begun that year, would be speedily settled once Russia's Baltic fleet arrived in the Far East. In fact, the Japanese fleet, under Admiral Togo, destroyed all but three of Russia's ships in the Straits of Tsushima in May 1905. With the defeat of Russia a novel phase in international relations began. The 'victory of little Japan over great Russia' explained Basil Matthews in 1924, 'challenged and ended the white man's expansion'. For Matthews it signified 'the end of an age and the beginning of new era' (p. 28); whilst for Inge (1933, p. 156) it marked 'one of the turning points of history'. In *The Rising Tide of Color Against White World-Supremacy*, a book that quickly became the best-known example of white crisis literature on both sides of the Atlantic, the American Lothrop Stoddard (1925, first published 1920) phrased the matter in even more cataclysmic terms. With 'that yellow triumph over one of the great white powers' (p. 21), he wrote, 'the legend of white invincibility was shattered, the veil of prestige that draped white civilisation was torn aside' (p. 154) .

The end of white solidarity?

The significance of Russia's loss also turned on another matter: the formal alliance of Britain with Japan. In *The Conflict of Colour* (1910) Putnam Weale offered a stinging critique of the British government's 'sensational step of allying herself with Japan' (p. 113). For Putnam Weale the Anglo–Japanese Alliance (1902) amounted to a self-defeating form of racial treason:

> The secrets of supremacy have been revealed; and other countries, led by what England has done, are beginning to accept in their extra European affairs what may be called the same clumsy doctrine of *pis-aller* (p. 117).

An ideal of international white solidarity was a logical outcome of the emergence of whiteness as a social and political force. Yet it remained a doomed and crisis-prone ideal, continuously vulnerable to the manifold difficulties inherent in employing a vaguely defined, highly idealised, yet utterly material, category as a significant geo-political identity. These difficulties are clearly illustrated by the attempt to employ the notion of 'white community' during and in response to the Great War.

Within the literature of white crisis, the First World War was routinely termed a 'fratricidal war'. The danger the poet Sir Leo Chizza Money (1925) wrote about in *The Peril of the White* 'is not Yellow Peril, or a Black Peril, but a peril of self-extermination' (p. 148): for 'whites in Europe and elsewhere are set upon race suicide and internecine war' (p. xx). Money's concern with white solidarity led him to attack both Stoddard and Inge for their attention to intra-white racial differences (what Money calls 'Nordiculous theory'). '[I]t is suicidal', he told them, 'to encourage racial scorns, racial suspicions, racial hatreds amongst the small minority that stands for White civilisation' (p. 149). However, both Stoddard and Money were in agreement on the political implications of the war: that the only way white solidarity could be secured was by creating a European political union. 'Europeans must end their differences' argued Money. It is time, he proposed, to 'federate all the States of Europe' (p. x).

Yet, such a clear solution to the crises of whiteness was immediately undermined by these authors' ruminations on the traitorous nature of huge swaths of white people, most notably Russians and the working classes. Other authors added women and effeminate men to this list of suspects (Rentoul, 1906; Whetham and Whetham, 1911; Curle, 1926; Champly, 1936). Even the physical environment could not be relied upon to support white ambitions. During the same period academic geographers had become pre-occupied with the 'limits of white settlement' across the 'hot tropics' and other climatically unsuitable parts of the colonial world (Woodruff, 1905; Trewarthara, 1926). The grand aspirations of white dominion and solidarity, and the consequent scale of white vulnerability, made any specific attempt to see a solution to the crises of whiteness appear inadequate. It was within the arena of class conflict, though, that the literature of white crisis exposed the limits of white community most thoroughly.

The class limits of white community

The literature of white crisis is a literature of white supremacism. Yet it is also a literature in which the mass of white people are treated with suspicion and, often, open contempt. This paradox provides the clearest evidence that this is not merely a literature about crisis but in crisis: its central myth is constantly found to be failing, to be unworthy. Whiteness is, unintentionally, exposed as an inadequate category of social solidarity. For if the white nation is split between the 'British sub-man' (Freeman, 1921) and Stoddard's 'neo-aristocrats' then the idea of white community necessarily appears, at best, a memory of a bond now passed into history.[5]

The problem is compounded by the fact that the suspect nature of most white people is not a minor chord within any of the texts under discussion. It is usually the key site of argument and evidence. For Inge (1922) civilisation is always the property of a small elite: it is 'the culture of a limited class, which has given its character to the national life, but has not attempted to raise the whole people to the same level' (p. 228). Without this cultured few, whiteness is an empty vessel, deprived of intelligence and direction. The 'brainy and the balanced have always controlled our world', agreed Curle; 'when they cease to do so, our White Race must pass into its decline' (1926, p. 213).

The elite are represented as an inter-breeding group possessing different values to the masses; almost a race within a race. Thus the most profound challenge for whiteness located by these authors concerns the weakening of this group's grasp on power. Indeed, the imminent possibility of being swamped by inferior whites is identified time and again. Money (1925), echoing a concern made familiar by the eugenics movement (Pearson, 1897) and sustained across the political spectrum, noted that 'in Europe and America alike, the White races appear to be dying off from the top downwards', adding, 'in Britain, in especial, the most intelligent people are refraining from rearing families'.[6]

Freeman's (1921; also Freeman 1923) 'sub-man', is the same person as Stoddard's (1922) 'Under-Man' and Curle's (1926) 'C3' type. He is white yet the enemy of whiteness; an enemy who is both a racial throwback and a harbinger of an anarchic future. In *The Revolt Against Civilisation* Stoddard (1922) offers a detailed depiction of the Under-Man as a discrete group, with his own traditions, interests and agenda. '[T]he basic attitude of the Under-Man', says Stoddard, 'is an instinctive and natural revolt against civilisation' (p. 22). The Under-Man 'multiples; he bides his times' (p. 23) waiting for his opportunity. This time, Stoddard concludes, has now come: the 'philosophy of the Under-Man is to-day called Bolshevism' (p. 151), which is 'at bottom a mere "rationalising" of the emotions of the unacceptable, inferior and degenerate elements' (p. 203; see also Armstrong, 1927). For Curle 'the masses', or 'the Unfit', although less prey to communism than Stoddard suggests, are equally as primitive. A new class and racial war is in the offing, he tells us, between the masses who will 'soon…be in control of legislation' (p. 215) and who, out of a sense of self-preservation, seek to thwart eugenic legislation, and 'the one man or woman in twenty-five' who possess 'what is good in the British' (p. 62).

The difficulty of asserting both white solidarity and class elitism was resolved, in part, by asserting that the 'best stock' of the working class had long since climbed upward. Thus the white elite's racial connection to the white masses could be claimed to be real but atrophied. For Ireland

> over a period of several centuries there has occurred a striking and progressive decline in the cultural contribution from the 'lower' classes in the United Kingdom, and, of course, a corresponding relative increase in the contribution from the 'upper' and 'middle' classes (Ireland, 1921, p. 139).

Two origin myths of the white bourgeoisie were employed to secure this argument. One identifies their geographical and social roots in the hardy and muscular country life of pre-industrial rural England. The other locates them as the progeny of natural winners, that is as being the inheritors of a fighting stock that was able to demonstrate superiority before the struggle for existence was compromised by state welfare and interference. The former position is commonly encountered through depictions of the degenerative nature of the city, a position expressed concisely by Galton in 1883: [T]he towns sterilise rural vigour' (p. 14; see also Masterman, 1901; White, 1901; Haggard, 1905; Cantlie, 1906). Pearson (1894, pp. 164–165) explained that the towns 'have been draining the life-blood of the country districts', the 'vigorous country-man' becoming absorbed into 'the weaker and more stunted specimens of humanity' who fill the towns. Thus the 'racial gift' that rural migrants bring to the town is soon squandered. It is an analysis that both roots the elite firmly within a white, rural past and condemns urbanisation and industrialisation as enemies of the race.[7]

Viewing the world through what Taguieff (1995) calls the '*reductio ad Hitlerum*' concerns of contemporary anti-racism, it is tempting to categorise such views as proto-fascist. In this way the opinions of Pearson, Inge, Putnam Weale, Money, Curle *et al.*, appear to achieve at least partial fulfilment within the neo-aristocratic totalitarian regimes of the 1930s and 1940s. However, this line of ascent overlooks the fact that the literature of white crisis tells us more about the contradictions and failure of racial supremacism than about its political possibilities. Once the bulk of whites had been dismissed as, in some way, inadequate, the problem of how to construct a positive programme to save white society became acute. Indicative of the seriousness of the problem is the fact that many of the texts under discussion conclude with utopian flourishes; far-fetched proclamations of racial re-birth. Freeman's (1921) and Inge's (1922) plans for 'experimental communities' of superior whites are illustrative. Freeman envisaged such settlements in Britain, whilst Inge warned that they would need to be established in remote colonies (he suggests, Western Canada, Southern Chile or Rhodesia) in order to avoid cross-class contamination. In either location, the settlements would consist of non-degraded whites who could live, work and reproduce in isolation. Such plans clearly suggest that the only way of saving 'the race' is to escape white society. In so doing they condemn whiteness as inadequate to the task of defining a meaningful identity for the elite.

The idea of a white race is central to this genre, yet it constantly fails these authors. Or, rather, they fail to believe in it sufficiently for it to be effective and sufficient. It is unsurprising that the literature of white crisis was soon forgotten, the titles of its key texts coming to look, from the late 1930s onwards, startling and eccentric. Yet there is another story running both alongside and within this genre. For there are powerful hints in each of the texts considered of how another category of identity, that of the West, could offer firmer foundations for 'our identity', particularly for an elite identity. However, before we can consider the 'rise of the West', it is necessary to note some of the other factors that helped ensure the eclipse of whiteness as an explicit and unembarrassed reference within Western public debate.

Explicit white supremacism: decline and eclipse

The early twentieth century is often cast as a period of intense 'race consciousness' (Guterl, 1999; Horne, 2004). What is so fascinating about the literature of white crisis is that it shows the *limits* of white supremacism. More specifically, it illustrates the difficulty of sustaining commitments to racial solidarity, racial supremacism and class hierarchy as a coherent and stable belief-system. Such a world view is not merely prone to crisis but manacled to it. There exists related evidence to suggest that politicians and other public commentators in Britain were loosing faith in the ideal of whiteness. A reasonable case can be made for the immediate wake of the First World War as a key moment for the serious questioning of white imperial destiny (Irvine, 1972). Pannikar (1953, p. 201) says of this time that, 'With the solitary exception of Churchill, there was not one major figure in any of the British parties who confessed to a faith in the white man's mission to rule.'

If they had sought to, such doubters could have received intellectual support from liberal anti-imperialists, the most prominent of whom was J.A. Hobson. In *The Crisis of Liberalism*, Hobson had warned that:

Deliberately to set out upon a new career as a civilised nation with a definition of civilisation which takes as the criterion race and colour, not individual character and attainments is nothing less than to sow a crop of dark and dangerous problems for the future (Hobson, 1972, p. 244, first published 1910).

The theme that Hobson stresses – that racial ideology breeds contempt and conflict – provided the most potent challenge to the explicit assertion of the white ideal. As this implies, the retreat from race and, more specifically from whiteness, had a much broader potential political constituency than liberals and left-wingers concerned about human equality. Summarising his research on British scholarly and popular attitudes to colonialism in the 1930s, Füredi (1998) notes that 'a clear correlation was drawn between those who were racially conscious and those who were anti-white' (p. 121). What Füredi is highlighting is an increasing tendency to associate 'racial consciousness' with a consciousness of racial oppression. Thus it became the task of British colonial policy, not merely to rhetorically 'deracialise' colonial encounters but, at least to appear, to oppose the meaningfulness of the very idea of racial hierarchy. This process was considerably encouraged by a desire to challenge the global influence of the Soviet Union, whose anti-racist credentials were taken seriously, even by ardent anti-communists. Thus, later attacks on racism – more specifically, on Nazi racism – were able to draw on an existing desire to 'move on' from race as a centrepiece of public discourse. As this implies, opposition to Nazi racism did not create the official acceptance of anti-racism. But it did help secure it. 'There is', noted one senior British official in the wake of the clear opposition to race discrimination offered in the United Nations Charter (1945), 'something like official unanimity of opposition to this species of primitive prejudice' (Corbett, 1945, p. 27).

Criticism of the race concept was already well established in scientific circles by the 1930s. However, its credibility became fatally compromised once knowledge of genetics had advanced to the point where race was irrelevant to the scientific classification of human difference (see Barkan, 1992). Within Britain, Hogben's *Genetic Principles* (1931) and Haldane's *Heredity and Politics* (1938) provided the first sustained scientific refutations of racism. It was a position popularised by Huxley and Haddon in *We Europeans* (1939, first published 1935). Huxley and Haddon suggested that 'the word *race* should be banished, and the descriptive and non-committal term *ethnic group* should be substituted' (p. 220). The notion that the word 'ethnic' (and, by extension 'ethnicity') is to be preferred because it enables one to avoid implying 'connotations of homogeneity, of purity of descent, and so forth' (p. 221), helped to demote racial labels, such as white, to an ever more anachronistic terminological currency.

Thus the public legitimacy of the white ideal drained away. Yet, even at its zenith, white identity was in crisis. With hindsight its decline and eclipse appears foretold in its own propaganda: for even the most ardent advocates of white solidarity found the idea inadequate. We may also detect something else from this : that white identity does not possess a discrete history – for contemporaneous with this crisis, another form of identity was emerging and gaining acceptance, both within and alongside the literature of white decay.

The West's West: beginnings

The historical lineage of the West is traditionally chartered from the break-up of the Roman empire, into western and eastern parts. The disintegrating western empire gradually came to be drawn together into what was later termed 'Western Christendom', a diverse community centred on Rome and Papal authority (Brown, 2003). Following schisms with the Eastern church in the eleventh century and the mutual excommunication of the leaders of the two faiths in 1054, Western Christendom achieved a clearer identity. Thus the sacking by Western crusaders of Constantinople, the capital of the Eastern church, in 1204, reinforced a *established* sense of suspicion between the two Christian traditions.

The early history of Western Christendom provided vague geographical parameters for the West. But it contains precious few indications of the emergence of the kind of wider, political and cultural, understanding of the West that we are familiar with today. If we want to find early associations that contain echoes of contemporary usage, we must look first to the rapidly changing world of sixteenth-century Europe. For it was then that the unity of Western Christendom was challenged by the Protestant Reformation. Protestantism created a new schism in the Christian world, a split that suggested the use of the secular term, 'West', as a non-contentious category for what was once called 'Christendom'. It was a word that papered over the cracks in Western Christianity (Federici, 1995). This secular usage was soon overlaid and complicated by the geography of the Reformation. For

Protestantism was firmly associated with northern and western European countries and Catholicism with the south. Thus 'the West' began to be adopted within Protestant lands as a self-designation, one that carried specific religious connotations.

However, a third connotation was also emerging. For a westward looking, colonial project was developing amongst those European powers facing the Atlantic. In the words of Delanty (1995, p. 43), a 'westernization of Europe' followed as 'Columbus replaced Charlemagne as the harbinger of the new age'. Combined with its Protestant connotations, the notion of an imperial and colonial West might be imagined to have secured the status of 'the West' as the key geo-political term both of the ages of discovery and Enlightenment. Yet it remained surprisingly peripheral: its usage largely prosaic and ideologically unelaborated. The West was, at best, a supplementary expression, used when talking about Europe. As this implies, it was 'Europe', not 'the West', that replaced 'Christendom'.

Hegel gave an influential fillip to traditional links and established ideas when, in the early nineteenth century, he outlined his occidentalist vision of Enlightenment. In a famous passage from *The Philosophy of History* (1991, first delivered as lectures in 1822) Hegel explained that '[t]he History of the World travels from East to West, for Europe is absolutely the end of History' (p. 103). The notion that human freedom cannot exceed its modern, Western incarnation emerged from Hegel's association of Protestantism with rationalism. The Reformation was 'the all-enlightening *Sun*' (p. 412), ensuring that '[t]he German Spirit is the Spirit of the new World' (p. 341). When Hegel talked about History travelling to the West, it was towards a Protestant horizon that he saw it going. However, despite elaborating at length on the Oriental world, Hegel had little to say about the West as a unity. When he turned to the Occident in *The Philosophy of History* he promptly fragmented it into three distinct civilisations (Greek, Roman and German). Hegel had scant interest in developing an explicit or overarching sense of Western identity. The ease with which he dispenses with the West is indicative of its continuing marginality as an idea.

In Britain, throughout the early-mid-nineteenth century there appears to have been little serious interest in elaborating the idea of the West or imagining something called 'Western civilisation'. Nevertheless, the association between the West and social dynamism and progress can be witnessed developing into a stereotype. The phrase 'the Western world' is used by Marx (1992, p. 319) in 1853 when commenting upon British colonial policy in Asia. The same context, if different political conclusions, occasioned the use of the term by Macaulay eighteen years earlier, in 1835 (Macaulay, 1970). These were not merely descriptive usages. Clichés of Eastern social rigidity and conservatism and Western dynamism had already become firmly entrenched. It is a stereotype to the fore in Marx's depiction, in *Capital*, of Asiatic 'unchangeableness'. The radical British MP, Joseph Cowen summed up these conventions pithily in a speech to the House of Commons (4 September 1880) when he depicted 'the conflicting civilisations of East and the West – the one iconoclastic and progressive, the other traditional and conservative' (Cowen, 1909, p. 87). What we have, then, by the mid-nineteenth century is a word and an idea of growing but still unclear power and potential. It carries traditional religious and political connotations and these were, fitfully, being put to use to interpret Europe's rise to global power. What we do not have is an explanation of why, from the late nineteenth century, and particularly from the first two decades of the twentieth, the West, became a *central* idea, a ubiquitous category in the articulation of the modern world.

The notion that 'Western society is a unity' (Toynbee, 1923, p. 4), that the West has its own discrete history, that it is 'an intelligible field of study' (Toynbee, 1934, p. 36), that it is, moreover, a 'perspective', an ethno-cultural repertoire, is a creation of little more than the last hundred years. It is a relatively recent invention that exceeds the term's older meanings. The development of this contemporary West can be explained in terms of the impact of specific events. The Bolshevik revolution, the rise of US hegemony, and the loss of colonial power are the most important of these; each acting to make the idea of the West seem more important, more necessary. An emphasis on these three events is favoured by GoGwilt (1995) in his valuable genealogy of the idea of the West. It is also a model that can be found at work in other parts of this book, such as in Chapter 2 where the impact of Bolshivism is addressed and in Chapter 6 where the identification of the West with the USA is discussed. However, what such an approach tends to miss is that new identities emerge in the context of existing ones. Neither people nor nations are blank slates upon which 'events' are written. Rather it is through and in the context of existing identities that new ones develop. Such a *relational* approach to the topic of the West produces different points of focus depending upon where in the world one is looking. But in Britain, the clearest path is through whiteness.

The Western path out of white crisis

It cannot be claimed that the contemporary notion of the West emerged out of the literature of white crisis, certainly not in any direct or simple fashion. However, this old word for a new idea did represent a partial resolution of this literature's failed attempts to marry social elitism with racial solidarity. The idea of the West had clear advantages. Usually defined as a civilisation, rather than a race, the West could connote a socially exclusive cultural heritage as well as a broad territorial community. This function is apparent both within the literature of white crisis and from the emerging literature about the West that also developed from the 1890s.

The utility of the West for white supremacists

The literatures of white crisis and the West overlap. The habit of using 'white', 'Western' and 'civilised' as synonyms can be found in both types of work. However, what is most striking about the literature that employs 'the West' as its principal category, is its ability to sidestep the contradictions of racial logic, especially the problems associated with the assertion of racial solidarity in a class stratified society. The West is defined as a set of principles or values inherent within (or associated with) 'European' or 'Western Christian' heritage, culture and history. It is not defined explicitly as a natural unit but as a cultural force; an entity of such sophistication that, whatever its future, it appears as more socially and intellectually advanced than all other civilisations.

This reading of the West may also be glimpsed *within* the literature of white crisis. It remains there as a marginal device, its latent significance overshadowed by the assumptions and prejudices of white supremacism. Yet, although infrequent, its presence tells us a great deal about the utility of the idea. It is particularly revealing that when the *higher aspirations and cultural achievements* of 'white civilisation' are being depicted they are often called Western. Referring to white colonial control, Money (1925) notes that 'Contemplating the glories of western art, philosophy and science, we feel justified in holding dominion' (p. 166). Thus, racial power is legitimised by reference to social forms that slide away from clear racial designation. The abstract and lofty terrain of 'Westerness' is also communicated by its association with the grandest scale of international political machinations (Putnam Weale, 1910; Inge, 1919, 1922, 1933). When these authors write of 'the Western world' they appear to be exhibiting a concern that 'white' is too small and reductive a word. Thus, despite the centrality of the latter category to their analyses, a sense of frustration with its prosaic, lumpen quality emerges between the lines.

A related illustration of the way 'the West' is used to help resolve the contradictions of racism is found in the tendency to deploy the term when grappling with the distinction between European and Asian races as well as between Russia and Western Europe. The idea of the West is found most frequently in Stoddard when he is seeking to differentiate these entities.[8] Significantly, 'the West' is used but left unexplained. It is a useful device, a quick fix, for when whiteness no longer functions. Another example of the usefulness of the idea of the West, is that it allows the contributors to this literature to broach the issue of global Europeanisation. The 'philosophy and social atmosphere of the West', notes Putnam Weale (1910) may be 'totally different' (p. 130) to that of the East, but that has not stopped the Japanese from 'borrowing and adopting the civilisation and inventions of the West' (p. 135). Whilst whiteness can only be mimicked (see especially Champly, 1936), 'Westerness' can be borrowed and adopted. Race is fixed but culture is fluid: whiteness cannot be acquired but 'Westerness' can. Yet this, evidently useful, distinction is not *fully* available to these authors. For they make the classic racist assumption that culture is a racial attribute. Westernisation, then, is a possibility that disrupts their racial logic. It holds a fascination for them but is, fundamentally, theoretically indigestible. Thus, Pearson, Inge, Putnam Weale, Money and Curle, all have to maintain that, at root, Westernisation is a sham, a superficial spectacle: non-whites can never acquire the authentic 'ways of whiteness'. Of course, this manoeuvre, designed to save race as an explanatory principle, exposes another aspect of its unsustainability. For commentators from outside this genre were already empirically substantiating Westernisation as an inescapable and profound aspect of global change. In Marvin's (1922a, p. 17) novel and, hence, clumsy formulation, the Japanese are 'now fit to be called the Westerns [*sic*] of the East'. The Westernisation of Turkey and China provided other influential illustrations of a process that challenged the basis of white racism and provoked Toynbee (1931) to identify the emergence of a new 'world culture'.

The literature of white crisis exposed the limits of whiteness at the same time as providing glimpses of the developing utility of the idea of the West. However, to understand just how useful and important the West might be, we need to turn to another, initially relatively small, body of British social and political commentary. For as whiteness was in crisis, 'the West' was being actively promoted as the central geo-political category of the modern world.

Western voices: the emergence of a key concept

The idea of the West that developed in the late nineteenth and early twentieth centuries was a varied concoction. It has the bubbling energy of something new and urgent, the miscellaneous character of an idea not yet refined by years of use. The West at this time could be made to mean many things. Before the Bolshevik revolution, its political character was highly mobile: the acme of Western civilisation was imagined to be, amongst other things communism, lassiez-faire capitalism, anarchism, authoritarian statism and many other positions besides. It would be misleading to isolate one single authority on the meaning of the West from this period. Below, I tune into four different British voices, and one German, who both employed and promoted the idea of the West. Each of these voices also shows us how 'the West' partially or completely marginalised whiteness and race.

Ramsay MacDonald

From the late nineteenth century, the idea of the West became closely associated with the delineation of social and political principles. The content of these principles varied considerably but what remained constant was the alignment of the West, relative to the prosaic and empirical nature of the discussion on whiteness, with self-consciously intellectual, often highly abstract, debate. The tendency towards discussing the West in terms of general principles meant that it provided a fertile terrain for political opinion and criticism. As this implies, the West, unlike whiteness, has been understood as amenable to the language and politics of reflexive social criticism. Indeed, a central device of many works on the West is auto-critique, in which the West is seen as 'failing to live up to' its own high standards or potential.

The left, in particular, found in 'the West' an attractive and useful terminology of political address. The leader of the Independent Labour Party, and subsequently Labour Party leader and British Prime Minister, Ramsay MacDonald (1866–1937), was amongst a group of liberal and radical critics who articulated an ethical lexicon of Western responsibilities in the 1890s and 1900s (Porter, 1968). MacDonald's speech to the West London Ethical Society in 1901, titled 'The propaganda of civilization', provides a fine example. 'The superior claims of Western civilization', MacDonald explained, are founded mainly on two circumstances – the first is our abhorrence of violent human suffering; the second, the value we place upon settled government (MacDonald, 1901, p. 460).

The first of these 'circumstances' may be taken to evidence the continuing influence of an identification of the West with Christian values. However, it is also suggestive of the possibility of the detachment of religion from humanitarianism and the development of a secular discourse of human rights. The second 'circumstance' MacDonald identifies is rooted in the association of Western civilisation with rational systems of legal and accountable justice. MacDonald argues that the former 'circumstance' is not 'lived up to' in practice, whilst the latter should not be imposed upon non-Western societies.

Although sometimes conflating Westerners with whites, MacDonald's speech suggests he has little use for, or interest in, the latter category. The idea of the West offered him a political terminology capable of sustaining the language of critical judgement and detached critique. By contrast, to cast Western 'principles' and 'values' as 'white' would naturalise them, removing them from politics and placing them on the terrain of blood loyalty and pre-intellectual solidarity. The West, then, is an idea that enabled *political* discourse. However, the deracialisation that it offered has usually been incomplete. Thus we must also note that MacDonald does not permit the possibility of Westernisation. Indeed, he maintains that '[c]ivilization cannot be transplanted' (p. 463): to be sustainable civilisation must be organic to a 'people' or 'race'.

Benjamin Kidd

A different vision of the West was developed by the British civil servant and, in the words of his biographer, 'spiky individualist' (Crook, 1984, p. 3), Benjamin Kidd (1858–1916). Kidd introduced the notion of 'our Western civilisation' in *Social Evolution* (1894).[9] But it is within *Principles of Western Civilisation* (1902), a lesser known but more intellectually ambitious book, that the concept finds its first detailed examination in English. It is immediately apparent from this rather verbose work that the 'principles' to which Kidd refers are not those that were later to become familiar, at least within the West. The West is not defined in terms of democracy, capitalism, or, indeed any liberal value but, rather, as a form of spirit, or consciousness, that is intellectually far-seeing and militarily enforced. Kidd regards the true promise of the West to lie in its potential to subjugate the present in the service of the future. '[T]he significance of Western civilisation', he argues, has been related to a single cause; namely, the potentiality of a principle inherent in it to project the controlling principles of its consciousness beyond the present (p. 289).

Laissez-faire, for Kidd, was 'a surviving form of barbarism' (p. 455) because it was unable to look beyond present needs. Kidd predicted the

gradual organisation and direction of the State...towards an era of such free and efficient conflict of all natural forces as has never been in the world before (p. 469).

Kidd's 'Western principles', then, are those that ensure the West's total victory in a world of ceaseless struggle and domination: 'We are par excellence the military peoples, not only of the entire world, but of the evolutionary process itself' (p. 458).

Kidd's racial vocabulary is vague. It can be inferred that he sees a racial content to being Western and that Western civilisation for Kidd is, for some unstated reason, white.[10] However, Kidd's West is a decidedly non-corporal, non-material entity. The 'Western mind', he writes,

is destined, sooner or later, to rise to a conception of the nature of truth itself different from any that has hitherto prevailed in the world (p. 309).

Kidd's propensity for such cloudy abstractions led to his contribution appearing marginal to what was, at the time, the more mainstream debate on whiteness. Inge (1922) accused him of being an 'irrationalist' and *The Principles of Western Civilisation* bewildered and annoyed many of its reviewers (see Crook, 1984). Yet Kidd's aversion to empirical detail and fondness for sweeping theorisations enabled him to render irrelevant the contradictions that were causing such anguish within the white crisis literature. By by-passing direct engagement with race, Kidd was able to ignore issues of racial purity, solidarity and sustainability and, hence, questions of class character and quality. For Kidd, 'Western principles' and 'our Western civilisation' were transcendental forces whose inherent superiority lies in their orientation to the future, as well as in their, literally, merciless enforcement. The success of the West in 'the modern world-conflict' was thus certain: '[I]t is the principles of our Western civilisation...and no others, that we feel are destined to hold the future of the world' (p. 340).

Francis Marvin

Kidd sustained whiteness as a prosaic fact. He treated the West as a higher and more important reality. This dynamic may also be seen at work within the 'Unity History Schools'. Organised by Francis Marvin (1863–1943), the Schools were sparked by the profound sense of cultural collapse and disunity precipitated by the Great War. Under Marvin's tireless guidance, the Schools became champions of the utility and coherence of the idea of the West. Between 1915 and 1931 ten School conferences were held, mostly at Woodbrooke, near Birmingham.[11] Drawing together major academics and public figures concerned with the fracturing of European community, they had the overarching aim of seeking to identify the unifying aspects of Western civilisation in almost every sphere of life. The topics where unity was explored were of an extraordinary variety: science, law, philosophy, education, art, music, pre-history, economics, and many more. Where unity was looked for, it was found.

Throughout these debates, race has an uneasy presence. It is both explicitly rejected as a source of unity, yet constantly creeps back in the form of a felt, pre-intellectual reality. Thus, on the one hand, the sociologist Hobhouse (1915, p. 165) reflected a widely accepted sentiment, when he noted at the first of the Unity History Schools, that 'The civilization of the West is fundamentally not one because the peoples of the West are one racially'. Another participant, the Oxford historian Myres (1915, p. 55), explained that race 'has been anything but a factor of unity' and warned against speaking 'on platforms of Europeans as "white men"'. Yet, in Marvin's editorial introduction to *Western Races and the World* (1922; this being a collection of papers from the fifth School), he ignores the implications of the book's title and equates Westerners with a single race, called whites. Indeed, in a passage that implies that Marvin was not listening very attentively to his colleagues, he attempts to rescue the British 'sub-man' from unfair criticism. '[T]aking the subman as he is, it is a notable fact', he blandly assures his readers, 'that any white man, thrown among blacks, even if he is quite ignorant…will promptly assume, and easily retain, a position of command' (1922a, p. 11).

Oswald Spengler

The rejection of race at an intellectual level, but its retention as a felt reality, is also seen in the work of Oswald Spengler (1880–1936). Spengler took the non-rationalist agenda apparent within Kidd even further, leaving aside evolutionary theory to distinguish the West as an autonomous form of being or Destiny. In this way the empirical concerns of the study of white crisis are made to appear inept and minor. Yet, whilst undermining race as science, Spengler allowed its further mystification as an experienced social reality. For example, whilst Spengler (1926) is condescending about racial science – as soon 'as light is let through it, "race" vanishes suddenly and completely' (p. 129) – he concludes that race:

> is not accessible to a science that weigh and measures. It exists for the feelings – with a plain certainty and at first glance – but not for the savant's treatment (p. 130).[12]

Spengler's *Der Untergang des Abendlandes* (1918, 1922), translated as the *Decline of the West* (1926, 1928), offered an anthropomorphising model of cultures as having life cycles of growth and decay. The Western life cycle had, Spengler said, entered its stagnant and sterile final stage (what he called 'civilization') in the nineteenth century. Another thesis Spengler propounded was that the term 'Europe' was a meaningless 'empty sound' that masked the difference between Russian and Western civilisation. 'It is thanks to this word "Europe" alone and the complex of ideas resulting from it', he complained, 'that our historical consciousness has come to link Russia with the West in an utterly baseless unity' (1926, p. 16). British Spenglerians, Goddard and Gibbons, concurred: 'not only does Russia not think like Western Europe but it never has done' (Goddard and Gibbons, 1926, p. 48). Such statements were designed, in part, to provide a sense of historical depth to a sensibility that also had much shallower roots. More specifically, they allowed an explanation of the popularity of communism in Russia that connected it to the primitive and non-European qualities of that country.

Arnold Toynbee

For Arnold Toynbee (1889–1975) race was largely an irrelevance. The twelve volumes of Toynbee's *A Study of History* (published 1934–1961) account for the genesis, growth, breakdown and disintegration of about thirty civilisations. Amidst their three million or so words, there is little mention of race. By contrast, 'the West' is the lynch-pin of Toynbee's endeavours: its development provokes and shapes his enquires whilst its impact on other societies occupied not only key volumes of the *History* but spilled out to dominate Toynbee's public and political interventions (Toynbee, 1923, 1931, 1953). Like Spengler, he argued that 'Europe' was a 'misnomer', since it appeared to link the West to the separate civilisation of Eastern Orthodoxy (Toynbee, 1954). However, unlike Spengler, Toynbee was a perceptive observer of his times, and understood that the West was a flexible category; that its most fundamental parameters remained in motion. It is Toynbee's fascination with the interaction of the West with the rest of the world that ensure his continuing topicality. Explaining the formation of a new 'world culture', Toynbee (1931) noted that, whilst before 1914, Westernisation was carried out as a minimal programme, after the war, non-Western peoples, especially in the East, 'have been seized by a furore of iconoclasm' (p. 764):

> Apparently the Turks and the Chinese have come to the conclusion that the world of the future is destined to be unified on a Western basis, not only on the superficial economic plane, but right down to the deeper levels of social life (p. 765).

For Toynbee, pre-scientific fallacies, like race, were a hindrance in understanding the rapidly shifting world of the twentieth century.[13] At the same time, his work exemplifies how the West could be used in ways that sustained supremacism. Rather than claims of racial superiority, Toynbee offered assertions of cultural, moral and spiritual progress. It is a final testament to Western superiority and achievement, Toynbee noted a few years after the end of the Second World War, that it alone should be capable of formulating and creating a multicultural synthesis of world cultures. It is a synthesis in which the West both disappears and finds its highest calling:

> the past histories of our vociferous, and sometimes vituperative, living contemporaries – the Chinese and the Japanese, the Hindus and the Muslims, and our elder brothers the Orthodox Christians – are going to become a part of our Western past history in a future world which will be neither Western nor non-Western but will integrate all the cultures which we Westerners have now brewed together in a single crucible... By making history we have transcended our own history. Without knowing what we have been doing we have taken the opportunity offered to us. To be allowed to fulfil oneself by surpassing oneself is a glorious privilege for any of God's creatures (1948, pp. 90–91).

Toynbee's combination of humility and arrogance, in which the West erases itself in the process of its compete victory, has proven a recurrent trope of later accounts of Western triumph (see Chapter 6). It is also testament to the utility of deracialisation. The cumbersome and literal language of race could be abandoned for a more refined discourse of principles and values.

MacDonald, Kidd, Marvin, Spengler and Toynbee: five influential founders of the idea of the West in Britain. Compared to the contributors to the literature of white crisis, each of these men appear recognisably of our own time and as well as of their own. Although race retains a presence in much of their work, it is neither prioritised nor accorded intellectual status. This realignment of public debate meant that the 'white masses' could be ignored. The sights of those who contributed to the emerging literature on this topic were 'higher' and certainly more abstract. They had found a language through which to talk about 'us' that appeared to marginalise problems concerning who exactly, empirically, 'we' were. Even more remarkable, the West became a comprehensible collective identity that connoted a certain group of people, who just happened, by and large, to be of European heritage, without it appearing to be mired in the racial mythologies of the past.

Yet, I must not leave any room for the mistaken assumption that white racism was eclipsed by the rise of the West. The term 'Western' remained and remains racially coded, burdened with the expectation that the world will never be 'free', 'open' and 'democratic' until it is Europeanised. Moreover, it must not be forgotten that my focus in this chapter has been on the West and whiteness within *public debate* in Britain. Whilst an assertive white identity may have become marginal within public discourse, within private and everyday forms of interaction and communication it maintains a considerable currency (Back, 1995; Frankenberg, 1997). Its continuing use reflects the maintenance of racial power relations and gives the lie to the idea that the rhetorical deracialisation of public life means that racism no longer matters. White privilege is no less real today than it was one hundred years ago. Yet the nature of that privilege has changed. It has become less visible, less acknowledged. Its alignment with biological racism has also weakened. In a previous book, *White Identities: Historical and International Perspectives* (Bonnett, 2000), I showed that white supremacism is highly adaptive; indeed, that it has moved faster than anti-racist politics. Drawing on examples from contemporary Latin America, China and Japan, I sought to show how whiteness has increasingly shed its links with notions of European biological difference and superiority, and become embroiled with images of an affluent, Western consumer lifestyle. Whiteness has been pushed to the sidelines in public debate in Britain. Yet, within and through the global circuits of symbolic capital it is being, not simply sustained, but re-invented. [14]

Conclusions

Interrupting the polite hum of dinner party conversation, Tom Buchanan, the wealthy cad at the heart of *The Great Gatsby*, is moved to exclaim that 'Civilization's going to pieces'. The startled guests are treated to Buchanan's particular view of world events: 'If we don't look out the white race will be – will be utterly submerged. It's all scientific stuff; it's been proved.' F. Scott Fitzgerald has his character cite as evidence a book called '"The Rise of the Colored Empires" by this man Goddard'.

On one level this incident is evidence merely of Fitzgerald's familiarity with one of the many incendiary racial tracts of the early 1920s (namely, *The Rising Tide of Color Against White World Supremacy* by Lothrop Stoddard). However, Buchanan's opinions are clearly designed to evoke something bigger. They are employed by Fitzgerald to create a tone of moral panic, a pessimistic atmosphere sustained by the existence of a far-reaching debate on the collapse of white prestige.

One of the distinctive attributes of this debate, in the USA as in Britain, was that it signalled both a crisis for, and the zenith of, white identity as a public ideal. Whiteness was celebrated before 1890 but rarely with such concerted fervour and never with such an elaborate repertoire of scientific and social justifications. Whiteness was celebrated after 1930 but, increasingly, those who did the celebrating were not drawn from the leading social and political commentators of the day. That white identity's moment of triumph should also be its moment of peril is no coincidence. Having become established as the symbol of extraordinary achievement and superiority, as the talisman of worldwide social authority, whiteness was vulnerable to any sign of challenge or social disturbance. The fact that white supremacism relied on the authority of the natural, of biological fact, compounded its unsustainability. For once the white race is accepted as an objective reality, its attributes must be represented objectively, without the interference of social factors, such as class prejudice. In other words, all white people have to have the characteristics of whiteness: they must all be superior, they must all be fit to rule. Yet there was no subject that the white supremacists discussed in this chapter felt more strongly about than the inadequacy of the masses. Their racism demanded social egalitarianism; their social elitism demanded something quite different. Something like the idea of the West perhaps?

There is some truth in the latter contention but it is also too neat, too glib. We cannot assume that, because it was in the context of the crisis of white identity that the idea of the West began to become attractive, that this crisis therefore 'produced' or 'led to' the idea of the West. This point needs to be insisted upon, whilst at the same time the contemporaneous and novel character of the concept of the West that was emerging is recognised. Something new was being born. The literature of white crisis illuminates some of the reasons why, as well as nearly all the reasons why whiteness was inadequate to the challenges, not merely that lay ahead, but of the moment.

The idea of the West helped resolve some of the problematic and unsustainable characteristics of white supremacism. Yet it carried its own burden of tensions. One of the most fundamental of these exposes a similarity of outlook between the proponents of whiteness and the West, for both are projects with an in-built tendency to crisis. From the early years of the last century (Little, 1907; Spengler, 1926), through the mid-century (Beus, 1953; Warburg, 1959; Burnham, 1964) and into the present day (Coker, 1998; Barzun, 2001; Buchanan, 2003), we have been told that the West is doomed (see also Herman, 1997). Although specific causes for this fate are usually at hand, a more general reason may also be adduced. For like whiteness, the idea of the West has been conflated with modernity and global mastery. These vast ambitions create a state of vulnerability. When Western colonialism was at its height, it was said that the West was in its death throes. When communism spread in East Asia, and as Asian and African countries achieved independence, it was said, perhaps with more justification, that the West was in retreat. Yet even minor phenomenon, like the rise of youth culture or the decline of classical music, have been interpreted as signalling the end of Western civilisation. As with the white crisis liter-ature, almost everything and anything, big or small, has been fed into the omnivorous pessimism of the West's doom-mongers.

The dread of decay that arises from the West's global claim closely echoes the panicky sensitivities of the white crisis literature. However, this similarity should not be pushed too far. The literature of white peril was not mirrored by a contemporaneous white triumphalist literature. But this is exactly what we see in the case of the West. For every book announcing its death, another is published claiming its ascendancy. In its own prolix way, Kidd's *The Principles of Western Civilization*, was the first British example. Later, more hesitant fanfares from the height of the Cold War, such as *Must the West Decline?* (Ormsby-Gore, 1966) and *Is the Liberal West in Decline?* (Kohn, 1957), were contemporaneous with more vigorous statements on *The Rise of the West* (McNeill, 1963). However, even McNeill's portrait of the West's flexibility and receptivity to cultural influences is tame compared with the triumphalism of end of century announcements, such as *The Triumph of the West* (Roberts, 1985) and *Why the West has Won* (Hanson, 2001; see also Fukuyama, 2001). The mood of strutting confidence is elaborated in other recent titles, such as *The Ideas that Conquered the World* (Mandelbaum, 2002) and *The End of History* (Fukuyama, 1992). The contrast with whiteness is stark: only military effort and direct domination would allow the white supremacists a sense of conquest and finality. For the majority of Western triumphalists all that needs to happen is that the world 'opens up', begins to see things 'our way' and acts accordingly.

Further reading
The retreat from race
To understand the erosion of idea of race in Britain it is necessary to study the rejection of the concept within the sciences as well as within social science. It is also useful to address changes within the wider political culture of a society moving towards a post-imperial identity. The following books cover much of the most relevant material:

Elazar Barkan *The Retreat of Scientific Racism: Changing Concepts of Race in Britain and the United States Between the World Wars* (1992, Cambridge, Cambridge University Press). A thorough, well-supported study of the scientific rejection of the race concept.

For the social sciences (especially anthropology) George Stocking's *Race, Culture, and Evolution* (1982, Chicago, University of Chicago Press) remains valuable for nineteenth-century and early twentieth-century debates in the USA and Britain.

For a fascinating and original discussion of the official rejection of race within British public discourse between the World Wars, see Frank Füredi's *The Silent War: Imperialism and the Changing Perception of Race* (1998, London, Pluto).

The broader cultural and political forces that have animated a rejection of race are depicted in *Anti-racism* by Alastair Bonnett (2000, London, Routledge). This work provides an international overview of anti-racism in both Western and non-Western societies.

Whiteness
The burgeoning field of white studies is producing some valuable historical research. The analysis of how different European groups 'became white' in the USA currently dominates the field. Two of the most important contributions have been David Roediger's *The Wages of Whiteness: Race and the Making of the American Working Class* (1991, London, Verso) and Matthew Jacobson's *Whiteness of a Different Color: European Immigrants and the Alchemy of Race* (1998, Cambridge, Harvard University Press). The following texts are also useful, being particularly attentive to the changing nature of whiteness, both historically and internationally.

Bonnett, A. (2000) *White Identities: Historical and International Perspectives*, Harlow, Pearson.

Dyer, R. (1997) *White* London, Routledge.

Levine-Rasky, C. (ed.) (2002) *Working Through Whiteness: International Perspectives*, New York, State University of New York Press.

Nayak, A. (2003) *Race, Place and Globalization: Youth Cultures in a Changing World*, Oxford, Berg.

The idea of Western civilisation

The focus of most critical work on the idea of Western civilisation is upon challenging Western racism and colonial authority. Three clear, polemical, statements that are worth reading are:

Bessis, S. (2003) *Western Supremacy: The Triumph of an Idea*, London, Zed.

Davies, M., Nandy, A. and Sardar, Z. (1993) *Barbaric Others: A Manifesto on Western Racism*, London, Pluto.

Patterson, T. (1997) *Inventing Western Civilization*, New York, Monthly Review Press.

A different critical line is taken by David Gress in *From Plato to NATO: The Idea of the West and its Opponents* (1998, New York, Free Press). Gress challenges conventional lineages of the West in order to sustain a vision of a 'New West' that can synthesise 'the modern triad of democracy, science, and capitalism' (p. 48) with the religious and cultural sense of community of the 'Old West'.

Arthur Herman's *The Idea of Decline in Western History* (1997, New York, Free Press) also offers a rebuke to critics of the West, who he casts as cultural pessimists. However, the most useful critical work on the West is neither anti- nor pro-Western but approaches it historically and geographically. For example, Robert Young's *White Mythologies: Writing History and the West* (1990, London, Routledge) provides a sophisticated but accessible interrogation of the presence of the West in structuralist, post-structuralist and post-colonial social theory. A shorter and simpler deconstructive examination of the 'formations of the West and its Others' is provided by Ali Rattansi in '"Western" racisms, ethnicities and identities in a "postmodern" frame', in A. Rattansi and S. Westwood (eds) *Racism, Modernity and Identity on the Western Front* (1994, Oxford, Polity). More basic again is Stuart Hall's popular and influential essay 'The West and the rest: discourse and power', in S. Hall and B. Gieben (eds) *Formations of Modernity* (1992, Cambridge, Cambridge University Press).

Western occidentalism

For further information on how the idea of the West has developed in the West see Christopher GoGwilt's *The Invention of the West: Joseph Conrad and the Double-Mapping of Europe and Empire* (1995, Stanford, Stanford University Press). This is an exceptionally valuable contribution, with an 'Epilogue' that provides 'A brief genealogy of the West'. GoGwilt's intriguing phrase – 'the double mapping of Europe and Empire' – is designed to suggest that the political segregation of Europe and the emergence of colonial criticism acted together to produce the West as a fragile crisis-prone identity of imperial retreat. 'The rhetorical force of the term "the West"', he notes, draws not only from the reconstruction of European history refashioned in the inverted image of Russian history, but also from the construction of a European history articulated in response to and within the specific contexts of a whole range of non-European cultural histories (p. 236).

Another essential work is James Carrier's edited collection *Occidentalism: Images of the West* (1995, Oxford, Oxford University Press). The essays in this volume include not only Western and non-Western studies of the West, but revealing studies of Western anthropologists who have relied on stereotypes of non-Western occidentalism (for example, Carrier's essay 'Maussian occidentalims: gift and commodity systems').

Chapter 2

Communists Like Us: The Idea of the West in the Soviet Union

Introduction

The idea of the West was fundamental to the Soviet Union. The USSR inherited a long tradition of Russian debate on the nature and merits of Westernisation. The Bolsheviks developed and adapted this tradition. In the process they helped establish the West as a politically self-conscious and recognisable entity: a place defined as non-Communist and anti-Soviet.

This chapter traces a transition in Soviet politics. It is a transition from imagining the West to be the home of socialist revolution to seeing it as the home of bourgeois reaction. It is also a transition from understanding Marxist revolution as a form of Westernisation to understanding it as antithetical to Western values.

These arguments form the core of the current chapter. However, they are supplemented by a somewhat more provocative position. For I will also be offering a portrait of communism in the USSR as a simultaneously ethnicising and politicising form of modernity, an 'ethno-politics' defined and developed in relation to changing constructs of the West. This argument also implies a transition in Soviet politics, albeit of a less clear-cut nature. It is a transition from the proletariat being connoted and idealised as Western and European to the proletariat being defined as Russian and non-Western. Below, I set out some of the background to this argument.[1]

From the early 1920s onwards, 'the West' began to be employed in Soviet[2] discourse as a repository of social ills. By claiming that racial and ethnic discrimination were ailments of the Western, capitalist world, Soviet leaders let it be known that to identify such problems within the USSR was counter revolutionary. In the aftermath of Soviet rule, a desire has arisen for more honest assessments. For the relationship between communism and ethnic politics is far from

40

being a matter of merely regional importance or of interest only to Soviet and post-Soviet specialists. This aspect of twentieth-century history raises concerns that go to the heart of how we understand the socio-economic contexts that enable and sustain racism and ethnocentrism. More specifically, consideration of the 'Soviet experiment' is capable of calling into question concepts such as 'Western modernity' and 'racialised modernity', and of offering a challenge to those who cast the politicisation of identity as an inherently emancipatory process.

A desire to portray the USSR as a continuation of or, at some point, as reverting to, Tsarist imperialism and, by extension, to offer the Soviet empire's 'survival' in the mid- and late twentieth century as a colonial anachronism, threads its way through a great deal of Western and post-Soviet commentary.[3] The same parallel invites a simple reversal of the once orthodox anti-racist image of the Soviet Union, a trend that, in the English-speaking world, has been encouraged by the development of a considerable literature on Soviet anti-Semitism (Baron, 1975; Kelman, 1979; Miller, 1984). However, although the temptation to represent the USSR as a kind of mutant off-spring of European colonialism and racism may, in some cases, be politically understandable, it is profoundly misleading. The Soviet Union was a colonial state, but of a new type.

The ideologies that animated the USSR's development reflected and legitimised ethnicised forms of intellectual and physical domination. Yet far from being mere faint echoes of a normative, Western colonial paradigm, these ideologies provided a fundamental challenge to them. Western colonialists and neo-colonialists may have been mistaken in fearing that the Soviet Union was, indeed, the beacon of equality that its leaders proclaimed it to be. However, their instinct that the USSR was different, that it offered a distinct way of understanding 'progress' and 'civilisation', was essentially correct. Indeed, their mistake in not seeing the 'racism' within the USSR was less a failure to see the country's similarities with the West, than an inability to appreciate just how unlike the West Soviet society really was. For whereas modernity in the 'capitalist West' tended to be simultaneously depoliticising and racialising (typically, if not exclusively, around the idea that white, European heritage people were the natural bearers of modernity) in the USSR, it was simultaneously politicising and ethnicising (typically, although again not exclusively, around the idea that 'Russian'[4] urban workers were the natural bearers of communism).

The West versus communism

Writing in the early 1930s, Gramsci (1971, p. 447) noted an intriguing recent phenomenon: 'because of the historical content that has become attached to the geographical terms, the expressions East and West have finished up indicating specific relations between different cultural complexes'. Yet, both the 'historical content' and the 'cultural complexes' Gramsci mentions are vulnerable not only to re-interpretation but to a profound sense of inadequacy in the face of societies who appear to be both Eastern and Western, or neither. There are no more telling example of this state of uncertainty than Russia and the USSR.

The racial attributes of Russia and the USSR excited considerable comment from foreign observers throughout the twentieth century. At the beginning of the century, imperial Russia was widely accepted as part of the fraternity of European colonial powers. The shock that greeted the country's military defeat by Japan in 1905 was widely articulated in terms of the frightening potent it offered for the global survival of white dominance. However, the notion that the European status of the country was superficial also continued to be voiced. Napoleon's aphorism – 'Scratch a Russia, find a Tatar' – summed up an ambivalence that for many Western critics provided the framework through which to understand the revolutions of 1917.

Of course, this last sentence assumes the prior existence of 'Western critics'. It is one of the conceits of the West that it was always there; judging events but not constituted by them. In Chapter 1 I looked at the emergence of the idea of the West in Britain in relation to whiteness. I also noted that a history of the West may also usefully focus on particular events that defines its use and form. There is no event more important in the history of the West than the Russian revolution. Although the idea of the West had long been in use in Russia, its widespread employment in Western Europe was slow in coming. However, from 1917 onwards, it gained considerable currency, eventually becoming inseparable from a political identity of anti-communism and pro-capitalism.

By the late 1920s the equation of the West with multi-party democracy and capitalism had became common within both the West and the Soviet Union. From this association a number of other connotations grew, connecting the West with non-authoritarian government and an open society. This chain of association was strengthened by the alignment of communism, fascism and Nazism as varieties of authoritarianism. Thus communism, fascism and Nazism could be run together as anti-Western.[5] In *Our Threatened Values* Gollancz (1946) provided an interesting permutation of this position, repeatedly drawing communism and Nazism together as non-Western: 'For Nazis, western values are, I repeat, evil', Gollancz writes, 'for communism they are, for the time being at least, irrelevant' (pp. 62–63). This type of characterisation helped to render even further redundant the kinds of crisis of class character and solidarity discussed in the previous chapter. Within a world divided between authoritarianism and Western 'open society', the whiteness of Russia or the Nazis appeared as a minor commonality that obscured the 'real differences'.

However, the theme of race was sustained by right-wing critics of the USSR. Central to this attack was the contention that Bolshevism was an ideology of racial treason. For Stoddard (1925, first published 1920), Bolshevism was 'the arch-enemy of civilisation and the race. Bolshevism is the renegade, the traitor within the gates, who would betray the citadel' (p. 221). This kind of revulsion and bewilderment helped kindle older suspicions about Russia, suspicions which emphasised that communism in general and Bolshevism in particular reflected 'the dominance of [Russia's] half-Asiatic Slavic peasantry' (Grant, 1925, p. xxviii). The American journalist Chamberlin (1987a,b, first published 1935, 1940) who emerged, after a brief period of sympathy with the revolution, as one of its most vociferous US critics, repeatedly voiced this conviction. Noting the supposedly Asiatic subservience and indifference to suffering characteristic of the Russian peasantry, Chamberlin sought to position Bolshevism as both an exploitation and a political extrapolation of these attributes. Lenin's 'distinctly Mongolian cast of features' (1987a, p. 139) and Stalin's Asian heritage[6] were offered as further testament to the non-European character of the Soviet Union. One of the implications of such commentary was that, unless 'the Russians' regained a pro-Western leadership, they would experience a kind of racial atavism, and 'sink back' into becoming a 'truly "dark people"' (1987a, p. 248).

The dark character of Soviet society appeared confirmed by its atheism. Throughout Western anti-communist commentary, godless materialism is associated with the extinction of personal and civic morality. The related equation, of Western civilisation with Christian civilisation, does not represent a continuation of pre-modern notions of Western Christendom, but a direct response to the rise of the USSR (and, to a lesser extent, Nazi Germany). In the years following the end of the Second World War, this religious emphasis took on particular significance. Indeed, in the year the Cold War began in earnest, 1948,

President Truman proclaimed that Americans 'are a people with faith' and that 'The faith of our people has particular meaning at this time of history.' In Britain, as Kirby's (2000) studies of British and US foreign policy have shown, a Christian definition of the West was seen to have a particular, strategic, value in papering over the political tensions between a socialist inclined Europe and a capitalist USA.

The racial and political exoticisation of the USSR established it, for many twentieth-century Western observers, as an indecipherable entity; in Churchill's much quoted phrase, 'a riddle wrapped in a mystery inside an enigma'. The post-Soviet era has not dispelled such constructions. Indeed, they are maintained within the rhetoric of Russia's post-communist 'return to Europe'[7], as well as within the ubiquitous practice of referring to the Soviet era as a 'moratorium' or 'hiatus' (for example, Neumann, 1996). Such readings of the Soviet era portray racial discrimination as emerging into view (and experiencing an upsurge after being 'buried' by communism) as Russia returns to 'normalcy'. As we shall see, in order to move beyond notions of Soviet 'hiatus' and Western 'normalcy' it is necessary to let go of the privileged status of the latter as an objective arbiter of Soviet reality, and begin to understand the invention and deployment of the idea of 'the West' within Russia.

Russia's West

The notion of 'the West' was developed in Russia, from the mid-eighteenth century on, as one of the key terms in an ongoing debate on the country's destiny and identity. Although the political meaning of the word was mutable, it became an indispensable tool in the argument about whether Russia should be Europeanised.[8] It was a controversy of little or no concern to earlier generations. Summing up the historical record of the previous two centuries, Mark Bassin tells us that 'There is little evidence',

> that the Russians of the sixteenth century or seventeenth century endorsed or were even particularly cognizant of the conceit brewing among the Europeans that the quality of their civilisation was "the best in the world", as Samuel Purchas put it ... and almost none of any subjective Russian desire that they should be counted as a part of this civilisation (Bassin, 1998, p. 67).

Indeed, before the mid-eighteenth century, those later to be cast by the 'Westernisers' (*zapadniki*, a Russian neologism) as fellow Europeans, were often not distinguished from Tatars or Turks. As this implies, Russia's conquest of Siberia in the sixteenth and seventeenth centuries was not understood as an act of European expansion. In marked contrast, the self-consciously imperial 'drive' southwards in the late eighteenth and nineteenth centuries was legitimised by reference to differences between civilised, European, Russians and semi-barbarous, non-Christian, Asiatics (Brower and Lazzerini, 1997). The eighteenth-century Russian geographer Vasily Tatischev was clear: Russia was European and Europe 'by virtue of its [material] abundance, its scholarship, its strength and its glory, as well as the moderation of its climate... dominates without question' (cited by Bassin, 1991, p. 5). Tatischev's designation, in the 1730s, of the Urals and the Caucasus as, respectively, the eastern and southern termini of Europe is of interest, not merely because of its survival to the present day[9], but because it reflects the emergence of a clear desire amongst the Russian elite to establish Europe and Asia as separate entities.

Thus the notion was established that a discrete, identifiable culture of economic and technological advance and rationality existed to the West and that, through Westernisation, the underdeveloped European qualities of Russia itself could be brought into view and any Asiatic trace could be erased. Although, by 1917, this perspective was also common amongst Marxist revolutionaries, it was first established in the eighteenth century as part of wealthy Russians' attempt to cast themselves within an increasingly normative image of European culture and colonialism. As this suggests, in attempting to establish Russia as European, the Westernisers were also fixing the majority of the country as peripheral, uncivilised and Asian. Emphasising the colonial dynamic contained in this formula, Becker points out that what came to be seen as the proximity of Asia to Russia was understood,

> not as a threat to Russia's European identity but rather as an opportunity to prove that identity. In bringing to her Oriental subjects the fruits of Western civilisation, Russia would be demonstrating her membership in the exclusive club of European nations (Becker, 1991, p. 50).

The rise of biological racism – especially white and Aryan supremacism – during the mid-to-late nineteenth century in Russian academic and political circles helped sustain this Eurocentric, imperial trajectory (Hauner, 1990). However, the desire to identify Russia with the West, and as another white power, existed in opposition with other forms of ethnocentrism. To a degree unique among other major European nations, the assumption that European civilisation was inherently superior to all others, or even a meaningful category, was actively contested. Russia's defeat by Britain, France and Turkey during the Crimean

War (1853–1856), combined with a persistent unease at the prospect of Russia ever really being accepted as fully European[10], encouraged those voices that condemned Westernisation as the spirit of alienation, materialism and superficiality.

Throughout the mid- and late nineteenth century, Slavophile and pan-Slavic critics poured scorn on the empty and instrumental world of the occident. The irony of this criticism is that its rejection of Europe had all the hallmarks of romanticism, nationalism and ethnic primitivism, ideologies developed in Western Europe from the late eighteenth century. Indeed, later incarnations of this current have the unmistakable ring of avant-garde provocations. Alexander Blok's poem 'The Scythians', written in 1918, may be taken as an example (the Scythians were a tribe of cruel savages, depicted by Ovid in *Tristia*). Replete with stereotypes derived from the European colonial project, it turned the fears of a swarming, cruel and animalistic 'yellow peril', or 'pan-mongolism', voiced by Vladimir Solov'ev, into a bold and positive identification with Asia,

> Of you, there are millions. We – are numberless, numberless, numberless.
> Just try to fight us!
> Yes, we are Scythians! Yes, we are Asiatics!
> With slanting and greedy eyes (Blok, 1918, cited by Bassin, 1998, p. 76).

Once it became apparent to them that revolutionary Russia would be a hostile environment for their views, the group of intellectual émigrés to which Blok's name is sometimes associated, known as the Eurasianists, continued to foment their primitivist agenda in exile (Riasanovsky, 1967). The first years of communist power reveal, however, an interesting dynamic within their work. For although they soon identified the revolution as a Westernising force, they also found something thrillingly anti-European about its challenge to the old order. As Blok's poem suggests, and as the passage from Sergei Esenin below reiterates in even cruder language, the sense that the revolution could also be cast as an overcoming of the West, an affirmation of the masculine, primitive capacity of Russia to destroy an effete Europe, helped animate the Eurasianist imagination.

> Let us be Asians, let us stink, let us scratch our buttocks shamelessly in sight of everyone. Even so, we don't have such a putrid smell as they have inside. No revolution is possible here. Everything is at a standstill, a dead end. Only an invasion of barbarians like us can save and reshape them. The march on Europe is necessary (Esenin, 1923, cited by Hauner, 1990, p. 55).

The fact that Blok and Esenin take a kind of perverse pleasure in conjuring a fantasy of the Russian masses as posed to sweep Europe away echoes what was becoming a familiar rhetorical mode of the avant-garde. Yet, it also hints at the way that, by positioning the Russian people as possessed of some unique, atavistic, energy, the Bolshevik revolution could be detached from the discourse of Westernisation, and integrated into stereotypical notions of 'Asianism'. It did not take much encouragement for Western anti-communists to also make this association nor for the pro-Western forces that came to power in Russia in the immediate wake of the fall of the USSR.

Yet, for the Bolsheviks themselves, far from auguring the victory of chaos and primitivism, November 1917 was a revolution of and for progress, rationality, science and civilisation. Indeed, at least initially, its ethno-political agenda privileged the politicised urban worker not only as a bulwark against Asia but also as a conduit for Western socialism.

The revolutionary West

Today the association of the West and Westernisation with the development of capitalism is so commonplace as to go unnoticed. It is a link that was continuously secured by the mutually defining relationship built up between the USSR and the USA, and their respective allies. This highly circumscribed view of what the term 'the West' connotes had a far less dominant position at the start of the century. 'The West' then was a more politically plural category[11]. Indeed, in Russia, the political affiliation of Westernisers was likely to be socialist and revolutionary.

This phase of Russian/USSR politics ended in the mid-late 1920s with the realisation that the West was not going to ignite in revolution and that the USSR would have to go it alone. The Bolshevik's difficulty in accepting or understanding the failure of radicalism in the West may, in part, be explained by reference to a more fundamental difficulty, namely of grasping that what was happening in Soviet society represented an original re-shaping of modernity. Early Bolsheviks talked of carrying Western enlightenment into a backward society. Yet, they were not importing but creating; establishing new models of identity as well as new types of reified community. As we shall see, 'the proletarian' emerged from this process as the central simultaneously politically and ethnically marked category, the symbolic bearer of socialist modernity to 'less advanced' peoples.

The Bolsheviks' attitude towards the West was tinged with ambivalence. It was the orthodox Marxism of the Mensheviks that acquired for them the tag 'European'. By contrast, the Bolsheviks were occasionally cast as 'Slavophile Marxists'. The Bolsheviks' emphasis on the need for a vanguard to lead the working class, their practice of evoking a (potentially) revolutionary peasantry, combined with their insistence that Russia did not need to go through the same stages of capitalist development as the 'more advanced European' nations, are all indicative of the heretical nature of their Marxism. However, their suspicion of the rigid application of a Western socialist template was not the same thing as suspicion of Westernisation. An unwillingness to 'humbly follow the prepared models' (Trotsky, 1980, p. 378, first published 1932) was combined with a powerful faith in the West as the source and real home of socialist revolution.

Lenin's (1964a, p. 68, first published 1917), goal was 'a state of the Paris commune type', a destination that required Western guidance and leadership. 'The European workers', he noted in 1905, will show us 'how to do it' (Lenin, 1962, p. 92). In late 1916, Lenin (1964b, p. 59, first published 1924) held that 'Only the advanced countries of Western Europe and North America have matured for socialism.' Indeed, the notion that Russian socialism could not survive without a Western revolution to support and lead it was still able to be openly expressed in the mid-1920s. Trotsky contended in 1925: 'that we have continued to exist is due to the fact that Europe has not remained what it was' (cited by D'Agostino, 1988, p. 96), an allusion to the 'moral support' provided by revolutionary European workers for the USSR.

The rejection of the West, and the associated rise of Russian nationalism, from the late 1920s onwards, has tended to overshadow the intensity and complexity of the Westernising spirit of earlier Bolsheviks. For Lenin and Trotsky, Russia was ripe for Westernisation; it was something that needed to happen not merely for the revolution to succeed but for it to be thinkable. In his typically imperious style Lenin decreed in 1918 that,

> it is our task...not to spare dictatorial methods in order to hasten the copying of Westernism by barbarous Russia even more than did Peter, not shrinking from barbarous methods of struggle against barbarism (cited by Neumann, 1996, p. 106)[12].

Western progress: Asian backwardness

The Bolsheviks' association of barbarism and slavery with Asia was, in part, a reflection of their faithful reading of Marx, who expressed similar views (Marx, 1969). However, it also represented the continuation of the views of the Russian elite. The conviction that progress was European and conservatism Eastern was mapped onto an existing imaginative geography of the West being modern, enlightened and civilised and the East being the antithesis of all three.

'Asianism' (Aziatchina) represented everything that was old and rotten, everything that needed to be ripped out of both Russia and her colonies. Mixing images of political reaction, with those of decay and infestation, Trotsky looked forward to the development of a clean, new Western civilisation. 'The revolution' he wrote in 1923, 'means the final break of the people with Asianism, with the seventeenth century, with holy Russia, with ikons and cockroaches…an assimilation of the whole people of civilisation' (quoted by Carr, 1958, p. 144).

'Asianism' was explained politically, as the feudal and backward ideology of 'Oriental despotism'. The entrenched nature of Bolshevik Eurocentrism made the ethnic content of the term not merely difficult to discuss but impossible to see. This myopia was compounded by the wider difficulty already mentioned, of grasping the originality of the revolution as an event that, far from simply extending Western, emancipatory traditions, established new and distinct ways of being modern. One of the most important aspects of this originality was the forging of *ethno-political* identities. As we have seen, this process contained clear moments of pro-Westernism. Although these attitudes were widespread amongst the revolution's leaders, they could only rarely be claimed to represent an unambiguously *racial* identification of Europeans as a superior human type. What emerged, instead, was an ethno-political investment in 'communists', 'proletarians', and 'revolutionaries', of whatever ethnic or national group, as inherently more Western, more European, more 'like us', than 'backward' elements. The missionary zeal this fusion of beliefs excited is captured by Diuk and Karatnycky (1993) in their description of the way that, following the incorporation of imperial Russia's Asian colonial territories into the Union after the Civil War, young Bolsheviks,

> went into Soviet Central Asia to promote the Bolshevik creed on a mission to spread enlightenment and dispel years of illiteracy and backwardness. Official records of the era abound in pictures of Kazakh herdsmen marvelling at the phenomenon of an electric light bulb, and of Uzbek women seeing the light of day for the first time after emerging from behind the Muslim veil (p. 177).

Making nations of the Western type

Communist modernity was presented and offered as a political and politicising process of social evolution. The civilising function of Western socialist culture was unquestioned. However, the status of other forms of ethnicity, more specifically, of national identities, was actively debated. The Leninist orthodoxy which emerged on this topic turned on the political function of non-Russian nationalism in the USSR in the context of the need to disseminate class consciousness. Unlike Siberia and Russian East Asia, which were considered to be assimilated parts of Russia[13], Soviet Central Asia was deemed to need to be propelled along a track of 'state-sponsored evolutionism' (Hirsch, 2000, p. 203). Its destination was a de-ethnicised, de-nationalised, internationalist communist identity. However, in order to get this far, and in order to keep its 'backward' populations politically engaged, it was considered a strategic necessity to have a period of national identification. This phase was designed to allow these former subjects of Tzarist imperialism to articulate their oppression as recognisable ethnic entities (as opposed to the unclassifiable, disparate 'tribesmen' encountered by Soviet administrators). These new national units were considered a necessary stage of political development, a stepping stone towards a modern, Westernised class consciousness.

Soviet attempts during the 1920s to establish, recognise and incorporate non-Russian nationalities were far-reaching. Slezkine (1996, p. 203) describes the period 1928–1931 as witnessing 'the most extravagant celebration of ethnic diversity that any state has ever financed'. Martin (1996) goes even further when he depicts the early USSR as *An Affirmative Action Empire*. Soviet positive discrimination in favour of non-Russian languages, cultures and economies, on top of the efforts made to indigenise the heavily Russian regional party structures, were startling and bold. In both scale and range, they far exceeded the government-sponsored assertions of federal ethnic pluralism and 'multiculturalism' developed in the West over fifty years later. However, the goal of Soviet nation-making was to assimilate diverse societies into a single, recognisably European, narrative of political evolution. A critical memo, written in the early 1920s, to the Central Executive Committee on the creation of Soviet republics in Soviet Central Asia, called this process the 'Europeanisation of the East', describing it as 'an adoption of a nineteenth-century West European tradition, alien to the region' (Bartol'd cited by Hirsch, 2000, p. 214). As a rebuke to an increasingly authoritarian regime this summary is certainly apt, but it misses the novel, political function of the Soviet 'nation-making' project (for discussion see Simon, 1991; Suny, 1993; Slezkine, 1996). Entities such as Uzbekistan Soviet Socialist Republic , Tajik Soviet Socialist Republic, Kirgiz Autonomous Soviet Socialist Republic as well as other, more ancient, countries granted republic status (for example, Armenia and Georgia) were never going to be sustained by the Soviet leadership as ethnically distinct nations. Their function was to contain and, finally, to help neutralise and eradicate any form of consciousness that differed from the dominant and unmarked ethno-political categories of communist rule.

'The aim of Socialism', Lenin (1935, p. 270) noted in 1916,

> is not only to abolish the present division of mankind into small states, and all-national isolation, not only to bring the nations closer to each other, but also to merge them.

'The essence of the national question', explained Stalin (cited by Gleason, 1990, p. 14) in 1921,

> is to liquidate the economic, political and cultural backwardness of the nationalities... We do this in order to give the backward peoples the opportunity to catch up with central Russia.

Stalin elucidated further:

> when the younger generation of communists on the periphery denies to take the play of independence for a play [they] are stubbornly taking words about independence at face value (cited by Kryukov, 1996, p. 373).

As Stalin's remarks imply, such was the enthusiasm with which these measures were carried out, that some party members outside Russia appear to have lost sight of their assimilative raison d'être. Yet, despite such early 'excesses' and the boldness of the Soviet 'multicultural' experiment, the political employment of non-Russian nationalism by the Bolsheviks sustained an unmistakably colonial regime. Thus although the claim that, as Stalin phrased it in 1927, 'the October Revolution has ushered in a new era, the era of colonial revolutions' (Stalin, 1954, p. 248), contains much truth, it remains a bitterly ironic testament to both the invisibility and thoroughness of Soviet internal colonialism.

Proletarian civilisation

As Slezkine (1996, p. 210) suggests, 'by equating ethnicity with development' the Soviet state ensured that the politics of modernity was also an ethnicisation of the political. Any form of suspected actual or potential resistance to assimilation into an atheist, scientific and Eurocentric

Soviet state, was perceived as a symptom of 'backwardness' that needed to be expunged. It was in this way that Soviet communism facilitated the representation of whole communities as unwanted and corrupting class elements.

In order to further understand how Soviet rule fused politics and ethnicity, it is necessary to look in more detail at the most privileged category of social identity within Bolshevik communism, the proletarian. It may be objected here that one of the unorthodox aspects of Bolshevik Marxism was its attention to the peasant. 'Land to the peasant' was, as Worsley (1984, p. 128) reminds us, 'the really decisive Bolshevik slogan'. Being 'hostile to the peasant' was a popular accusation against political enemies. Yet despite the considerable amount of lip service paid to the importance of the peasantry as a potentially revolutionary force, the normative role model of what a real revolutionary looked like wielded the hammer not the sickle. For Trotsky, '[t]he proletariat in power will stand before the peasants as the class which has emancipated it' (1962, p. 203; originally published 1906). For Lenin, cited with approval by Stalin (1954, p. 263) in 1927, 'the alliance of the proletariat and the peasantry [exists] in order that the proletariat may retain its leading role and state power'.

'The preference accorded by "Great Russian chauvinism" to the Great Russian', Carr (1966a, p. 377) tells us, 'accorded all too easily with the preference given in Marxist orthodoxy to the proletariat, and could easily disguise itself in Marxist trappings' (1966a, p. 377). The Soviet proletariat was not Asian but European. Urban industrial workers were largely confined to Soviet territories in the West. Moreover, the population of urban centres across the Union tended to be dominated by European Russians. This confluence of history, politics and ethnicity was cemented by the enforcement of what Slezkine (1996, p. 221) calls a vision of an 'urban Utopia' as the destiny for all of the Union's nationalities. It also led to the stereotyping of peasants and proletarians as two types of humanity with fixed political attributes and trajectories. Indeed, when considered alongside his many declarations on peasant and Asian 'backwardness', Trotsky's advocacy of internal colonialism begins to resemble a crude racism.

Thus, whilst the open scorn for 'the exceedingly low cultural level in the countryside' (Stalin, 1954, p. 312), and the 'unstable' and 'treacherous' sensibilities of the peasantry (Trotsky citing Lenin; Trotsky, 1980, p. 386), was articulated as political critique, it was rooted in a mutually reinforcing mixture of Eurocentrism, communism and colonialism. The peasant famines of the early 1930s, which had a proportionately greater impact on non-Russian Soviet territories were, in part, a product of this noxious brew.

Summary

The early years of the revolution saw the employment and deployment of the concepts 'the West' and 'Westernisation' as positive and necessary models for revolutionary Russia. The 'revolutionary West' was defined in relation to 'backward Asia', more specifically, the cancerous presence of 'Asianism' in Soviet society. However, the deployment of these categories should not be taken to imply that Bolshevik modernity was, in fact, imitative of the West. The revolution set in motion a new type of colonialism and a new type of modernity, each being premised on the simultaneous ethnicisation and politicisation of identity. This process offered a profound challenge to the racialised hierarchies current with West European modernity. Yet it contained its own logic of ethnic discrimination and exclusion. It is now necessary to consider how and why notions of the West changed under Stalin.

The Western enemy

> The official order is to evince the greatest horror of the West. Everything is evil there: trains are late, stores are empty, no one has money, people are poorly dressed, the highly praised technology is worthless. If you hear the name of a Western writer, painter, or composer, you must scoff sarcastically, for to fight against 'cosmopolitanism' is one of the duties of a citizen (Milosz, *The Captive Mind*, 1985, p. 43, first published 1953).

From the mid-to-late 1920s 'the West' was increasingly cast as synonymous with 'capitalist countries'. The 'moral support' for the Soviet state offered by some Western workers did not compensate for the brute fact that the revolution had not spread to the West. This was a calamity for Bolshivism. The Bolshevik project was premised on internationalism and, more specifically, on the Western revolution. It was thought impossible for an authentically communist state to survive in the midst of hostile capitalist powers. The absence of revolution, or even effective mass revolutionary movements, to materialise in the West, changed the nature of Soviet politics. It allowed Stalin to turn his back on the West and develop a form of nationalist socialism in which Russia was proclaimed to be the home of world revolution.

'The whole world now admits', Stalin declared in 1930, 'that the centre of the revolutionary movement has shifted from Western Europe to Russia' (Stalin, 1955, p. 25). This position, which was retained in its basic form throughout the period of 'neo-Stalinist compromise' (which lasted to the mid-1980s), simultaneously strengthened the already existing Russocentric attributes of Bolshevik identity politics whilst necessitating a selective de-Westernisation of Soviet heritage. Claims of a socialist 'separate path' were accompanied by the withering of 'affirmative action' initiatives to pluralise the communist project. This period also witnessed convoluted attempts by Stalin, as well as Stalinists of his and subsequent generations, to both call on and repudiate the legitimising authority of Western civilisation. In an exchange that typifies the management of this tension, Stalin responded in 1931 to a fawning interviewer's attempt to compare him with the most famous Westerniser in Russian history, Peter the Great, by noting that 'the latter was a drop in the ocean, whereas Lenin was a whole ocean' (Stalin, 1955, p. 107).

Stalin's hostility to the West turned on the latter's anti-Soviet nature. It did not imply any active identification with the East. It is true that, drawing on his Georgian background, Stalin did, occasionally, depict himself as Asian (he told the Japanese foreign minister in 1941, 'you are Asiatic, so am I'; cited by Stephan, 1982, p. 36). However, far more indicative is this recollection by Stalin's daughter, Alliluyeva (1968, p. 127): 'I know no other Georgian', she said of her father, 'who had completely sloughed off his qualities as a Georgian and loved everything Russian the way he did'. The mutually defining relationship that Stalin elaborated was not East versus West, but Russia versus the West. It was an antagonism that was able to maintain a claim on Russia as a modern, civilising society as well as the image of Soviet Asia as in constant need of progressive intervention. Despite incidents which suggest that being Russian did not necessarily offer any protection from ethnic discrimination under Stalin (such as the persecution, in the late 1930s, of migrant Russian railway workers suspected of having ties with China), overall Stalinism tended to draw together the politicisation of identity with Russian ethnocentrism.

Criticism of the 'corrupt culture' of the West began to be articulated in explicitly ethnic terms. The distinction between Westerners and Soviet people was codified through the proliferation of, officially sanctioned, negative stereotypes of Western culture. In particular, Western 'decadence', 'imperialism', 'reaction', 'aggression' and 'greed' became naturalised; increasingly fixed as essential components of a threatening other. The notion of 'capitalist encirclement', associated with Stalin but maintained under various guises within subsequent neo-Stalinist regimes, came to be central to the depiction of 'Soviet man' as an embattled and specific ethno-political entity whose only possible stance towards 'bourgeois nations' was one of stoic resistance against attack.

Soviet modernity was identified as a separate civilisation, a society whose leaders were proud to claim that their country had its own, distinctively communist, technology, science, literature, ethical code and so on (see also Kotkin, 1995). Such claims relied on a comparison with Western forms of technology, science, literature and ethical code. The assertion of 'red science' provides an example of the attempt to define Soviet society as the antithesis of the West. 'Red science', promoted by the Institute of Red Professors and other organisations, relied on the denouncement of all other forms of science as Western and bourgeois. Although Lysenkoism is an extreme example of this current it was far from being unique (cf. Joravsky, 1986). Rejecting conventional geneticists as 'reactionary and decadent, grovelling before Western capitalism', Trofim Lysenko (cited by Sakwa, 1999, p. 299) won the support of Stalin[14] for his claims that enormous gains in crop yield could be achieved, not by crop selection, but by altering crop characteristics by exposing them to different climatic conditions. However, as Krementsov (1997, p. 179) notes, '[t]he core of this model' was not a scientific contention but 'the juxtaposition of "Soviet" and "Western" science'. In the West, where the prevalent ideology asserted the value of science as politically neutral, Lysenko's ideas were seized upon as an instance of the bizarre and irrational nature of communism. However, in the context of Soviet modernity, Lysenkoism becomes explicable. It provided a reflection of a culture that looked to anti-Westernism as a foundation of communist identity.

The development of Russian nationalism in Soviet identity politics was accompanied by an increasingly explicitly dominant relationship between Russia and other parts of the Soviet Union.[15] In contrast to Western forms of colonialism, Russian power did not bring significant material benefits to the general populace of the 'motherland'. Moreover, the process of 'nation building' continued in many parts of the USSR (Suny, 1993). Nevertheless, Russia had a special place within Stalinist 'universal suppression' (Sakwa, 1990, p. 252). Soviet colonialism was simultaneously and sometimes starkly Russian and communist: the Stalinist, Russocentric version of the established pattern of ethno-political domination. This mutually supportive relationship was apparent on many levels, both cultural and economic. As regarding the former it is indicative that, from the early 1930s onwards, Russian history, culture, language, Cyrillic script, as well as Russian national heroes, began to be accorded pan-Soviet status. The Russians became the Union's 'elder brothers': in *Pravda*'s (1937, cited by Fowkes, 1997, p. 69) terms 'the first among equals'; in Stalin's, 'the most outstanding nation of all the nations forming the Soviet Union...the leading force of the Soviet Union' (Stalin, 1999, p. 287, from a speech delivered in 1945). Non-Russian national anthems provide a concise illustration of the imbalance of power and status between Soviet nations. The Azerbaijanian anthem proclaimed, 'The mighty Russian brother is bringing to the land the triumph of freedom; and with our blood we have strengthened our kinship with him.' The Uzbek national anthem began 'Hail Russian brother, great is your people.'

Under the 'neo-Stalinist compromise', through which successive leaders maintained the Union's economic structure whilst pushing through reformist or counter-reformist political measures (it is conventional to place Krushchev and Gorbachev in the former category and Brezhnev, Andropov and Chernenko in the latter), ethnicised communism was maintained until the last few years of the USSR. However, because so much had been vested in what, in the post-Second World War era, became an unwieldy and rigid socio-economic model, the practice of offering Sovietisation and modernisation as synonymous terms began to appear questionable. During and after the so-called 'years of stagnation' associated with Brezhnev, modernisation began to take on other, distinctly non-communist, connotations. Indeed, it increasingly came to mean copying or assimilating Western techniques, even to the point of introducing market-led solutions. By the time Gorbachev became General Secretary in 1985, faith in the Soviet version of modernity had become largely a matter of rhetorical gesture. The solutions to Soviet problems were located in the West.

The 'kidnapped West' and Russia's 'return'

> We shall meet again in Petersburg,
> as though we had buried the sun there
> (Mandelstam, 1974, written in 1920).

The USSR's territorial gains during the Second World War were quickly perceived in the West as comprising, in Milan Kundera's phrase, 'un occident kidnappé'. Throughout the Soviet era there also existed a tendency within some 'Eastern Bloc' countries, as well as within the western nations of the USSR, for popular resentment against Russia to be articulated in terms of suspicion of the latter's non-Western and, hence, Asiatic, credentials. One may get a sense of these sentiments from the comment of the Estonian politician Tiit Maade who, in 1989, noted that the Russians were a wild, untamed people who spread remorselessly outwards. Maade went on to explain that these attributes derived from the systematic raping of Russian women by Asian invaders during the Mongol invasions (Neumann, 1999). Within the post-Soviet era an official position has arisen within the Baltic states, as well as within other non-Asian ex-Soviet nations, to the effect that these countries may be distinguished from Russia by virtue of their indestructible and organic Western essence, a core identity that survived, in a state of political hibernation, during the years of Russian domination.

The claim to be part of the 'Western club' is made by way of a related contention, of not having been contaminated by communism and the East. In 1992 the Ukrainian foreign minister Anatoliy Zlenko (cited by Dawisha and Parrott, 1994, pp. 70–71) asserted a fundamental difference between Ukraine, as 'a wholly European country', and the Russian 'Eurasian state'. Such geo-historical readings are designed, in part, to flatter the West, whose leaders often appear to enjoy their new role as arbiters of which, once errant, nations merit 're-admission' to the Western family. Returning to the example of Estonia, we may note, for example, that changes to the country's law on foreign nationals in 1993 were enough to convince Carl Bildt, the Swedish Prime Minister, that 'Estonia has secured its ties with the values and institution of Western democracies. It is highly regarded by all those who consider Estonia as a secure and well-off European country' (cited by Smith *et al.*, 1998, p. 109).

On the diplomatic stage, the language of 'securing' a place within the West has become a common rhetorical formula. Any lingering memories of the once politically plural implications of Westernisation are not allowed to complicate the meaning of the 'security' being offered. The process of 'admission' is presented as an irrevocable political decision, a final closure not just on communism but on any other departure from late capitalism and its allied forms of democracy. Within Russia, although Westernisers have sought to 'Asianise' communism, this 'othering' has not been eased, as it has in every other post-Soviet society, by the additional association of communism with Russian domination. Without this resource, Westernisation can easily be connoted as the anti-patriotic and craven ideology of a new capitalist elite.[16] It also makes Westernisers vulnerable to the charge of being dismissive of Russian history and popular sentiment (see, for example, Krivorotov, 1990; Novikov, 1991; also Pozdnyakov, 1991). Indeed, anti-Western nationalists in Russia are able to be simultaneously populist and have a sophisticated grasp on the hollowness of attempts to conflate the West with modernity. It is, then, unfortunate but unsurprising that the urgent task of questioning and deconstructing the West in Russia has, in large measure, fallen into the hands of isolationist voices. For example, it was the anti-Semitic nationalist writer Igor' Shafarevich (1989) who explained in 1989 that the Westernisers' vision of Russian being prey to 'Asiatic' authoritarianism relied on a historical misreading. More specifically, Shafarevich was able to assert that the ideological roots of totalitarianism lay in the West (he singles out the work of Hobbes) and that communist tyranny, far from reflecting an Asian presence, was a consequence of incorporation into Western culture.

As the date of Shafarevich's remarks implies, the process of Westernisation was felt and challenged by critics before the fall of the USSR. More specifically, hostility to Gorbachev's reforms was often couched in terms of their supposed Western origins and content. These reforms did, indeed, reflect a loss of faith in a distinctive vision of Soviet modernity (although this was a vision that had been extinguished long before Gorbachev came to power). Gorbachev attempted to re-orient the USSR and Russia towards western Europe. Thus Gorbachev developed the association between the 'opening-up' of the country, its democratisation, and the need for the USSR to be positioned within what he called 'Europe, our common home' (Gorbachev, 1987).

However, Gorbachev's phrase 'Europe, our common home' is also revealing for another reason. For, despite the charges of Westernisation brought against him, Gorbachev brought to an apogee Soviet leaders' attempts to differentiate Europe and the West. Maintaining the conventional geo-political rubric, he cast the West as a negative and ideological force. This association was compounded by the notion, increasingly familiar since the end of the Second World War, that the West was led by the USA. Europe, by contrast, was connoted as the natural home of Soviet citizens. This distinction contained a clear ethnic message: the West was a political device, a set of anti-communist and pro-capitalist mechanisms and prejudices (led by or associated with the USA), whilst Europe was an organic, pre-political entity. Addressing a both national and international audience in 1987, Gorbachev enthusiastically affirmed that 'Europe is our common home', protesting that:

> Some in the West are trying to 'exclude' the Soviet Union from Europe. Now and then, as if inadvertently, they equate 'Europe' with 'Western Europe'. Such ploys, however, cannot change the geographic and historical realities. Russia's trade, cultural and political links with other European nations and states have deep roots in history. We are Europeans... The history of Russia is an organic part of the great European history. (Gorbachev, 1987, p. 191)

This passage acts as a refutation of the idea that the USSR/Russia is Asian. It both 'forgets' to mention Asia and conflates the USSR with Russia. It is indicative of the way Gorbachev sought to contain the USSR's and Russia's Asian identity as either an aberration, an exotic supplement or a geo-political detail of merely strategic relevance.

Although post-Soviet Russia is still, territorially at least, predominantly an Asian country, its leadership has tended to adopt a similar stance towards the East. Asia is represented as a place to engage diplomatically and, occasionally, to economically emulate, but not as an inherent part of what Russia is. Speaking in April 2001, President Putin (cited by Traynor, 2001) noted that 'a course of integration with Europe will be one of the main directions of our foreign policy'. Moreover, whilst a distinction between 'the West' and 'Europe' continues to be employed, resistance to the West as a political entity has become increasingly redundant. For, whether or not the West is in favour amongst the leadership of the Russian Federation, it appears that the collapse of faith in communist modernity has been accompanied by an absorption of the idea that modernity equals Western modernity. Progress, rationality, enlightenment and civilisation are no longer explicitly and fervently politicised, as they were during the early and mid-Soviet period. 'There will be no more revolutions or counter-revolutions' Putin (cited by Traynor, 2001) assures his audience. The attributes of modernity are approached in a similar way to that found in most other countries, as facets of the seemingly natural and entwined processes of privitisation, democratisation, and, increasingly, economic flexibility.

The demise of communist ethno-politics entails a general withdrawal from the notion that identities are political achievements. Whereas for the early Bolsheviks the West was the inspiration for a project that acted to re-create the meaning of modernity, a project that was always as much political as it was ethnic, the emphasis now is upon the depolitisation of identity; that is, upon its return to 'normalcy'.

The 'burgeoning of racism' in the Russian Federation following the disintegration of the USSR (Roman, 2002; cf. Bahry, 2002) has often been discussed in terms of an explosion of emotions pent up by an authoritarian regime. This explanation is partly persuasive but its constant repetition has had the effect of making it difficult to note the existence of other contributing factors. One of the implications of this chapter is that the transition from ethno-politics to racism is causally related to the transition from communism to capitalism. If we accept this idea we are inevitably led to two others. First, that contemporary racism in Russia is not a re-animated genetic strain released from the Stalinist permafrost, nor is likely to die out if and when the country grows increasingly Western. Secondly, that, in terms of its adverse impacts on people's lives, racism in Russia is not necessarily worse than communist ethno-politics: to politicise people's lives can be just as devastating as racialising them.

Conclusions

Although often cast as a rhetorical device of the Brezhnev era, the notion of 'Soviet man' encapsulates the ambitions of the Bolshevik ethno-political project. It was the goal of the October revolutionaries to produce a new human type, a confidant and committed communist worker who could rise above pre-modern or bourgeois loyalties to locality or community. Yet, as we have seen, the creation of 'Soviet man' was itself an ethnicised and ethnicising project: he was manufactured in the image of the Western and/or Russian industrial worker. This agent of progress was the talisman of modernity for party members spreading the message of modernity into the reaches of the Soviet empire.

The post-Cold War triumphalism associated with contemporary articulations of Western modernity appears to be making people increasingly forgetful of the scale of the challenge posed by the Bolshevik revolution. Communism was not merely an alternative; a parasitic off-shoot from the main branch of Euro-American capitalist hegemony. It represented a re-shaping of the meaning of modernity; a re-organisation of modernity around a new set of ideas and practices for the creation of identity. Indeed, even this depiction fails to do justice to the significance of the revolution. For the growing popularity of the idea of the West in the twentieth century is a direct reflection of the desire to organise a collective identity defined in opposition to 'communist menace'.

Ironically, whilst debate on the idea of the West has played a marginal role in Western constructions of Western modernity, it has been central to the formation of Soviet modernity. Both the Westernising and Russocentric forms of Soviet modernity discussed in this chapter relied on the idea of the West to map their pathways through communism. The West was central to the Soviet project. The early identification of the revolution as a Westernising process carried ethnocentric implications that easy to see for a world attuned to thinking about the impact of the West on 'the rest'. However, the move from pro- to anti-Westernism in the USSR, did not augur a decline in ethnocentrism, merely its transformation. Soviet anti-Westernism and Soviet colonialism developed hand-in-hand. The idea of the West, as both model and as anti-model, has been deeply involved throughout the twentieth century's patterns of prejudice.

Further reading

The West: visions of the USSR/Russia

Engerman, D. (1999) 'William Henry Chamberlin and Russia's revolt against Western civilization', *Russian History/Histoire Russe*, 26, 1, pp. 45–64.

Naarden, B. (1992) *Socialist Europe and Revolutionary Russia: Perception and Prejudice, 1848–1923*, Cambridge, Cambridge University Press.

Neumann, I. (1999) *Uses of the Other: 'The East' in European Identity Formation*, Minneapolis, University of Minnesota Press.

Wolff, L. (1994) *Inventing Eastern Europe: The Map of Civilization on the Mind of the Enlightenment*, Stanford, University of California Press.

USSR and Russia: visions of the West

Bassin, M. (1991) 'Russia between Europe and Asia: the ideological construction of geographical space', *Slavic Review*, 50, 1, pp. 1–17.

English, R. (2000) *Russia and the Idea of the West: Gorbachev, Intellectuals and the End of the Cold War*, New York, Columbia University Press.

Hart, P. (1998) 'The West', in N. Rzhevsky (ed.) *The Cambridge Companion to Modern Russian Culture*, Cambridge, Cambridge University Press.

Neumann, I. (1996) *Russia and the Idea of Europe: A Study in Identity and International Relations*, London, Routledge.

Sodaro, M. (1990) *Moscow, Germany, and the West: From Khrushchev to Gorbachev*, Ithaca, Cornell University Press.

USSR and Russia: visions of the East

Bassin, M. (1991) 'Russia between Europe and Asia: the ideological construction of geographical space', *Slavic Review*, 50, 1, pp. 1–17.

—— (1998) 'Asia', in N. Rzhevsky (ed.) *The Cambridge Companion to Modern Russian Culture*, Cambridge, Cambridge University Press.

Hauner, M. (1990) *What is Asia to Us? Russia's Asian Heartland Yesterday and Today*, Boston, Unwin Hyman.

Hirsch, F. (2000) 'Towards an empire of nations: border-making and the formation of Soviet national identities', *The Russian Review*, 59, pp. 201–226.

Diverse modernities

The last ten years or so have witnessed the discovery of non-Western modernity in Western scholarship. Indeed, the examination of 'alternative', 'multiple' or 'co-existing and co-eval' modernities has come to represent cutting-edge research in area studies, post-colonial studies and political theory. This chapter echoes the view, expressed elsewhere in this book, that modernities are best understood as co-evolving and co-existing within a global context of unequal power relations. The most sophisticated example of this thesis to date has been Harry Harootunian's

Overcome by Modernity: History, Culture and Community in Interwar Japan (2000, Princeton, Princeton University Press).

This approach can be contrasted with the 'multiple' and 'alternative' modernities perspectives. The latter posits forms of oppositional modernity working within and against Western modernity. This perspective chimes with the emphasis that post-colonial studies has come to place on the transgressive and subversive nature of the non-Western encounter with the West. Thus the 'Afro-modernity' portrayed in Michael Hanchard's essay 'Afro-modernity: temporality, politics, and the African Diaspora' (1999, *Public Culture*, 11, 1, pp. 245–268) and in Paul Gilroy's *The Black Atlantic: Modernity and Double Consciousness* (1993, London, Verso) is a countercultural phenomenon, a product of African agency operating through but in opposition to a hegemonic Western modernity.

'Multiple modernities' perspectives also see the West as the normative site of production for modernity. However, the additional claim that distinct 'civilisations' have distinct religious cores (cores which provoke dissimilar pathways through modernity) provokes a very different research agenda. See Shmuel Eisenstadt's *Fundamentalism, Sectarianism, and Revolution: the Jacobin Dimension of Modernity* (1999, Cambridge, Cambridge University Press). It is interesting to note, in passing, that whilst the notion of 'alternative modernities' is allied to the academic left, 'multiple modernities' has strong links to business strategy research. See Sachsenmaier, Riedel and Eisenstadt's *Reflections on Multiple Modernities* (2002, Brill, Leiden).

The preoccupations of the 'multiple modernities' school have echoes with a variety of recent and influential calls to question the link between modernity and Westernisation. The idea that 'civilisation' is a useful category of analysis and that civilisations have religious cores, combined with a critique of the West's claims on modernity, are all central to Samuel Huntingdon's *The Clash of Civilisations* (1997, London, Simon & Schuster). A possible correlation between the rise to public prominence of this kind of thinking and the emergence of a 'post-September 11' geo-political sensibility, is suggested by later, polemical, interventions, such as Roger Scruton's *The West and the Rest* (2002, London, Continuum), and John Gray's *Al Qaeda and What it Means to be Modern* (2003, London, Faber & Faber). For both the conservative (Scruton) and the liberal intellectual (Gray), it is time the West moved beyond its traditional, jealous, claim on the ownership of modernity.

Chapter 3

Good-bye Asia: The Westernisers' West, Fukuzawa and Gökalp

Introduction

'Westerniser' is rarely used as a compliment. It smacks of slavish imitation, of wishing to replace indigenous society with an illegitimate import. Westernisers are associated with a passive, uncritical enthusiasm. Conversely, to be critical of the West appears more active, more engaged, more independent.

This chapter takes issue with these stereotypes. It offers a portrait of Westernisers as deploying and employing their own vision of the West not in order to submit to the authority of the West but in order to preserve national autonomy.

I will be drawing on the work of Japanese and Turkish nationalist intellectuals from the late nineteenth and early twentieth centuries in order to understand the development and deployment of the idea of the West within 'non-Western' national identities. The notion that two such distant nations could be brought into the same frame of analysis may strike a discordant note to some, especially to those who have grown used to the heavily policed demarcations of contemporary area studies. It may be of interest to mention, therefore, that the comparison of Turkey and Japan as Westernising states was once reasonably common (Bellah, 1958; Ward and Rustow, 1964). Moreover, reformers in late nineteenth- and early twentieth-century Japan and Turkey made the same comparison (for example, Fukuzawa, 1973; Gökalp, 1981). Within the Turkish Union and Progress movement, for example, the idea that a 'non-Western', non-Christian, country could enter and be accepted within the arena of Western civilisation was seen to have been evidenced by Japan's 'rapid rise'.[1]

However, whilst wishing to defend the possibility of comparing Japan and Turkey, the present chapter does not attempt anything quite so ambitious. I will not be claiming to provide a representative survey of national opinion but, rather, focusing on two individuals. They are the Japanese Westerniser Fukuzawa Yukichi, whose work was first published in the late nineteenth century and the Turkish nationalist and critical proponent of Westernisation, Ziya Gökalp, who was most active in the first two decades of the twentieth century. Each has some claim to be regarded as the principal interpreter of the West within their particular era and within their respective countries. However, their engagement with the relationship between nationhood, modernity and Westernisation also establishes them as figures of global importance. Certainly, the often awkward questions they raised and the fraught line they trod between nationalism and anti-colonialism, establish their political and intellectual status neither as colonial imitators nor resisters, but as something more complex and original.

Aside from the general assertion of the importance and value of analysing the employment of the idea of the West by Westernisers, I shall be developing another argument. For the relation between 'non-West' and West is not staged simply or purely in the form of a binary opposition by the two intellectuals discussed here. Both my case studies evince the centrality of other categories that shape and sustain the stereotyping of the West. In particular, both Fukuzawa and Gökalp deploy a form of orientalism in which Asia is cast as a separate and primitive realm, to be distinguished from both the West and their own nations.

The uses of the West

Vigorous debates about the meaning of the West, and whether Westernisation was a good or bad thing, were going on in Turkey and Japan, well before the idea of the West was at the centre of debate in Western Europe. Throughout the world there are certain clichés about the West that have come to play an important role in the formation of national and pan-national 'non-Western' identities. The supposed individualism and materialism of the West, along with its secular and instrumental culture, are some of the better-known characteristics identified in almost every corner of the globe. Using the capitalised term 'Civilisation' as a synonym for the West, and lower case 'civilisation' to denote other, non-hegemonic, traditions, Prasenjit Duara makes the following observation of the 'basic' use of the West in Asia:

> The basic approach involves combining elements that are a) identical to and b) the binary opposite of the constituents of Civilization. One strategy is to rediscover elements identical to Civilized society within the suppressed

traditions of civilization: Confucian rationality, Buddhist humanism, Hindu logic, and so on. Another strategy identifies the opposite of the West in Asian civilization: 'peaceful' as opposed to 'warlike', 'spiritual' as opposed to 'material', 'ethical' as opposed to 'decadent', 'natural' as opposed to 'rational', 'timeless' as opposed to 'temporal', and more. Finally, the nation authorizes its opposition to imperialist Civilization by synthesizing or harmonizing the binaries after the equivalence has been established. Thus Western materialism will be balanced by Eastern spirituality and modernity redeemed (Duara, 2001, p. 108).

Duara is arguing for an appreciation of the dialectics of modern regional identities. This model usefully highlights the interaction of conflicting visions of the West. However, dialectics has its own momentum, one that tends to obscure the jagged and unresolvable nature of different representations of the West.

More specifically, Duara's approach neglects the utility of different representations of the West for different social groups. What may be functional to the sustainability of the national unit is not necessarily an appropriate focus in the context of social and political struggle over the idea of the West, struggle that is unlikely to produce a clear synthesis.

A similar point may be made about attempts to frame non-Western uses of the West within the terminology of hybridity. Like dialectics, hybridity is a model with its own logical momentum. It suggests the mating of two distinct stocks to create a partially original third form.[2] The implication that the interweaving of West and non-West creates, not a synthesis, but a site of creation and tension may be of value and is, in part, sustained by the two case studies introduced here. However, I will not be labelling either Fukuzawa or Gökalp as hybrid thinkers. Such a categorisation would mislead by insinuating that, relative to Western intellectuals, these men were imitative thinkers. It would also encourage an unhelpful *a priori* politicisation of their work, implying that what is most interesting about Fukuzawa and Gökalp is their role as cultural emancipators and transgressors. In this way, the social and political particularities that need to be understood in order to make sense of Fukuzawa and Gökalp would be displaced by a flattening and homogenising emphasis on the achievement of hybridity. In fact, as we shall see, far from producing a liberatory 'third space', the uses of the West considered here encouraged the production and naturalisation of ethnic stereotypes and nationalist authority.

Sun Ge has helped refocus debates on orientalism onto the Asian use of ideas of East and West. 'In the hands of the Asians' she notes,

Orientalism 'it is not positioned against the Western world from the perspective of the East, but rather against an image of the West constructed in Asia' (Sun, 2000b, p. 14). What is being described by Sun is not al-'Azm's (1981, p. 19) 'orientalism in reverse', in which Easterners succumb to 'the dangers and temptations of applying the readily available [i.e. Western] structures, styles and ontological biases of Orientalism upon themselves and upon others'. [3] Sun's analysis does not posit, empirically or theoretically, either orientalism or occidentalism as inherently Western devices. A similar contrast may also be drawn with Chatterjee's (1986) insistence upon the 'inherent contradictoriness in nationalist thinking' in post-colonial contexts between the adoption and refutation of Western orientalism. Both Chatterjee and al-'Azm assume a primacy and determining power for Western conceptions of itself and its others. Sun's point – which is endorsed in the following case study – is that 'the West' can be seen as having multiple sites of creation: there is no ur-text of either occidentalism or orientalism.

Fukuzawa Yukichi: occidentalism and nationalism in Japan

Fukuzawa Yukichi (1834–1901) is the most well known and influential of the nineteenth-century Japanese Westernisers.[4] Born in 1834, as a child Fukuzawa studied *rangaku* (Dutch learning) at a school in Nagasaki, at a time when the Dutch were the only Westerners allowed even limited entry into the country. In 1862 he was part of the Takenouchi mission to the West, the first of a series of official Japanese investigations of Western society, industry and economic development. His glowing account of what he saw was published in 1866 ('Conditions in the West', 1958) and became an immediate best-seller. Fukuzawa later wrote the primary school textbook, World Geography (1959, first published 1869), which drew on similar material and explicitly placed Europe at the centre of world civilisation.

One indication of Fukuzawa's influence is that between 1866 and 1878 all nine of the best-selling books in Japan were either Western translations or about the West, and that the latter were popularly referred to as 'Fukuzawa books'. Fukuzawa is also credited with writing 'a crucial text that marks the beginning of modern thinking in Japan' (Sakamoto, 1996, p. 116). This work is *An Outline of a Theory of Civilisation*. It was published in 1875 (Fukuzawa, 1973; see also Fukuzawa, 1934, 1969, 1985, 1988) and is Fukuzawa's most substantial intervention on the nature and meaning of the West.

In *An Outline of a Theory of Civilisation* Fukuzawa identifies the West with civilisation and suggests that Japan must re-invent itself as Western for the sake of its own future. His message was uncompromising: merely copying the exterior or superficial aspects of Western civilisation was not enough.

> [W]e must not import only the outward forms of civilization, but must first make the spirit of civilization ours and only then adopt its external forms...The cornerstone of modern civilization will be laid only when national sentiment has thus been revolutionized, and government institutions with it. When that is done, the foundations of civilization will be laid, and the outward forms of material civilization will follow in accord with a natural process without special effort on our part, will come without our asking, will be acquired without our seeking. This is why I say that we should give priority to the more difficult side of assimilating European civilization. We should reform men's minds, then turn to government decrees, and only in the end go out to external things (Fukuzawa, 1973, pp. 17–18).

As this passage suggests, the survival of Japanese traditional culture was of little significance to Fukuzawa. This is not because he regarded 'Japaneseness' as unimportant but, rather, because, in the context of expanding and predatory Western global ambitions, he identified 'backward looking' cultures as doomed. Thus, in contrast to the far more fragile and novel sense of national identity being developed in other 'non-Western' societies (for example, by Gökalp in Turkey), Fukuzawa did not bracket off the country's 'inner spirit' as an untouchable and defining essence. The only essence he was concerned to protect was that of national independence, something that Japan had kept 'intact from earliest antiquity' (Fukuzawa, 1973, p. 27), but which was now under threat from Western imperialism and required a drastic social revolution to retain.

> Now, the only duty of the Japanese at present is to preserve Japan's national polity. For it to preserve national polity will be to preserve national sovereignty. And in order to preserve national sovereignty the intellectual powers of the people must be elevated...the first order of business in development of our intellectual powers lies in sweeping away blind attachment to past customs and adopting the spirit of Western civilization. (p. 28).

Fukuzawa argued that this process required a shift away from blind loyalty to the imperial line and a greater focus on Japan as an active national community. Within this national community the allocation of rewards and responsibilities should be a matter, not of custom or inheritance, but individual merit. The characteristic of the West that most excited Fukuzawa's enthusiasm was its open, transparent and rational system of social advance. It is an enthusiasm that draws us into consideration of the way Fukuzawa's idea of the West reflected the aspirations of a rising middle class in Japan.

Fukuzawa shared with many other, contemporaneous, Westernisers around the world, a social background of educated middle-class exasperation. In his autobiography (1934), he identifies his position 'in a family of low rank' (it was low samurai) as creating the conditions for his 'discontent' (p. 189) and 'naïve dislike of oppression' (p. 199). Indeed, Fukuzawa's constant theme in *An Outline of a Theory of Civilisation* is merit and intelligence; more specifically, the need for Japan to be run on the basis of education rather than lineage. Traditional culture is portrayed as a feudal fetter on class mobility. By contrast, Western culture is represented as both meritocratic in social structure and critical in disposition. 'If we seek the essence of Western civilisation', Fukuzawa observes, 'it lies in the fact that they scrutinise whatever they experience with the five senses, in order to discover its essence and its functions' (p. 111). Fukuzawa paints a landscape of intellectual and academic enquiry occurring 'right down to the remotest village' in the West. 'This process is repeated many times' he adds, 'in the end, a national opinion takes shape' (p. 79). Thus, for Fukuzawa, the West does not contain cleverer people but values clever people more. In Japan 'the people who felt [the need for meritocracy]

> were leading inconspicuous lives as doctors or writers, or were to be found among the samurai in this *han* or that, or among Buddhist monks and Shinto priests. All of them were learned men who could not realize their ambitions in society (p. 65).

Thus the West is used as a model for the re-distribution of power between the traditional elite and an aspirational class.

Such sentiments were to be channelled and reflected by the Westernising policies of the Meiji imperial regime.[5] As this relationship suggests, Fukuzawa was not embarked on a project of democratisation. During the nineteenth century, democracy was not closely associated with Westernisation, either in Japan or Europe. 'Progress' and 'civilisation' implied a more rational society but not necessarily a less authoritarian forms of politics. Indeed, it was clear to Fukuzawa that the West was successful, in part, because it was prepared to dominate non-civilised peoples, a habit that Fukuzawa encouraged the Japanese to emulate.

Good-bye Asia

Fukuzawa did not develop his ideas simply in terms of an opposition between Japan and the West. Although his usage was not consistent, Fukuzawa tended to cast both China and Asia as the opposites of the West whilst placing Japan as more capable of assimilating Western civilisation. Indeed, in terms of the structure of Fukuzawa's argument, China has as important a role in *An Outline of a Theory of Civilisation* as the West. It is China that is represented as static and passive; China that is cast as hopelessly archaic and vulnerable to national humiliation. Where these attributes are located in Japan they are cast as stemming from the age-old domination of Japanese culture by China.[6]

The following passage exemplifies this 'othering' of China, as well as hinting at the aggressive and nationalistic foreign policies that Fukuzawa's work was later taken to condone.

> Such phrases as 'be gentle, modest, and deferring to others', or 'rule by inaction', or 'the holy man does not have ambition'... all refer to inner states which in the West would be described as merely 'passive'... The Chinese Classics, of course do not teach only this kind of passive virtue. Some passages imply a more dynamic frame of mind. However, the spirit which breathes throughout those works stirs up in people an attitude of patient endurance and servility (Fukuzawa, 1973, p. 79).

The positioning of Japan as dynamic, as containing the seeds of social revolution, also animated another ambition in Fukuzawa, to introduce the concept of personal competition and the ideology of capitalist entrepeneuralism into Japanese society (Tamaki, 2001).

The most well-known slogan associated with Fukuzawa concerns the relation between Japan, the West and Asia. The title of his essay *Datsu-a nyu-o* (1997), first published in 1885, has been translated as 'On leaving Asia', 'Disassociating Asia' and, more simply, 'Good-bye Asia'. It suggests that Japan must now consider itself part of Western civilisation and thus 'dissociate' itself from its barbaric and doomed neighbours:

> We do not have time to wait for the enlightenment of our neighbors so that we can work together toward the development of Asia. It is better for us to leave the ranks of Asian nations and cast our lot with civilized nations of the West. As for the way of dealing with China and Korea, no special treatment is necessary just because they happen to be our neighbors. We simply follow the manner of the Westerners in knowing how to treat them. Any person who cherishes a bad friend cannot escape his notoriety. We simply erase from our minds our bad friends in Asia (Fukuzawa, 1997, p. 353).

However, this stance was not intended to suggest that Japan should cut itself off from Asia but, rather, that Japan was a nation of a different order, a higher type. Saying 'good-bye' to Asia meant, ironically, being more involved with it; not as an equal but in a similar fashion to other Western powers. This position was also developed by Fukuzawa to suggest that Japan was the natural leader and defender of weak and anarchic Asian nations against Western military might. As Sakamoto (1996) has shown, this attitude to Asia, whilst more explicit and clearly colonialist towards the end of Fukuzawa's life, was present throughout his work. He goes on to argue that Fukuzawa's work 'annuls the West/Japan dichotomy', leaving the 'civilisation/ non-civilization dichotomy' intact, and ' "Asia" [to function] as the negative Other of civilised Westernised/hybridised Japan' (p. 125). Sakamoto's real target here is the political naiveté of contemporary theories of hybridisation. He concludes that:

> the construction of a hybrid discourse, at least in Japan's case, led to the exclusion of another Other...To "go beyond" one dichotomy without creating yet another may not be an easy project (p. 126).

Clearly, Fukuzawa's work does not sustain a vision of hybridity as a kind of 'open' and reflexive third moment. In fact, I would cast doubt on the utility of conceptualising his work as an example of hybridity at all. Rather than importing or translating a ready-made idea of the West, Fukuzawa actively fashioned a certain representation of the West to suit his own (and, in large measure, his social class's) particular political ambitions. This process is best understood as a creative and original intervention in the history of the idea of the West. In this way we can position Fukuzawa alongside Kidd, Spengler and Toynbee in the West, as well as other intellectuals in the 'non-Western' world (such as Gökalp): all people engaged with the similar challenge of working out the meaning of modern national and international identities in an unequal world.

Ziya Gökalp: finding Turkey, inventing the West

> when a nation advances to the higher stages of its evolution, it finds it necessary to change its civilization too. The Japanese, for example, dropped the civilization of the Far East and took over Western civilization. A striking example in this connection is given by the Turks. The Turks have adopted three distinct and dissimilar civilizations during the course of their social evolution. When they were in the stage of ethnic-state organization, they belonged to the civilization of the Far East. When they passed to the stage

of the sultanistic state, they entered into the area of Eastern civilization. And today, in their transition to the stage of nation-state, we see the rise among them of a strong movement which is determined to accept Western civilization (Gökalp, 1981, pp. 270–271, first published 1923).

Ziya Gökalp (1876–1924) has a strong claim to be regarded as the chief ideologist of Turkey's creation as a modern nation. Gökalp began his political life as a student nationalist revolutionary. Appointed to a professorship of sociology at the University of Istanbul in 1912, he remained a key figure of Turkish nationalism. Exiled to Malta in 1918, but freed in 1921 after the nationalist victory, he was elected to the Parliament of the new Turkish republic in 1923. Perhaps best known for his poetical works, such as *Kizil Elma* (1915; The Red Apple), Gökalp had an extraordinarily diverse output. Sociology, history, poetry, fiction, autobiography were all put to work to further his central aim, the celebration of Turkish identity. Indeed, Berkes suggests that he 'laid the only plausible comprehensive cognitive map for Turkey's passage from a six-hundred year empire to a new nation-state' (Berkes, 1954, p. 375).

Gökalp's vision involved Turkey 'leaving Asia' and escaping an archaic past just as surely as Fukuzawa's involved Japan saying 'Good-bye Asia'. Indeed, in the essay cited above, which is titled 'Towards Western civilization', he tells us, rather bitterly, that 'Japan is accepted as a European power, but we are still regarded as an Asiatic nation' (1981, p. 277). Gökalp also shared with the Japanese intellectual an unsentimental appraisal of the *necessity* of Westernisation:

> We have to accept the civilization of the West, because, if we do not we shall be enslaved by the powers of the West. To master the civilization of the West, or to be mastered by the powers of the West: between these alternatives we must choose! (1981, p. 266, first published 1923).

A poet as well as an essayist, Gökalp often articulated his political thought in verse. Thus we find the same sentiment in the following lines: 'We were defeated because we were so backward, to take revenge, we shall adopt the enemy's science. We shall learn his skill, steal his methods' (cited by Heyd, 1950, p. 79).

Yet, as with Fukuzawa, Gökalp's notion of 'the West' and 'Asia' were far from being mere imports. Rather, these were categories animated and employed in the service of an attempt to create a novel political identity and national project, namely 'Turkishness'. The originality of his enterprise was even more marked in Turkey. For 'Turkishness' was not established as a national or even a clear ethnic category. It was developed with startling rapidity in the early twentieth century so as to exhibit all the attributes of modern national consciousness and to obliterate the supposedly archaic and doomed Ottoman identity. Gökalp's work represents a seminal contribution to the activities of a wider group of Turkish nationalists who, as Canefe (2002, p. 148) writes, were to go to 'great lengths to silence the Ottoman heritage of the new nation and its state in virtually every area of life, including memories of the previous demographic and cultural make-up of Asia minor'. This 'cleansing' process – both ethnic and historical – was construed as part and parcel of Turkey's establishment as a coherent, 'modern-looking' nation state.

Turkish culture, Western technique

The 'rise of the West' was understood by Gökalp to be founded on the rise of nationalism. Thus he interpreted it as sounding the death knell for 'pre-modern' multi-national, heterogeneous ideologies such as Ottomanism. 'Today the West as well as the East shows unmistakably that our age is the Age of Nations', Gökalp wrote in 1913: 'The most powerful force over the mind of this age is the ideal of nationalism' (1981, p. 72). It was a view that relied on a construction of the West that wilfully overlooked the imperial, cosmopolitan nature of Western nations (as seen, for example, in the French and British empires) and emphasised the cultural homogeneity of the modern nation state. Gökalp claimed that '[t]oday in Europe only those states which are based on a single-language group are believed to have a future' (p. 81, first published 1918). In this way, the pluralism associated with the Ottoman Empire was cast as an anachronism, a relic of Eastern civilisation. The ground was thus laid for the dramatic and forced Latinisation of the Turkish language as well as its use as the defining attribute of Turkish identity. The Turkish language could be employed as a tangible, social commonality that could enable an answer to the question that may be said to have animated Gökalp's entire project 'who is a Turk?'[7]

For Gökalp the Turks were the principal victims of the Ottoman empire; denigrated as commoners by a cosmopolitan elite. Thus the imperial successes of the Ottomans achieved little for the Turks:

> many times Turks have conquered continents. But in reality, we were the ones who were conquered. They became Hindus, Arabs, Persians, or Europeans according to the country conquered. A Turkish law and philosophy were not born…We have produced hundreds of famous poets, scientists, philosophers, but they produced their works in Arabic, Persian, Russian, and

Chinese... The Turk always sacrificed himself to others, and his own being remains incomplete (cited by Kirmaci, 1982, p. 436).

However, it is revealing that, in seeking to explain why the Ottomans were so successful, Gökalp suggests that it was because of the presence of a Turkish 'folk elite' (1981, p. 90, first published 1913) among their ranks. The notion of authentic Turkish culture as a folk or popular culture is key to Gökalp's thought and clearly differentiates him from Fukuzawa. To understand Gökalp we must appreciate that he placed considerable importance on the difference between culture and civilisation. The former was the authentic national spirit, and included such things as everyday language, customs and the creative arts; the latter was book based and offered a structure of technical and administrative practices that could encompass many different cultures. Thus Gökalp wanted Turkey to enter Western civilisation but not import Western culture. As might be imagined, this position was prone to inconsistencies. In fact, as if to excuse the charge of importing an alien civilisation, Gökalp offered a history of the West that emphasised its Turkish roots:

> Western civilization is a continuation of ancient Mediterranean civiliza-
> tion. The earliest founders of the Mediterranean civilization were Turanian
> peoples... These ancient Turks, who were attacked by Semites from
> the south and by Aryans from the north, were forced to turn temporarily
> towards the Far East. But this temporary Eastern affinity does not prove
> anything against out affinity towards Western civilization (1981, p. 267,
> first published 1923).

Despite this historical 'let-out clause', Gökalp spent considerable energy urging the identification of an utterly distinct, Turkish cultural form. This form was defined as 'not Oriental' and 'not Western' but as profound and unique. Gökalp's representation of Turkish folk culture was constructed in relation to images of the East and West. He paid particular attention to demarcating Turkish tradition from Eastern influence. The village structure of 'Arab villages' was cast as a primitive 'clan organisation', whilst 'Turkish villages are democratic communes' (1981, p. 139, first published 1923). In the area of the creative arts, Gökalp argued that the 'lifeless traditions' of the Orient (p. 264) were 'decadent', 'pessimistic': 'Over against these, are not the language of the [Turkish] people, rhythms of folk poetry, the people's aesthetic taste, folk literature, folk morality, the wisdom of the people all living traditions in general?' (1981, p. 265, first published 1923).

Gökalp instructed that the new elite of modern Turkey should be required to 'go to the people', in order to both communicate Western civilisation to them and receive Turkish culture from them. At the moment,

> [t]heir education merely serves to denationalise them. They need to compensate the shortcoming by mixing with the people, by living with them, by learning their language, by observing the way they use the vernacular, by listening to their proverbs, their traditional wit and wisdom, by noting their mode of thinking and their style of feeling (1981, p. 259, first published 1923).

It is in this way, Gökalp claims in his essay 'Towards Genius', that the West produced its men of national influence: 'Great men of genius, like Shakespeare, Rousseau, and Goethe, had acquired an education in the people' (1981, p. 264, first published 1922). This stance was also employed by Gökalp to differentiate himself from 'Westernists' who simply wanted to copy all things Western. In this regard he had as an anti-model the Westernising reforms of the Ottoman Empire in the nineteenth century (the Tanzimat, or 're-ordering', reforms, begun in 1839), as well as more contemporary modernisers. Such endeavours were doomed to fail he thought precisely because they remained unengaged with the authentic cultural life of the people.

Despite his view that socialism was a socially divisive political form and, hence, unsuitable for a united nation like Turkey, Gökalp's populist nationalism implied the possibility of a new organic relation between the government and the people and the replacement or marginalisation of traditional forms of authority. Although, the place of both Islam and the Orient in Gökalp's thought has proved controversial,[8] it is clear that he wished to dissociate Turkey from what he saw as the atrophied and elitist civilisation of the East and envisioned a modern, nationalist Turkey as demanding the strict separation of political and religious spheres. Yet, Gökalp was not anti-Islam. He saw Islam as integral to Turkish national culture and the splitting of state and religion as necessary to the survival of Islam as a vital force within Turkish culture. Gökalp's slogan 'Turkisation, Islamization, and Modernisation' (taken from his book of 1918, *Türklesmek, Islâmlasmak, Muasirlasmak*) captures this combination of forces. Although the phrase, like so much of Gökalp's thought, may be taken as an instance of hybridity, in which Western and non-Western elements come together to construct a third position, it is clear that Gökalp's position actively constructed, rather than merely mirrored, deconstructed or mixed, a series of stereotypes of self and other. As we have seen, this process established the 'Orient' (or 'East') as the most denigrated category, 'the West' as a model (but only within the technical sphere of civilisation) and 'the Turk' as an idealised ethno-national identity.

The more militantly secular currents gathering strength in Turkey towards the end of Gökalp's life (under the leadership of Mustafa Kemal) have conspired to render his vision of modernity as hesitant and politically merely 'in-between' the competing ideologies of the day. Yet Gökalp was attempting to work out a distinct version of modernity for Turkey, one that employed certain images of the East and the West rather than simply reflecting a process of Western domination. These creative and original aspects of Gökalp's thought mark out his work as an important nationalist statement of the meaning of the West.

Conclusions

'Western' has become one of the world's most ubiquitous prefixes. 'Western modernity' is commonly offered as a tautology: modernity being seen as something that the West created and then provided to, or forced on, others. The notion that the world may be divided into 'the West and the rest' sustains this interpretation. It also helps perpetuate the notion with the only significant dilemma for 'non-Western' societies is their relationship with the West. Framing this entire history of misinformation and ethnocentrism is the conceit that the West is a Western invention; that the rest of the world occupies the role of by-stander to Western effort.

A dissatisfaction with this approach has provoked a lively post-colonial debate on non-Western uses of nationalism. An interest in the paradoxes of using something 'foreign' to assert something 'indigenous' animates Chatterjee's (1986) and Tang's (1996) examination of non-Western nationalism. Tang's work on nationalism in China identifies how it both enforced 'subordination' to a European linear and Eurocentric view of modernity, whilst enabling a new Chinese national and global imagination to form, thus 'reassert[ing] space in cognitive principle' (p. 232). Thus Tang concurs with Chatterjee's point that:

> Nationalist thought, in agreeing to become 'modern', accepts the claim to university of this 'modern' framework of knowledge. Yet it also asserts the autonomous identity of national culture. It thus simultaneously rejects and accepts the dominance, both epistemic and moral, of an alien culture (1986, p. 11).

Chatterjee's and Tang's concern with ambivalence in respect to the West, a concern with being 'inside and outside' Western modernity, is of immense value. However, if one starts one's investigations with an interest in the way the idea of the West has been employed and deployed around the world, a wider sense of 'non-Western' agency also comes into focus. More specifically, the paradoxes or ironies of Fukuzawa's and Gökalp's theories come to seem less important than the utility of the West for the social and political projects they were helping to envision.

This chapter has sought to consider the way the West was made outside the West by examining its discursive uses by two, highly influential, theorists working in two countries that are still often regarded as non-Western. My principal aim has been to elucidate how and why these individuals constructed the West. However, whilst admitting the specificity of my approach precludes generalisations about Japanese or Turkish ideas of the West, it is hoped that this discussion will provide some preliminary pointers and ground-work for national and international studies of 'non-Western' representations of the West. Although I have not claimed them as 'voices for their nations', it is clear from the preceding analysis that Fukuzawa and Gökalp articulated creative and complex ways the West has been, not simply assimilated or absorbed, but actively created and deployed within specify national debates and struggles. It has also become clear that occidentalism has not occurred in isolation from the construction of other 'other' ethno-geographical stereotypes. Thus we have seen that the idea of Asia and/or the Orient was fundamental to the thinking of Fukuzawa and Gökalp, although for somewhat different reasons.

Fukuzawa and Gökalp deployed a form of orientalism in which the East is cast as a separate and primitive realm, to be distinguished from both the West and their own nations. Moreover, given the prevalence within post-colonial studies of the notion that the mixing of traditions produces forms of political consciousness somehow more critical and destabilising than the rigidities of Western colonialism, it is significant that the interpenetration of occidentalism, orientalism and nationalism described in this chapter did not produce anti-essentialist agendas. Indeed, if anything, these processes produced new and more militant nationalist and ethnic stereotypes. Fukuzawa and Gökalp were both true moderns, not only in their originality and iconoclasm but also in the ferocity of their prejudices.

Further reading

Non-Western nationalism

Many studies of global change assume that non-Western nationalism is a symptom of Westernisation which is, in turn, a simple process of cultural imposition or adoption. For example:

Latouche, S. (1996) *The Westernization of the World*, Oxford, Polity.

Von Laue, T. (1987) *The World Revolution of Westernization: the Twentieth Century in Global Perspective*, New York, Oxford University Press.

However, a more interesting starting point has been provided by postcolonial investigations of the uses of nationalism in the non-Western world. Of these the following are especially important:

Chakrabarty, D. (2000) *Provincialisng Europe: Postcolonial Thought and Historical Difference*, Princeton, Princeton University Press.

Chatterjee, P. (1986) *Nationalist Thought and the Colonial World: A Derivative Discourse*, London, Zed Books.

Harootunian, H. (2000) *Overcome by Modernity: History, Culture and Community in Interwar Japan*, Princeton, Princeton University Press.

Tang, X. (1996) *Global Space and the Nationalist Discourse of Modernity: The Historical Thinking of Liang Qichao*, Stanford, Stanford University Press.

Fukuzawa and Gökalp

The existence of a variety of Japanese sources of funding for the translation of important Japanese works means that a number of Fukuzawa's books are available in English. Although occasionally hard to find in British and American university libraries, the following are worth searching out:

Fukuzawa, Y. (1934) *The Autobiography of Fukuzawa Yukichi*, Tokyo, Hokuseido Press.

Fukuzawa, Y. (1973) *An Outline of a Theory of Civilization*, Tokyo, Sophia University Press.

Fukuzawa, Y. (1997) 'Good-bye Asia (Datsu-a), 1885', in D. Lu (ed.), *Japan: A Documentary History: The Late Tokugawa Period to the Present*, Armonk, M.E. Sharpe.

Gökalp's political thought is less widely available in translation, but an excellent compilation does exist of his most important writings:

Gökalp, Z. (1981) *Turkish Nationalism and Western Civilization*, Greenwood Press, London.

Japanese and Turkish visions of the West

Since the topic of Western influence is usually central to modern histories of Japan and Turkey, a comprehensive list of the literature concerning the relationship between Japan or Turkey and the West could easily encompass several volumes. Below, I provide a few starting points for those interested in the more specific topic of Japanese or Turkish visions of the West.

For Japan a wide-ranging introduction is Endymion Wilkinson's *Japan versus the West: Image and Reality* (1990, London, Penguin). Amongst recent valuable studies that illuminate Japanese prejudices and stereotypes about the West are:

Creighton, M. (1995) 'Imaging the other in Japanese advertising campaigns', in J. Carrier (ed.) *Occidentalism: Images of the West*, Oxford, Oxford University Press.

Dale, P. (1988) *The Myth of Japanese Uniqueness*, London, Routledge.

Hutchinson, R. (2001) 'Occidentalism and the critique of Meiji: the West in the returnee stories of Nagai Kafu', *Japan Forum*, 13, 2, pp. 195–213.

Naff, W. (1985) 'Reflections on the question of "East" and "West" from the point of view of Japan', *Comparative Civilizations Review*, 13/14, pp. 215–232.

The 'modern ambiguities' of Turkish national identity, within and against the West, are the subject of Sibyl Bozdogan and Resat Kasaba's (eds) *Rethinking Modernity and National Identity in Turkey* (1997, Seattle, University of Washington Press) and Ayse Kadioglu's paper 'The paradox of Turkish nationalism and the construction of official identity', *Middle Eastern Studies* (1996, 32, 2, pp. 1–11).

General helpful overviews of the relationship between Turkey and the West are David Barchard's *Turkey and the West* (1985, London, Routledge & Kegan Paul) and Heper Metin and Heinz Kramer's *Turkey and the West: Changing Political and Cultural Identities* (1993, London, I.B.Tauris).

Examples of the lively Turkish-language debate on the influence of the West include Niyazi Berkes's *Turk Dusununde Bati Sorunu* [The Problem of the West in Turkish Intellectual History] (1975, Ankara, Bilgi Yayinevi), Mehmet Dogan's *Batililasma Ihaneti* [The Betrayal that is Westernisation] (1986, Istanbul, Otuken Yayinlari) and Cemil Meric's *Isik Dogudan Gelir* [Light Comes from the East] (1984, Istanbul, Otuken Yayinlari).

Chapter 4

Soulless Occident/Spiritual Asia: Tagore's West

Introduction

The ideas of 'Western civilisation' and 'Western decadence' came to prominence, in Western Europe, in a sickly embrace at the turn of the nineteenth century. Surveying the various tracts on decline at this time, we often find an attitude of sophisticated cynicism. We see an intellectual community coming to equate profundity of insight with pessimism of outlook. Yet even the Great War could not remove the *complacency* that accompanied this perspective; the sense that to speak of Western decay was an act of provocation of an increasingly accepted and expected sort.

It is in the non-West that we find the most earnest and anxious accounts of the West's power to corrupt. If one wants to find depictions of Western decadence that are entirely serious, especially about the power of the West to extinguish cultures and disorient lives, than one must turn to those whose knowledge of the West is of something that came from outside, destroyed much and overturned everything. Such experiences produced a keen interest in the nature of Western civilisation, both as something to be emulated and to be resisted. We saw in the previous chapter that one response to the power of the West was to develop a grim determination to exploit its success: to use its weapons, its technology, in order to maintain independence. It is time to turn our attention to less optimistic visions of what an accommodation with the West entails.

Chapter 7 addresses those who have sought a complete rejection of the West; who appear to wish to have nothing to do with it. Inevitably, though unfortunately, the present chapter may appear to be charting a middle course, an equivocal path between Westernisation and all out resistance. It is true that many of the thinkers I will be addressing here did claim to be seeking a synthesis of East and West. However, their project is misunderstood if seen as representing merely a point in-between existing identities. Rather I take their work as a place of origin, as an act of creation.

Later in this chapter I argue against the ubiquitous assumption that the idea of Asia and, more specifically the idea of Asian spirituality, can be described as Western inventions. 'Simply put', says Palat (2002, p. 687), 'Asia's unity derives from, and derives only from, its historical and contemporary role as Europe's civilizational other'. I do not deny Western influence on the formulation of Asian unity, or that the idea of Asian spirituality developed, in part, as an inversion of Western materialism. However, none of these processes allow us to proceed to claim that the West is the original identity and that Asia is a mere alternative or parasitic off-shoot. Indeed, what we may call pro-Asian or 'Asianist' discourse shows a persistent tendency, especially in the first fifty years of the twentieth century, to define itself not as a fixed, inverted image of the West but as a mobile site of solidarity and as a transcendence of the West.

The Asian invention of Asia as a space of spirituality saw an effort to live and transcend cultural difference on an extraordinary scale. The Bengali poet and essayist Rabindranath Tagore (1861–1941) was at the forefront of this movement. Unlike most of the non-Western intellectuals discussed in this book, Tagore has a certain status, albeit very minor, within the post-colonial canon (Chakrabarty, 2000; Spivak, 2001, 2002). His role as a poet and novelist who adopted and transgressed the expectations of English literature, has allowed him to be cited as offering the kind of 'irreducible heterogeneity' (Chakrabarty, 2000, p. 178) that is so valued within this genre of commentary. Thompson (1991) and Nandy (1994) arrived at a similar judgement when they claimed Tagore as a precursor of post-modernism. However, if 'reducibility' is something to be disapproved of, then the attempt to reduce Tagore to a prototype of post-modernism should also be objected to.

In fact, the Tagore who I discuss here is not in the least post-modern. For it is not his ambivalent interventions in English literary tradition that concern me so much as his activities as a missionary for Asian unity. Tagore had a message to Asia and a mission to the world. It was a message that made contentious claims about the meaning of Asia. Yet it also offered Asian spirituality as a project in the making, something that needed to be willed into existence. Tagore's message about Asia was inseparable from his message about the West. The one defined the other. Tagore saw in the West and Westernisation an unacceptable version of modernity. Western modernity was a misguided form of modernity, Tagore argued, for it represented the despoliation of personality and individuality by an increasingly standardised and industrialised social system.

Asia is one: the West as spiritual void

We are used to the idea of Asia. So familiar, in fact, that it may be difficult to grasp the excitement and daring of the Japanese art critic, Kakuzo Okakura's (1862–1913) declaration in *The Ideals of the East* (2000, first published 1904) that 'Asia is one'.

Yet Asia is not a self-evident ethnic or physical entity. Indeed, the notion that there is some shared essence between all the different cultures of this vast and variously imagined land – or, at a more particular level, between, for example, Indian culture and Japanese culture – is an imaginative leap of startling proportions.

Tagore and Okakura claimed to detect an Asian essence in spiritual traditions that stretch across a greater portion of the continent, most notably in Buddhism. Yet to even begin naming commonalties immediately opens up the implausible nature of attempts to see Asia as a single entity. Buddhism, after all, is a minority religious current in Asia. Moreover, its absorption into regional cultures, from India to Japan, has taken very different paths. Thus any claim of contemporary solidarity based upon Buddhism becomes an act of historical retrieval, a reclamation and reinvention of a distant past. More general affinities, which might seem plausible to many Westerners, such as the idea that Asia, as a whole, is more religiously inclined than the 'secular West', are also highly dubious. Formal religious observance in the USA remains today, as it was when Tagore was alive, a far bigger part of everyday life than it is in East Asia. Indeed, the deeply rooted non-religious philosophical traditions of East Asia might make us wonder how Westerners ever managed to claim secularism as one of their defining characteristics.

We may, of course, find testament to Asian homogeneity in European orientalism: in the need that Europeans have felt to create a despotic, exotic or, indeed, enlightened 'other'. Western orientalism has a place in my account, largely because it had an impact in Asia itself, leading to 'self-orientalisation'. However, the widespread dissemination and adoption of the idea of Asia in Asia in the late nineteenth and early twentieth century was not simply a process of imposition. Indeed, to risk a generality, Asia is better understood to have been created, re-invented and re-valued by Asians themselves. The urgency behind this effort, the force that drew the region together, was not a self-evident cultural and ethnic bond but something both pressing and novel; namely the experience of domination by the West.

The rise of 'Asianist' consciousness is intimately associated with the consolidation and dissemination of stereotypes concerning what the West was like; more specifically, that the West was brutal, greedy and lacked a spiritual dimension. These concerns run throughout early self-consciously 'Asian' commentary, though they were put to use for different ends. The two most important of Asianist traditions may be categorised as 'national-political' and 'transcendental-cultural'. The former gave rise to pan-Asianism and was dominated by the ideology of nationalism. Thus, in Japan (with the rise of regional hegemonic ambitions in the early twentieth century), in China (after the revolution of 1911), and in India (with the emergence of the Greater India movement in the 1920s), the idea of 'Asia versus the West' was put to work to legitimise nationalistic regional ambitions. Although, as we shall see in the next chapter, pan-Asianism had other dimensions (both political and cultural), the persistent focus of its characteristic forms was upon the nation as the primary unit of change and modernisation. This national logic inevitably enabled the second kind of Asianist agenda mentioned, the transcendental-cultural, to appear as a more authentic and less self-serving attempt to envision Asia 'as one'.

Indeed, the association of pan-Asianism with colonialism and military power, especially in its Japanese forms, made it an object of suspicion and contempt for Tagore. He and other 'cultural Asianists' accused Asian nationalists of being just another symptom of the decadent influence of the West.

Tagore wished to resist the West through a process of education and transcendence. What cohered this enterprise was a desire to imagine Asia as possessing both a soul and a mind that was distinctively non-Western. Tagore's endeavour offered a vision of the West as a single civilisation defined by its technical achievements but also, and more profoundly, by its lack of a spiritual dimension. Tagore understood the 'spiritual' to refer to an open, meditative form of consciousness, a rejection of merely instrumental thinking and a sense of the transcendental potential and importance of individuals' unique experiences of existence. As this implies, Tagore was far less concerned with the absence of formal religion in the West than with a wider sense of how and why human life is valued.

The Ideals of the East

Okakura's *The Ideals of the East* is the classic statement of Asian unity. The first paragraph paints an epic scene. With bold, sweeping gestures the author reveals the grandeur of Asia:

Asia is one. The Himalayas divide, only to accentuate, two mighty civilisations, the Chinese with its communism of Confucius, and the Indian with
its individualism of the Vedas. But not even the snowy barriers can interrupt
for one moment that broad expanse of love for the Ultimate and Universal,
which is the common thought-inheritance of every Asiatic race, enabling
them to produce all the great religions of the world, and distinguishing them
from those Maritime peoples of the Mediterranean and the Baltic, who love
to dwell on the Particular, and to search out the means, not the end, of life
(2000, p. 1, first published 1904).

Paying homage after Okakura's death in 1913, Tagore said, 'from
him we first came to know that there was such a thing as an Asiatic
mind' (cited by Hay, 1970, p. 38). Yet, although the paragraph from
The Ideals of the East provided above has a majestic quality, it cannot be
said to ring true. Okakura says 'Asia in one', only to show why it might
be better seen as two. Moreover, the connecting theme he identifies
('that broad expanse of love for the Ultimate and Universal'), sits
uneasily with his definition of Chinese civilisation as Confucian, a
social philosophy with limited metaphysical pretensions. In the end
though, what is of interest is not whether Okakura can or cannot prove
that 'Asia is one', but his *effort to do so*; the desire and the need to see
shared patterns and find a space of solidarity.

The Ideals of the East was written in English, between 1901 and
1902, during Okakura's visit to India. Although Okakura travelled
extensively in Bengal, he spent much of his time as a guest in the Tagore
family mansion in Calcutta. Surendranath Tagore, the poet's nephew,
later described the atmosphere that surrounded the meeting of the
Japanese art critic and Tagore's circle as one of incredible excitement.
During 'wildly exhilarating evenings' (cited by Hay, 1970, p. 41) the
meaning and consequences of Western dominance and Asian identity
were formulated into a newly assertive ideology of East–West relations.
Indeed, a certain clamour of voices can be detected in Okakura's book,
especially in respect to the value that is placed upon India, China and
Japan as centres of Asian culture. The creaking quality and connective
leaps that characterise *The Ideals of the East* evidence Asia under
construction; it is an entity that has not quite passed into easy cliché.

The most glaring strain, the one that stands out rather grimly a hundred
years later and that made Okakura's work so vulnerable to Japanese
imperialist exploitation, concerns the privileged role that Okakura awards
to Japan. The book's subtitle, *With Special Reference to the Art of Japan*,
suggests that that country will be used for the purpose of illustration.
Yet Japan is not offered merely as an example but as a higher type,

a national personification of the utterly non-Western and, thereby, authentically Asian. The unconquered nature of the Japanese race is used to verify this status.

> The rock of our race pride and organic union has stood firm throughout the ages...The national genius has never been overwhelmed. Imitation has never taken the place of a free creativeness. There has always been abundant energy for the acceptance and re-application of the influence received, however massive. It is the glory of Continental Asia that her touch upon Japan has made always for new life and inspiration: it is the sacred honour of the race of Ama to hold itself invincible, not in some mere political sense alone, but still more and more profoundly, as a living spirit of Freedom, in life, and thought, and art (2000, pp. 19–20).

Japanese cultural mastery in Asia is secured, according to Okakura, by the fact that his country remains undominated, feeding from but unbowed by outside influence. There is no imperial intent in Okakura's patriotism, no desire to see Japan intervene to protect its neighbours for the sake of Asian independence. Nevertheless, *The Ideals of the East* exposes one of the central contradictions of the Asian ideal: that within a colonised landscape there emerges a hierarchy of authenticity, with distance from the West being used as a yard-stick by which cultural authority may be measured.

Dead monotony: the nationalist and urban West

Tagore confronted and, in part, resolved the dilemma of competing, national claims to authenticity by maintaining a highly suspicious attitude to the process of nation building. 'In the modern world' he wrote, 'the fight is going on between the living spirit of the people and the methods of nation-organising' (Tagore, 1922, p. 143). The West, said Tagore, was dominated by the 'Cult of the Nation', a cult which destroys human personality and enforces a narrow and selfish relationship between people. Tagore described this process as 'the professionalism [i.e. professionalisation] of the people' (p. 146).

For Tagore, the West was a mechanical, officious civilisation, the antithesis of the organic culture found within Asia. This distinction mapped onto another: the West was essentially urban, and spread itself around the world by way of urbanisation. Authentic Asia, by contrast, was to be found, not in any particular nation, but in the countryside. '[D]ead monotony is the sign of the Nation. 'The modern towns, Tagore wrote in *Creative Unity* (1922, p. 144), are everywhere the same, from San Francisco to London, from London to Tokyo. They show no faces, but merely masks.' It was a theme that Tagore returned to on several occasions, denouncing, as below in 1924, the Western relationship between town and country that he saw spreading throughout Asia:

> unlike a living heart, these cities imprison and kill the blood and create poison centres filled with the accumulation of death...The reckless waste of humanity which ambition produces, is best seen in the villages, where the light of life is being dimmed, the joy of existence dulled, the natural threads of social communion snapped very day (Tagore, 1924, p. 221–225).

Tagore cast Asia as a community of tradition that could and should modernise on its own terms. This also implied a vision of Asia as united by its status as a victim of Western modernisation, as a site of solidarity for those oppressed by inhuman versions of the modern. The humiliations of domination thus enabled a kind of resistance. In *Nationalism* (1991, p. 75, first published 1917) he advises 'we of the no nations of the world, whose heads have been bowed to the dust, will know that this dust is more sacred than the bricks which build the pride of power'. Thus Tagore gives a spiritual value to abasement: to be forced into humility, to be reduced to nothing, takes Asia nearer to the sacred and further away from the West.

This line of thinking put Tagore on a collision course with the muscular defiance of pan-Asian nationalists. For many pan-Asianists, Japan's victory in the Russo–Japanese war (1904–1905) was a source of immense pride. By contrast, Tagore was scornful of the way Japan had dramatically 'proved itself' by virtue of its military might. In one of the angriest passages in *Nationalism*, he argues that:

> the western nations felt no respect for [Japan] till she proved that the bloodhounds of Satan are not only bred in the kennels of Europe but can also be domesticated in Japan and fed with man's miseries. They admit Japan's equality with themselves, only when they know that Japan also possesses the key to open the floodgate of hell-fire upon the fair earth whenever she chooses (pp. 39–40).

It was Tagore's near contemporary, Muhammad Iqbal who was to offer, perhaps, the most memorable image of Western militarism as seen from Asia. In 1899, Tagore (1966, p. 234) had written that 'The last sun of the century sets amidst the blood-red clouds of the West.' But with the Great War an accomplished fact, Iqbal injected a telling note of simple horror: 'That is not the rosy dawn of a new age on the horizon of the West, but a torrent of blood' (1955, see also Siddiqi, 1956).

The West: not creative and not free

Tagore was not an anti-Westerner. His books swarm with fond images
of the English romantic poets and he was keenly alert to the utility of
science and technology in the alleviation of poverty and oppression.
Indeed, his reformist, conciliatory approach made him vulnerable
throughout his life to accusations of being a Westerniser. Yet, however
much Tagore protested his faith in a 'creative unity' of East and West,
his dialectical logic was constantly interrupted by the stereotype of the
West he had worked so hard to develop. What I mean by this is that,
because Tagore's West was a place of instrumentalism and soulless
anomie, it was also a place quite unsuitable for 'creative unity'. It was a
civilisation that did not want real contact with others and that was, at
root, inherently destructive. Citing the British trade in opium in China
as an example, Tagore noted that:

> The dominant collective idea of the Western countries is not creative. It is
> ready to enslave or kill individuals, to drug a great people with soul-killing
> poison, darkening their whole future with the black mist of stupefaction,
> and emasculating entire races of men to the utmost degree of helplessness.
> It is wholly wanting in spiritual power to balance and harmonise; it lacks
> the sense of the great personality of man (1991, p. 99).

Thus, Tagore roots the rise of mechanical and instrumental thinking
in the West's hostile and destructive culture. The West, he says, is
trapped by a vision of the 'perpetual conflict of good and evil, which
has no reconciliation' (1991, p. 47).

As this portrayal of the West suggests, Tagore, who travelled extensively and for long periods in both Europe and the USA, was cynical
about the claims he heard there about the value Westerners' placed on
personal freedom. In a open letter from New York, published in 1922,
he writes that 'In my recent travels in the West I have felt that out
there freedom as an idea has become feeble and ineffectual' (Tagore,
1922, p. 133). What Tagore saw in the West was not freedom but a
'spirit of repression and coercion', driven by the industrialisation of
social relations and the 'immense power of money' (p. 136). Tagore
was also clear that, as freedom had diminished, the personality and
individuality of Westerners has become superficial and vulnerable to
political manipulation:

> Man as a person has his individuality, which is the field where his sprit has
> its freedom to express itself and grow. The professional man carries a rigid
> crust around him which has little variation and hardly any elasticity. This

professionalism is the region where men specialise their knowledge and organise their power, mercilessly elbowing each other in their struggle to come to the front (1922, p. 145).

Tagore associated true freedom with the possibility of individual and social creativity, a process that he identified in the Asian relationship to the spiritual. Although critical of many areas where freedom and individual development are stymied in the East, he cites Buddhism and the epic poem of Hinduism, the Mahabharata, as an illustration of the possibilities of free expression:

> [the] great epic of the soul of our people – the Mahabharata – gives us a wonderful vision of an overflowing life, full of freedom of enquiry and experiment. When the age of the Buddha came, humanity was stirred in our country to its uttermost depth. The freedom of mind which it produced expressed itself in a wealth of creation, spreading everywhere in its richness over the continent of Asia (1922, p. 137).

Many contemporary readers of *Creative Unity* (1922) will notice that Tagore's concern with free expression breaks down when he addresses gender relations. Whilst admitting that this has become an important area in which Western culture claims and demonstrates a concern for human liberation, Tagore's response is to retreat into a series of explanations of why 'Woman has to be ready to suffer' (p. 168). It is both fascinating and depressing to observe how Tagore stretches his idea of freedom to accommodate the subjugation of woman. Mocking 'that an increasing number of women in the West are ready to assert their difference from men is unimportant', he contends that this phenomenon is a by-product of men being lured away from the comforts of the home by commercial enterprises and leisure pursuits. In Asia, by contrast,

> women have naturally accepted the training which imparts to their life and to their home a spirit of harmony. It is their instinct to perform their services in such a manner that these, through beauty, might be raised to the realm of grace (p. 161).

Thus, when it comes to women, freedom is not to be found in creativity or individuality but in sacrifice in the service of others: 'the Eastern woman, who is deeply aware in her heart of the sacredness of her mission, is a constant education to man' (p. 168). It is at such moments that Tagore's critique of the absence of liberty in the West suddenly shows its age and collapses. The most honest reaction is to not to deny or excuse this aspect of Tagore but to admit that he was a derivative and traditionalist thinker as well as someone with a more original project. It is the latter I am most interested in, though the question of its limitations, as we shall, has long excited his critics.

Tagore wanted to break the association, not just between freedom and Westernisation, but also between modernisation and Westernisation. 'Modernism is not in the dress of the Europeans, or in the hideous structures where their children are interned when they take their lessons' he argued, 'These are not modern but merely European' (Tagore, 1991, p. 34). 'True modernism', he continued,

> is freedom of mind, not slavery of taste. It is independence of thought and action, not tutelage under European schoolmasters. It is science, but not its wrong application in life.

As these sentiments suggest, Tagore did not romanticise poverty or cultural stasis. Yet Tagore's visionary geographical imagination was attempting to speak to and speak for a vast and diverse population. His attempts to forge a continent and identify its essence were based on presumptions about distant societies that Tagore knew less about than he did about Victorian Britain. Indeed, although Tagore was self-consciously aware of his own powerlessness in the face of the economic and military gains of the West, his project had an international intellectual reach and an ambition that parallels that of colonialism itself.

Who wants to be Asian? The failure of Tagore's mission to the East

Tagore's reception during his travels to Europe and the USA had been warm and rewarding. Tagore had been treated as an archetypal Eastern mystic, a profound figure, a man of genius to be revered and respected. W.B. Yeats one of his many literary champions, explained that the cynical West needed a natural and deep soul like Tagore:

> we fight and make money and fill our heads with politics...while Mr Tagore, like the Indian civilization itself, has been content to discover the soul and surrender himself to spontaneity (Yeats, 1913, p. xx).

Tagore found himself becoming a minor publishing sensation. The publisher's appendix of the first edition of *Creative Unity*, which appeared in London in 1922, lists no less than 23 other works by Tagore issued by Macmillan. Tagore won the Nobel Prize for literature in 1913 and was awarded a knighthood in 1915 (which he renounced in 1919, after the Amritsar Massacre). The West flattered Tagore; he appeared to be wanted and needed.

Yet, if the West loved Tagore, the East often appeared unconvinced by him. The difficulty of having a spiritual vision of Asia accepted *in Asia* was cruelly exposed during his lecture tours of Japan and China. Tagore made three trips to Japan (in 1916, 1924 and 1929; the most important being from 29 May to 3 September 1916) and one to China (12 April–30 May 1924). Tagore sought not just to bring a message of Asian spirituality and cultural solidarity but to enter into a relationship of mutual trust with other Asians. Yet these were, in many ways, misjudged visits. Indeed, the accounts of Tagore's progress are painful reading. They also make it clear that the meaning of the West and of Asia was a site of conflict, riven by claims and counter claims concerning political direction and cultural authenticity.

In China, and more especially in Japan, Tagore did find enthusiastic individual followers and a receptive wider audience. Indeed, many of those who attended his lectures on the meaning and spirit of Asia appeared to have some sympathy with his desire to transcend the confrontational nature of political debate apparent in both countries. However, the fact that there existed a mismatch between Tagore's vision of West and East with the kind of expectations and hopes that were being fuelled by the rise of nationalism and militarism in Japan and China, ensured that much of this sympathy had a wistful and patronising edge . The Japanese publisher Kuroiwa Shuroku commented that:

> Tagore's thought is a kind of resignationism . . . we must have entertainment from time to time, and Tagore's thought is like a refreshing drink. I suppose this is why it is so accepted by the Europeans, who are very busy (cited by Hay, 1970, p. 87).

Tagore's first lecture tour to Japan in 1916 aimed to bring both a message of Asian unity and exalt Japan as a prime example of what Asian culture could achieve. However, even before his trip Tagore had doubts about the country. Writing from Yokohama to his lifelong corespondent and intimate, the English painter William Rothenstein, he explained that he 'fully expected to find here one monotonous mist of the Modern' (Tagore, in Lago, 1972, p. 231). After his trip to Japan, Tagore set out other apprehensions concerning its Westernisation. 'What is dangerous for Japan', Tagore wrote, 'is not the imitation of the outward features of the West, but the acceptance of the motive force of western nationalism as her own' (1991, p. 36) . Indeed, in his letter to Rothenstein, Tagore is clearly beginning to think that, far from being the acme of Asianess, Japan is far less Asian than India or China. More specifically, he claims that Japanese culture lacks depth and that it is this very shallowness that makes it vulnerable to an unthinking replication of Western forms. The 'genius' of the Japanese, he says,

> has taken the course of the definite – they revel in the rhythm of proportion in lines and movements. But music is lacking in them and the deeper currents of poetry which deals with the ineffable. They have acquired a perfect sense of the form at some cost of the sense of the spirit. Their nature is solely aesthetic and not spiritual (in Lago, 1972, p. 232).

It may be wondered how and why Tagore persisted with his 'mission to Asia' in the light of such a dismissal. The answer, at least in part, takes us back to the fact that the development of an Asian ideal appeared to Tagore a vital task in the face of the onslaught of Westernisation: it was not a dilettantish flight of fancy but a necessary struggle against the odds. Moreover, this struggle was not just with Westernisation but with other, competing, interpretations of Asia and Asian unity.

Within Japan there was disappointment amongst nationalists that their famous visitor failed to make any clear connection between his own vision of Asia and Japanese pan-Asian ambitions. Reaction to Tagore was shaped by what was known about India. This knowledge provided nationalists with a convenient way of dismissing Tagore once it had become clear he was an unreliable ally. Thus Tagore's antipathy to nationalism was interpreted as a species of primitivism: the voice, as Tagore's loyal English follower, C.F. Andrews paraphrased it, of a 'defeated nation' (cited by Hay, 1970, p. 72). The prevailing view of Tagore, expressed in the Japanese press and by Japanese intellectuals during and after his trip, was framed by the contention that India was a *conquered* country. Tagore's critique of the West was cast as reflecting a passive, defeatist culture, one that had been humiliated and dominated. Tagore's spiritual definition of Asia, with its attendant emphasis on Western materialism, could, in turn, be dismissed a 'loser's philosophy'.

The philosopher and journalist Tanaka Odo offered some of the more trenchant attacks on Tagore's mission. In the September 1916 issue of the 'The Central Review', a leading Japanese monthly magazine, he wrote: 'I regret to say this to the propagandist of transcendentalism, but the worst thing for India is the very existence of transcendentalism' (cited by Hay, 1970, p. 109). The next month an even more hard-hitting article by Tanaka appeared. In 'Tagore came, and then went' in 'New

Opinion', Tagore is called a representative of a 'ruined country' who has failed to understand either Japan or the West.

> When he discussed our country's past, he overestimated the influence of Buddhism; and when he discussed our country's present condition, he expressed his abhorrence of European influence without sufficient reason... From the standpoint of modern civilisation or modern life, my opinion is based on deeper needs than is Tagore's... We are living in the midst of modern civilisation, which we cannot neglect or avoid, and we are living more freely and more fully than Indian people. Tagore's visit has been a failure because he had neither understood these things, nor did the Japanese who welcomed him help him to see the true nature of Japan's modern civilisation... We parted from one another without any spiritual contact in the true sense of the term. We were disappointed with Mr. Tagore, but I think he was even more disappointed with the Japanese (Tanaka, cited by Hay, 1970, p. 110).

Despite the criticism he received in Japan, Tagore remained convinced that a non-imperial, non-national sense of Asian solidarity could and must be formed. Indeed, it was in Japan that he had the idea to establish a World University, an international centre for research and cultural exchange that would grow out of the school at Santiniketan, in Bengal, that Tagore had started (these ambitions led to Visva-Bharati University, founded in 1921). Spelling out the aims of such an institution, Tagore wrote:

> To bring into more intimate relation with one another through patient study and research, the different cultures of the East on the basis of their underlying unity. To approach the West from the standpoint of such a unity of the life and thought of Asia (in Chakarabarti, 1990, p. 175).

Thus Tagore remained an enthusiastic missionary from the East and to the East when he went to China in 1924. Yet this trip was even more bruising than his journey to Japan. In large measure this was because Tagore was quickly identified by the newly emergent communist movement as the embodiment of reaction. Influenced by the early Bolsheviks and regarding Soviet Russia as a Western country, these communist critics saw the West as the natural centre of radicalism and progress.[1] This revalourisation of the West existed alongside and in relationship to more familiar ideas of the West as a home for imperialism and aggression. Hay explains that:

> The West, for... young Chinese intellectuals in 1924, was no longer one, but two: the old West of Britain, France, and the United States, and the new world of Bolshevik Russia, where revolution was said to be solving

what seemed to be social, political, and military problems similar to China's. Tagore appealed to China's youth to save the spirituality of the East from the materialism of the West. They replied in effect that spirituality had so enfeebled India that she had been conquered by the old West, and that to save China from a similar fate after they were importing materialist doctrines from the new West, the Soviet Union (1970, p. 245).

Shen Tse-min, a leading communist in Shanghai, was as clear as Tagore that there existed an East/West cultural divide. However, as a revolutionary, his loyalties were firmly with the West and against 'the Hindu' who he felt to be the personification of Eastern passivity. 'Western themes of development are based on energy', Shen wrote:

> If we were to listen to Tagore's doctrine we would be completely colonised. What we need is exactly the opposite of that doctrine. Resist! Fight until we bled!... We want none of Mr. Tagore's 'Eastern civilisation' (cited by Hay, 1970, p. 240).

The novelist Shen Yen-ping, also a man of the left, took a more condescending approach. In response to Tagore's vision of Asian spirituality he stated:

> This interests me – I, an Oriental, born and grown up in China – for (shall I admit it?) I don't know what Oriental civilisation is. I have searched in vain through books, Chinese and foreign, to learn what it is. I have read the works of Mr. Tagore, especially the lectures he gave in Germany. I said to myself that a man who comes to China expressly to preach Oriental civilisation will inform me better than anyone else could concerning the nature of this civilisation. Therefore I have carefully followed the reports of his lectures in Shanghai, Peking, and elsewhere... and still I don't know what Oriental civilisation is... Now, in all the documents I have found nothing but a poet's sleight-of-hand. Thus I am disappointed and unhappy as can be. Just a little more of this, and I will be ready to believe that this man is a swindler (cited by Hay, 1970, p. 201).

Tagore was also attacked by conservatives. Within this group, the *derivative* nature of Tagore's ideas provided a focus for criticism. The philosopher Wu Chih-hui pointed out that the Bengali's message was a mere echo of the well-known Chinese interpretation of Western civilisation developed by the nationalist statesman Liang Ch'i-ch'ao a few years earlier. As Hay has shown, this comparison was flawed. Whilst Liang was concerned with propagating a broad appreciation of the richness of Chinese civilisation in China, his was not an 'Asianist' or essentially spiritual project. This suggests that the fact that Tagore could be dismissed in such terms does not illustrate the derivative nature of his ideas but, rather, a desire not to take them seriously, a willingness to misrecognise Tagore's doctrine as something familiar and stale. More specifically, it highlights how certain resemblances with existing, familiar narratives of East and West, were alighted on to pigeon-hole and attack Tagore.

Moreover, the abuse meted out to Tagore by Wu, and other Chinese contemporaries of left and right, with its attention to the archaic, primitive and slave-like condition of India, indicates that this was, in part, a racial and racist discourse of derision. It is striking that, even though Wu points to the similarity between Tagore and Liang, a fellow nationalist who he clearly admires ('our great man of letters, Liang Ch'i-ch'ao'), his attitude to the former is one of bilious contempt. 'Mr Tagore', snarled Wu, is nothing but 'a petrified fossil of India's national past' and 'has retreated into the tearful eyes and dripping noses of the slave people of a conquered country'. His advice to Tagore was as follows:

> Please have your honourable mouth sealed up tightly. This interpretation of Eastern and Western civilisation is as shallow and ridiculous as a blind man's babbling (cited by Hay, 1970, p. 218).

From a more isolated camp, the arch-conservative writer Ku Hung-ming – who flaunted his attachment to the aristocratic ideal by maintaining his queue (a symbol of loyalty to the monarchy) – found the very idea of identifying China as an Oriental civilisation both inaccurate and unacceptable. China is 'not an Oriental civilisation like the civilisation of India and Persia' he complained. What Tagore cast as uniting China and India, namely Buddhism, was condemned by Ku as a cancerous and alien invasion. Buddhism had pushed and insinuated its way into China from India, he maintained, subverting the true spirit of the Han. Ku's analysis comprehensively turned the tables on both Tagore and the West. Positioning India as the home of irrationalism, he proceeded to align it with the West, noting:

> when the modern West once gets itself free from Mediaevalism, it will have the same civilisation as China...a civilisation of rationalism and science...if we really want to make progress, instead of reviving, we must get rid of this Oriental civilisation (cited by Hay, 1970, p. 206).

After his East Asian tours, Tagore concluded that East Asia was not spiritual, at least not in the way he had originally envisaged. In 1927, during a stay in Singapore, he admitted that:

the Philosophy of China... offers no stimulant of spiritual emotionalism, but is sanely practical, and sensitively mindful of the influence of human conduct upon its social surrounding (cited by Hay, 1970, p. 323).

Tagore's attitude to spirituality was anti-dogmatic and highly elastic, so it is unsurprising that this reappraisal of the Chinese attitude to life did not extinguish his vision of a spiritual Asia. However, it certainly stands in stark contrast to the reverence for the soulful Far East he had before he went there.

Tagore's attempt to bring the message of Asian spirituality to Japan and China, at a time when the political conditions in these countries offered stony ground for affirmations of peace and love, was unquestionably brave, but also naïve and, perhaps, arrogant. Commenting on his negative reception, one British observer in Shanghai, noted simply that Tagore 'is too truly international to suit the present phase of acute nationalism in this country' (cited by Hay, 1970, p. 187). Ironically it seems to have been this very internationalism, that encouraged many of those who came to listen to Tagore to (mis)recognise his depictions of East and West as 'old-fashioned' and backward looking. The ideologies of nationalism, socialism and communism had come to establish the parameters of political debate and, within them, it was easy to overlook the originality of Tagore's vision of Asian solidarity.

Although such misunderstandings seem, in retrospect, unsurprising, Tagore was able to interpret them as yet another manifestation of a wider sickness, namely Western alienation. He saw the Westernisation of the way people understand foreigners as a process that produces exoticisation, objectification and xenophobia. Moreover, this process was globally pervasive; it had become the common sense of cross-cultural communication. Thus, as the passage below suggests, Tagore worried that Western colonialism had become the paradigm for all human contact.

> The modern age has brought the geography of the earth near to us, but made it difficult for us to come into touch with man. We go to strange lands and observe; we do not live there. We hardly meet men: but only specimens of knowledge. We are in haste to seek for general types and overlook individuals (Tagore, 1922, p. 95).

For Tagore, the development of alienated, instrumental relations between people encourages a hollow cosmopolitanism, in which people are able to travel extensively, encountering many different cultures, yet never experience any vulnerability or desire for genuine exchange. '[O]ur knowledge of foreign people grows insensitive', writes Tagore

(1922, p. 95), coming to resemble the way that 'Western people' know about other people yet 'do not recognise any obligation of kinship'. Thus, Tagore's disappointment with his travels in Japan and China was probably tempered by a sense that meeting people – not stereotypes nor stances, but people – and forming connections with them, was an increasingly hard thing to do. Moreover, he was not attempting to start a movement in either country, but something more personal. Indeed, if we are to believe his letters to William Rothenstein, we must be prepared to accept that what he really wanted was to establish a kind of soulful kinship, to make and enjoy friendships. And in this regard at least, amid all the rancour, his China trip was not wholly unsuccessful. Here and there, as a guest in someone's home or as a traveller, he found genuine acceptance and affection, and it made a lasting impression on him. A few months before he died (on 7 August 1941) and when he was too weak to write, Tagore dictated the following, on his eightieth birthday,

> Once I went to the land of China.
> Those whom I had not met
> Put the mark of friendship on my forehead,
> Calling me their own.
>
> The garb of a stranger slipped from me unknowing.
> The inner man appeared who is eternal,
> Revealing a joyous relationship, unforeseen.
>
> A Chinese name I took, dressed in Chinese clothes.
> This I know in my mind;
> Wherever I find my friend, there I am born anew.
> (Hay, 1970, p. 333).

Asian spirituality: transcending the West

It has been said many times and for many years that Asia and its associated ideals are Western inventions. This paradox was offered, with some justification, as a *provocative* insight by Tagore's Chinese and Indian critics in the 1920s. Increasingly, though, it has become a cliché; one that explains so much so neatly that it appears to be irresistible. There is much to support the contention that, as Hay has it, '[p]aradoxically the idea that Asia possessed a uniquely spiritual civilisation was essentially a Western idea' (1970, p. 51). However, the historical detail to support this position can easily slip into a few gestural points that act to confirm something many people seem to *want to believe*:

that the West created the modern world, that the West is all-powerful. In his discussion of Okakura, Leo Ching puts the point with the kind of assurance and certainty that has become characteristic:

> The principle of [Asian] identity lies outside itself, in relation to (an)Other. If one can ascribe to Asia any vague sense of unity, it is that which is excluded and objectified by the West in the service of its historical progress. Asia is, and can be one, only under the imperial eye of the West (Ching, 1998, p. 70).

The theoretical heritage behind Ching's depiction is certainly weighty. Deconstruction, psychoanalysis, existentialism, and a dichotomising theory of human identity reaching from Hegel to Mead, are all put to work on what is, essentially, a political argument. In this way, philosophical abstractions are given historical resonance, and the non-West turned into the archetypal Other. Fanon and Sartre showed us how rhetorically powerful this combination of politics and philosophy could be. Yet how accurate is it? The political merit of casting the non-West as a shadow land, a landscape of victims, is controversial enough. However, I want to argue a more specific and empirical point: that the evidence that Asia or Asian spirituality are either essentially or dominantly Western ideas is far from compelling.

First, it is pertinent to note that Hay does not empirically support the notion that Asian spirituality is, as he claims, 'essentially a Western idea'. Indeed, Hay's conscientious itemisation of the various influences on Tagore rebels against this thesis, showing a variety of sources, both Eastern and Western, for this impulse. Hay also gives due attention to the creative and original aspect of Tagore's interventions. Indeed, one could make an argument from his research that Western identity (especially the notion that the West is secular and soulless) is, in large measure, an Asian idea. However, I am not going to be pinpointing cultural essences in this section but, rather, examining in more depth the evidence concerning the pattern of influences on Tagore. This examination does not lead me to imagine that the impact of the West can, in any way, be described as minor. It does, though, draw the West's influence *into* a wider analysis of how the idea of Asian spirituality was developed through a creative process of resistance and cultural adaptation.

Inventing Asia: lineages in East and West

To stage the creation of Asia as a Western drama would certainly be tidy. Moreover, it would allow Westerners to register a political concern for 'others', whilst saving them the effort of having to look at a vast range of inaccessible sources (i.e. to study what Asians actually said and did). Less cynically, it is clear that we cannot understand Asian spirituality without reference to the way European intellectuals 'used the East' or 'made the East' as a site of control and fantasy. This line of argument often starts with etymology, calling attention to the fact that the word 'Asia' was incorporated into Asian languages as a phonetic transcription of a European term. For Palat (2000) this process is sufficient to mark Asia as a foreign myth, something 'invented', in contrast to the ur-continent of Europe.

> Unlike Latin Christendom which provided a framework through the network of churches and dynastic alliances for Western Europe, there was no similar structure to provide a common sense of identity in the other 'continents'. There is no indigenous word for Asia in any of the languages of the people living in the lands between the Straits of Bosphorous and the Pacific coasts of China. *Aija* in Japanese and *yaxiya* in Chinese are phonetic transcriptions of the European term.

In fact, as we shall see, the story of the term 'Asia' is more complex than this. 'Asia' is reported to derive from a Babylonian term referring to the rising of the sun, 'asu' (to rise) (Toynbee, 1954). It may be rooted in the East, but 'Asia' seems to have been reintroduced to Asia through its Greek form. The maps of the Italian missionary and geographer Matteo Rico are often credited with bringing 'Asia', along with other continental divisions, to China, in the sixteenth century. However, the implications of this etymology remain controversial. I shall return to the conflicting evidence later.

A more concrete line of argument supporting the Western origins of 'Asian spirituality' might examine Okakura's and Tagore's position as part of a *Westernised elite*. Both men were educated in a cosmopolitan environment highly disposed towards Western learning. Tagore was from a very wealthy, Westernised family with a tradition of working closely with the British authorities. Okakura was from a Samurai background, a class and occupational group who provided a key conduit for Western political and military ideas in Meiji Japan. Both men were affected by European romanticism, a tradition that laid great store on the ability to experience moods of profundity and revelation in the face of unmediated nature; moods which acted as a criticism of the mechanical and shallow nature of the scientific spirit.

Tagore was also greatly influenced by the dissection of 'the fundamental antagonism between Eastern and Western civilisation' described in *Letters from John Chinaman*, written by an anonymous Chinese

official and published in English in 1901. In his review of the book
Tagore wrote: 'I have seen from it that there is a deep and vast unity
among the various peoples of Asia' (cited by Hay, 1970, p. 34). Here
though is more evidence confirming 'Western influence'. For the
anonymous 'Chinese official' was, in fact, G. Lowes Dickinson, a
fellow of King's College, Cambridge, a man who had never been to
China. Dickinson's act of mimicry needs to be seen as part of a tradition
within Western European literature of writing from the position of an
exotic outsider. Montesquieu's *Persian Letters* (1973, first published
1721) is one of the earliest and better-known examples. What is
distinctive about Dickinson's contribution was its emphasis on the
spiritual qualities of the East. In this he was reflecting a contemporary
enthusiasm for Asian mysticism amongst a sizeable minority of the
Western intelligentsia.[2]

Other lines of influence include the impact of Edwin Arnold's
hugely popular epic poem *The Light of Asia*, a panegyric on the life of
Buddha, which was published in 1879. This work, along with Arnold's
version of the Hindu epic the Bhagavad Gita, impressed and inspired
Gandhi during his time spent studying law in London during 1888–1891.
On a less elevated plane, the assertion that Asia constituted a racial and
political unity, 'a comity of Asia' (1905, p. xviii), was central to
Meredith Townsend's *Asia and Europe*, which Nehru was later to cite
as one of the influences upon his political imagination.

More such general 'Western influences' could be itemised. But even
more direct evidence concerning Tagore's own intellectual circle might
seem to clinch the case. I am referring to the role of Sister Nivedita.
Sister Nivedita was the name taken by Margaret Noble, a schoolteacher
from Northern Ireland who had travelled to India, as a disciple of
Swami Vivekananda, to pursue her interests in Theosophy. Nivedita's
powerful, clear vision of Asian spirituality had its clearest impact during
Okakura's stay in India. *The Ideals of the East* was, in some measure,
the product of her efforts. Referring to the crucial opening chapter of
the book, Hay notes that 'there are good reasons to believe these were
not Okakura's words' but Sister Nivedita's (Hay, 1970, p. 40). Her
biographer asserts that she 'completely revised and rewrote' (Reymond,
1945, p. 65) *The Ideals of the East* in such a way as to appeal to a Western
audience.

Although no Westerner directed Tagore's hand, the status of his work
as Western has long been asserted by his many Indian critics. Tagore's
use of Western forms (such as the novel), Western ideologies (such as
romanticism) and, most damaging of all, his enormous popularity in

the West, have all been offered as evidence that damages, fatally, his political and cultural pretensions to be either authentically Asian or Indian. The fact that Tagore was awarded the Nobel Prize for literature in 1913 and a knighthood in 1915, have been taken to secure his inauthenticity.

> Bengal has not given Rabindranath to Europe – rather Europe has given him to the Bengalis. By praising him, European scholars praise their own gift. I would feel more proud if our own poets had received such fame in foreign countries (Dinesh Chandra Sen, 1922, cited by Chakrabarty, 2000, p. 158).

Some recent critics have been more generous. Chakrabarty and Spivak have sought to draw out the ambivalances within Tagore and position him within a wider project of questioning and 'provincialising Europe'. Moreover, Chakrabarty pointedly observes that Tagore's songs and poems remained something of a private vice amongst those on the left who publicly condemned him.

However, we can also offer a more fundamental defence, one that suggests that the evidence that Tagore's and Okakura's notion of Asian spirituality was a Western import appears conclusive only if (a) we delete an even greater weight of material suggesting Eastern influence; and (b) if we fail to understand that the West was also an idea in the process of development.

This is not merely a question of positioning Tagore through the language of cultural autonomy; as someone who managed to eke out a little non-Western agency. Rather, I take Tagore to be amongst those who actively constituted the ideas of Western soullessness and Asian solidarity and spirituality. We have already seen how he developed a vision of the West as materialist, as an industrial civilisation that 'professionalises' and depersonalises its citizens. Yet he also offered a spiritual vision of Asia, that far from being a simple replica of the Western ideal of the static, timeless East, emphasised its own provisionality and role in creating a collective identity in the face of external aggression.

Bharucha (2001, p. 153) makes the point that, for both Okakura and Tagore, '"Asia" has not yet been completely imagined. If it is "one", it is also multitudinous. Profuse in its possibilities, it also remains unknown'. Drawing out the fact that most of *The Ideals of the East* deals with Japanese and Asian art history, Yumiko Iida (1997, p. 417) adds that 'Okakura presented "Asia" as external to the marks of inferiority imposed by the West, as a category beyond the intelligibility of Eurocentric discourse'. What these contemporary analysts are suggesting is that Tagore and Okakura were not merely taking an image of the soulless West and turning it on its head to make a soulful East. Nor can they be seen as re-heating a Western caricature of Asian otherness. Their engagement with Eastern religion was creative and synthetic, drawing on Western ideas, yet largely dominated by Asian spiritual movements themselves. Moreover, theirs was an open-ended project. The privileged point of reference was Buddhism, yet they were even more interested in imagining commonalties between Buddhism's meditative practice and doctrine of 'Infinite Wisdom and Love' (Tagore, 1922, p. 72) and Indian folk religion (cohered as Hinduism). 'In both of these religions', says Tagore, 'we find man's yearning to attain the infinite worth of his individuality, not through any conventional valuation of society, but through his perfect relationship with Truth' (1922, p. 76). It is precisely the original and mobile qualities of such a vision of Asian spirituality that attracted many Western followers like Sister Nivedita. Far from importing Asian spirituality to a grateful continent, she was engaged in a dialogue with Indian, Japanese and European friends, a dialogue that was developing but also transcending the expectations and categories of both Western and Eastern tradition.

What this implies is that it is necessary to take Sister Nivedita's self-identification as a *follower* of Eastern wisdom seriously. She was a devotee of the Bengali religious leader Swami Vivekananada (1862–1902), who was in turn inspired by Sri Ramakrishna (1836–1886). After tracing the patterns of influence between Indian and Western religiosity, Peter van der Veer (2001) has concluded that Vivekananada acted as a 'translator' of Ramakrishna's more esoteric beliefs into a less particular and more modern notion of Hindu spirituality. 'Asia', Vivekananada argued, 'produces giants in spirituality just as the Occident produces giants in politics [and] giants in science' (n.d., p. 6). It was a conviction that led him to spend five years as a Hindu missionary in Europe and the USA (during 1893–1896 and 1898–1900). Arriving home as something of a national hero, Vivekananada provoked his audiences with a vision of Indian thought conquering the world. As he told one audience in Madras:

> This is the great ideal before us, and every one must be ready for it – the conquest of the whole world by India – nothing less than that . . . Let foreigners come and flood the land with their armies, never mind. Up, India, and conquer the world with your spirituality! . . . Spirituality must conquer the West. Slowly they are finding out that what they want is spirituality to preserve them as nations. They are waiting for it, they are eager for it. Where is the supply to come from? Where are the men ready to go out to

every country in the world with the messages of the great sages of India?...Such heroic workers are wanted to go abroad and help disseminate the great truths of the Vedanta. The world wants it; without it the world will be destroyed. The whole of the Western world is on a volcano which may burst tomorrow, go to pieces tomorrow. They have searched every corner of the world and have found no respite. They have drunk deep of the cup of pleasure and found it vanity. Now is the time to work so that India's spiritual ideas may penetrate deep into the West (1966, p. 100).

Vivekananada's lectures had such an impact that a number of his foreign converts were prepared to follow him back to India. His work, though, is just part of a broader tradition of Eastern involvement with, and influence on, the West. Indeed, Clarke (1997) uses the term 'oriental enlightenment' to explain how Chinese, Indian and Japanese sagacity and learning inspired intellectuals in Europe from the sixteenth century.

Far from being testament to Western creativity, European enthusiasm for the Asian ideal was, in large part, a product of both direct and indirect Eastern agency. These Asian affirmations of the continent included major figures from Bengal and Japan that shaped the cultural heritage of Tagore and Okakura. In Bengal, Rammohan Roy (1772–1833), who Tagore was to cite as a 'foundation' for his own views of East and West (Tagore, 1921), and, later, Tagore's father, Debendranath Tagore (1817–1905) and his disciple Keshub Chunder Sen (1838–1884), identified Asia as the spiritual home of humankind. In Japan, Iida (1997, p. 412) records that, as early as 1715, Arai Hakuseki had offered a 'proto-type of the notion of Asia' when he contrasted the East as 'spiritual civilisation' to the 'material civilisation' of the West. This contrast was elaborated in the nineteenth century as part of debate between pro-Westernisers, such as Fukuzawa (see Chapter 3) and his anti-Western critics.

Tagore's willingness to perform the role of venerable Eastern sage before the British and American public, should also be examined in a little more detail. The sentimental, wooden style of Tagore's English translations of his poetry accentuated the cliched nature of his mysticism. They may, then, be taken to represent an act of self-orientalisation before a Western audience. However, in a detailed and persuasive reading of Tagore's 'foreign reincarnation', Nabaneeta Sen explains how Tagore *knowingly and strategically* allowed himself to '[cater] to a rare mystic taste in the Western mind' (1966, p. 281). He was prepared to translate his poetry into purple prose, even though this would inevitably 'contribute to the irreparable loss of his reputation' (p. 278) outside India. Sen's assessment is that Tagore 'deeply believed at that moment, that his responsibilities as the "carrier of the Eastern Light" to the unhappy

West were greater than his private responsibilities as an artist' (p. 281). This, then, was strategic self-orientalisation for a practical purpose and for a particular audience. It is a project that suggests that the image of 'Tagore, the Eastern mystic', far from being a product of Western fantasies, was designed by Tagore in order to change and shape the West's view of itself and Asia.

Finally, let us return, briefly, to etymology; to the term 'Asia' itself. In the citation from Palat mentioned earlier, it is noted that the Chinese term for Asia, *yaxiya*, is nothing but a European import. This is the accepted wisdom and often presented as a solid foundation for the more general thesis that the West invented Asia. It seems a concrete example. However, I am returning now to this seemingly minor point of vocabulary because more thorough research appears to be leading to a different conclusion. Recent studies by the Finnish East Asian specialist Pekka Korhonen suggest that this 'solid foundation' is based on assumption rather than fact. Korhonen argues that the 'modern reader, whose thinking has been influenced by Edward Said's concept of Orientalism' (2002, p. 254), tends to seize upon proof of Western dominance wherever she or he looks. It appears, however, that although Matteo Ricci may have devised his own maps, he was not responsible for translating the names upon them. Indeed, as an admirer of the East he is unlikely to have been responsible for the Chinese characters for Asia, which are written as 'Inferior-Trifling-Inferior'. The Chinese translation makes it clear that Asia was considered to be a marginal place, an area that surrounded but did not include China. Korhonen's interest in this question arises from his concern that 'the Chinese of the twenty-first century may have to be content with relating to the rest of Asia with a pejorative regional name that they themselves chose four centuries ago, not for themselves, but for their neighbours' (2002, p. 267). For our purposes, it is the fact that the Chinese name for Asia was one 'they themselves chose' that is significant.

The idea of Asia and the ideal of Asian spirituality can be told as a Western story. It is a neat tale and has long found a receptive audience. Yet it is empirically inaccurate and confused. Tagore's vision of Asia was not the flip side of an established Western notion of the West. It constantly strove to transcend the West, driven by the need to establish a space of solidarity that is better understood as something mobile and new than as 'non-Western' or 'anti-Western'. Moreover, the idea of the West developed by Tagore and his Asianist contemporaries and predecessors has had a considerable impact. The notion that Western civilisation is secular and, moreover, soulless, alienated and mechanical still forms part of the background common sense on the topic. It is a powerful critique precisely because it draws attention to the shallow nature of the West's achievements. It makes Western freedom seem thin and regimented. Unlike Western critics (such as Weber, Simmel and the 'Western Marxists' of the Frankfurt School) who were to offer a similar critique of industrial culture, Tagore is constantly attentive to the colonial and Western nature and context of alienation and objectification. In particular, he calls attention to the way Western power, whether capitalist or communist, is united both by an industrialising vision of modernity and by a casual contempt for the non-Western world. Tagore imagined that his vision could assist in the development of a new Asian modernity. However, as we shall see in the next chapter, Asian spirituality is today a residual discourse. Other, more powerful, imaginative geographies of Asia's relationship with the West have arisen that demonise the latter, not for its lack of soul, but rather for its lack of stamina in the global marketplace.

Conclusions: Tagore and modernity

The conflation of modernity and the West conspires to make the West seem interesting and everywhere else boring. It ensures that the non-West is understood as imitative or old-fashioned. Thus, no matter how modern Tagore may have said he was, the mere fact of his being Indian has contributed to his marginal status within contemporary academic debate in the West.

Yet the chains of association that link the West to modernity are more fragile than it is sometimes imagined. Consider the link between modernity and living in a disorienting, fast-moving, creative society. This association inspires a heady belief that Westerners live in a perpetual social vortex; that Western lives are interesting because they are forever being spun around and about. In academic terms, this assumed linkage has inspired literatures on the transgressive politics and aesthetics of Western modernism as well as on Western countries as 'risk societies'. Indeed, the themes of uncertainty and reflexivity, along with the challenge of living in 'post-traditional' communities, have become staple topics within Western social theory. They are usually employed to describe the state of consciousness that accompanies post-Fordist capitalism. Thus Ulrich Beck's distinction between modernisation as the 'disembedding and second the re-embedding of traditional social norms by industrial social norms' and 'reflexive modernisation' as the 'disembedding and second the re-embedding of industrial social norms by another modernity'

(Beck, 1994, p. 2) is designed to capture both a Western historical process and a recent transition.

Yet, there is something amiss here. Something obvious. Compare Britain and India. The former is a country which had its last revolution in the seventeenth century, its last invasion in the eleventh and which has developed a relatively highly stable national identity, national language and class structure. The other is a country both ripped asunder and welded together by an utterly foreign colonising power until 1947 and, both before and since, subject to massive upheavals in social composition, identity and class structure. Which of these is a risk society, a post-traditional society? If social 'disembedding' is to be associated with modernity then it is India, not Britain, which is modern.

The challenges of being alienated both from one's 'own traditions' and from hegemonic authority have been negotiated by those subject to Westernisation and colonisation for centuries. By limiting the possibility of reflexivity and 'alternative modernity' to a post-industrial landscape, Beck renders the diverse modernities and patterns of critical consciousness seen outside the West as an irrelevance (see also Lash, 1999). Previous chapters have already indicated that this attitude is misjudged. However, I want to make the more specific point here that Asian spirituality, as understood by Tagore, can be understood as a form of reflexive modernisation. My desire to make this association arises from a sense of frustration at the way the critiques of Westernisation and Eurocentric modernity that Tagore articulated are today ignored because they are assumed to be merely anti-modern, the resistance of 'marginal man' to an inevitable process.

Since Tagore was opposed to an industrial model of society and, since he did wish to defend certain traditional values, it is understandable that he does not appear in the kind of historical overview offered by Beck. Yet, Tagore considered himself a defender of the modern. As noted earlier he considered that '[t]rue modernism is freedom of mind, not slavery of taste. It is independence of thought and action, not tutelage under European schoolmasters. It is science, but not its wrong application in life' (Tagore, 1991, p. 34). What Tagore was concerned with is the identification of progress and modernity with the West, the very mistake that continues to render provincial so much Western social theory. It is unfortunate in this regard that the issue of 'how modern' Tagore's poetry and prose were continues to be judged on the template of Western artistic modernism and has tended to dominate discussion of his 'modern sensibility' (Chatterjee, 1996). This leaden approach obscures more fundamental questions, namely: how does the idea of

Asian spirituality produce the West; and how does it offer or intimate a different form of modernity?

It is in the arena of Tagore's travels and networks within Asia that we find some of the answers to these questions. We have seen how Tagore's idea of the spiritual developed mystical and meditative Buddhist and non-doctrinal Hindu traditions, where emphasis is placed on inner reflection and the removal of dogmatic conceit. It is an individualistic exploration that has the restless quality of a perpetual and dissatisfied seeking for 'unity' and 'reconciliation'. 'In dogmatic religion', Tagore tells us, 'all doubts are laid to rest'. Tagore's own understanding of religion is, he says, 'indefinite and elastic': it offers 'no doctrine or injunction' and 'never undertakes to lead anybody anywhere to any solid conclusion; yet it reveals endless spheres of light, because it has no walls round itself' (1922, p. 16). This language of spiritual self discovery found a considerable following and influence in the West, partly because it appears to offer transcendental experience without succumbing to the rigid anachronisms of conventional Christianity. However, there is little that is 'alternative' or hedonistic about Tagore's approach to the spiritual. It represents, rather, a reflexive, self-questioning approach to the problem of modernity, an approach that hopes to embrace modernity without being over-impressed by the instrumental and materialist logic associated with its Western incarnation.

Given the waves of nationalism and militarism that inundated the last century, it is not surprising that Tagore's ambitions now appear to us naïve and doomed to fail. Yet, there remains something about spirituality and the critique of the soulless, alienated nature of 'the Western world', that refuses to entirely go away. Such ideas appear lodged in our political and geographical consciousness. If and when they are finally dislodged by the complete 'industrialisation' of personality, Tagore's journeys to East Asia will appear literally incomprehensible. That we still, somehow, see what he was trying to do and still, somehow, understand that Asia once offered a kind of hope, is testament to the unsatisfying nature of the technological visions and consumerist blueprints of the early twenty-first century.

Further reading

Tagore on the West and nationalism

The most readily available of Tagore's political works is *Nationalism* (1991, London, Macmillan). Also worth searching out is Tagore's study of the future of the East and West relationship, *Creative Unity* (1922, London, Macmillan).

Two important secondary works on Tagore's attitudes to nationalism and Asia are:

Hay, S. (1970) *Asian Ideas of East and West: Tagore and his Critics in Japan, China, and India*, Cambridge, Harvard University Press.

Nandy, A. (1994) *The Illegitimacy of Nationalism: Rabindranath Tagore and the Politics of Self*, Delhi, Oxford University Press.

Rabindranath Tagore: The Myriad-Minded Man is a comprehensive recent biography by Krishna Dutta and Andrew Robinson (1995, London, Bloomsbury).

Asia's Asia: Asia's West

Okakura's classic statement is available in a recent edition: *The Ideals of the East, with Special Reference to the Art of Japan* (2000, ICG Muse, New York and Tokyo). The growing critical literature on the meaning of Asia is highly diverse, with many regional and national variations. The following small selection is biased towards Chinese and Japanese accounts:

Bharucha, R. (2001) 'Under the sign of "Asia": rethinking "creative unity" beyond the "rebirth of traditional arts"', *Inter-Asia Cultural Studies*, 2, 1, pp. 151–156.

Harootunian, H. (2000) *Overcome by Modernity: History, Culture and Community in Interwar Japan*, Princeton, Princeton University Press.

Howell, D. (2000) 'Visions of the future in Meiji Japan', in M. Goldman and A. Gordon (eds) *Historical Perspectives on Contemporary East Asia*, Cambridge, Harvard University Press.

Karl, R. (1998) 'Creating Asia: China in the world at the beginning of the twentieth century', *The American Historical Review*, 103, 4, pp. 1096–1118.

Palat, R. (2002) 'Is India part of Asia?', *Environment and Planning: Society and Space*, 20, pp. 669–691.

Sun, G. (2000) 'How does Asia mean? (part I)', *Inter-Asia Cultural Studies*, 1, 1, pp. 13–47.

—— (2000) 'How does Asia mean? (part II)', *Inter-Asia Cultural Studies*, 1, 2, pp. 319–341.

Tanaka, S. (1993) *Japan's Orient: Rendering Pasts into History* Berkeley, University of California Press.

Tang, X. (1996) *Global Space and the Nationalist Discourse of Modernity: The Historical Thinking of Liang Qichao*, Stanford, Stanford University Press.

Chapter 5

From Soulless to Slacker: The Idea of the West from Pan-Asianism to Asian Values

Introduction: forget Tagore

In 1931, Buddhadev Bose felt able to announce that 'the age of Tagore was gone' (cited by Chakrabarty, 2000, p. 160). Bose's pronouncement was certainly prescient. As we shall see in this chapter, Tagore's ideal of Asian spirituality was soon to be overshadowed by other, newly emergent, ideologies.

The transition from predominantly colonial to post-colonial regimes across Asia that occurred from the late 1940s onwards, ushered in new generations of leaders keen to assert modern, forward-looking, national agendas. A future of national development and national modernisation was envisaged, a future that would ensure that the humiliations of the past could be overcome. The rise of Asian independence corresponded with a shift in the way the West was imagined. Most obviously, the association of power, of political and economic decision making, with the West, could be challenged, not just by Japan and China, but by countries across the continent. It was felt, not unreasonably, that new nations can forge new paths and, correspondingly, that however much they may borrow or emulate the West they would do so through choice and on their own terms.

It was predictable that, as the levers of power became decolonised, and the institutions and ideologies of nation building took an ever more dominant position, the post-national, anti-political, aspirations articulated by Tagore would appear increasingly utopian. The industrialised, bureaucratised and soulless quality of the West became a minor note within Eastern critique of the West. Indeed, the themes of creativity, freedom and individual personality, which Tagore saw as being crushed in the West, were the very things that, for those who came to espouse 'Asian values' in the late twentieth century, were held to characterise the West. These 'values', given a negative spin, were associated with chaos and offered as attributes that explained Western decline and decadence. The West was transformed: not so much soulless as work-shy; not a ghastly, efficient machine stamping conformity and alienation across the planet but an individualistic, anti-social and bloated creature that could no longer 'keep up' with Asia. It is a curious transition: for it turned Asia into the scold of the West for not possessing the very qualities that Tagore most despised.

Perhaps the final proof of Tagore's marginality is the increasingly elegiac tone of Indian commentaries on his work. The reverential conferences that honour his name (Colussi, 1991), the hushed prose of panegyrics to one of India's great men (Sharma, 1987; Chakarabarti, 1990; Chatterjee, 1996), suggest that this is a figure beyond criticism and an intellectual and political irrelevance. Ashis Nandy explains that, once Tagore

> had dreamt, like Gandhi, that India's national self-definition would some day provide a critique of western nationalism, that Indian civilization with its demonstrated capacity to live with and creatively use contradictions and inconsistencies would produce a 'national' ideology that would transcend nationalism. However, even before his death, nationalism in India proved itself to be not only more universal but also more resilient than it had been thought. Today, fifty years after Tagore's death and forty years after Gandhi's, their vision of patriotism has almost ceased to exist, even in India, and for most modern Indians this is not a matter of sorrow but of pride (Nandy, 1994, pp. 83–84).

And yet, perhaps not quite. For the distinction between Asian spirituality and Western soullessness is not quite dead. Despite being cast into a strange, sentimental, limbo, it retains a certain symbolic power. What it symbolises is *cultural depth*. It was a depth explicitly claimed by pan-Asianism and, at least, acknowledged by the proponents of Asian values. Asian spirituality remains attached to – or, perhaps, we should say clings to – the idea of Asia. Moreover, despite its relegation to a symbolic backwater, it continues to offer a disruptive, subversive sense that if Asia has a meaning worth defending it cannot be based on the disparagement of Western individualism or laziness. As this implies, the movement towards 'Asian values' has been characterised by ambivalence. This is particularly apparent when we look at one of its ideological predecessors, pan-Asianism.

Pan-Asianism: Eastern redemption, Western nationalism

The most forceful expressions of pan-Asianism were seen in China in the 1920s and in Japan from the 1920s through to the end of the Second World War. In both cases we find a curious mix of images of East and West, with Asia being offered as a site of redemption to the materialist West, yet also as the home of an aggressive 'Western-looking' nationalism that could beat the West at its own game. Thus Fukuzawa and Tagore were combined and traduced by a geo-political current that acted to cohere and conceal (and thus to resolve) Westernising and anti-Western forces. In this way, pan-Asianism acted to heal the tension between, on the one hand, nationalist and Westernising impulses and, on the other, the desire to forge a regional and ethnic solidarity against the West.

The term 'pan-Asianism' might suggest that it was a movement that offered a natural home for Tagore's ideas. It is true that pan-Asianism, especially in its principal Japanese form, was suffused with the rhetoric of the divine. However, this was a fascistic divinity, a religion of authority and obedience, centred upon the god-like status of the Japanese Emperor and the necessity of collective submission to his authority. Furthermore, Japanese pan-Asianism became tied to the notion that Asia could only come together under Japanese political and military leadership. Chinese pan-Asianism was also bound up with nationalism. In China, however, this combination was employed to bring a diverse nation together. The fact that the Republic of China (1911–1912) was officially declared the Republic of the Five Races is indicative of official concern with the management of China's ethnic (and, potentially, national) hetero-geneity. Pan-Asianism provided an ideology that drew Han and non-Han Chinese peoples into a single national project. Moreover, when the founder of the Nationalist Party, Sun Yat-sen, delivered his lecture on 'Greater Asianism', in Kobe, Japan, in December 1924, it was clear that pan-Asianism was also being used to assert the regional centrality of China. Sun drew a distinction between the unethical and belligerent conduct of the West and the peaceful, ethical and rational system of Chinese tradition, which he offered as a model of Eastern virtue.

The ideology of Asian spirituality has a convoluted relationship with pan-Asianism. It may be witnessed working both within and against pan-Asian nationalism and imperialism. An illustration of the complex utopian energies this combination produced can be found in the plans for the (re)foundation of Koryo in 1920 by nativist Korean and far-right Japanese pan-Asianists. As described by Duara (2001), Koryo was to be located in the Jiandao region, on the Korea–China border, as both an anti-Western *and* Western polity. Describing the constitution of Koryo, Duara writes:

> Confucianism was to be the national religion; property was to be owned collectively...Citizenship was to be equal without discrimination on the basis of ethnicity or race...Thus its ideology contained elements of a return to East Asian traditions which self-consciously embedded an opposition to the modern Western or Westernised state. At the same time it also proclaimed modern notions of republicanism and equality (p. 112).

Koryo was more an ideological than a practical endeavour. Its importance lies in its role as a precursor for Manzhouguo, the Japanese controlled state in Manchuria, in north-east China, that existed between 1932 and 1945. In Manzhouguo religious and spiritual currents were put to work within and against Japanese imperial pan-Asianism. Duara's (1997, 2001, 2003) research has begun to illuminate this flow of forces for English language readers. His focus on what he calls the 'redemptive societies' operating in Manzhouguo and other Japanese controlled areas of China, allows us to see how pan-Asian spirituality could be sustained as both a fascistic and anti-authoritarian, spiritual tendency. Groups such as the Morality Society (founded in 1918), Society for the Great Unity of World Religions (founded 1915) and the Society of the Way, with its partner organisation, the Society of the Red Swastika, pre-existed the Japanese invasion. In 1932 they already had memberships measured in the millions. Their basic creed amounted to a critique of Western materialism: more specifically, the need to retain and promote Asian spirituality alongside and in synthesis with Western technological civilisation. Such redemptive groups indicate the popular support available for the notion of Eastern spirituality. This suggests that the negative reception Tagore experienced in China (Chapter 4) was neither inevitable nor necessarily representative of broader Chinese opinion. However, the redemptive societies also show how easily Asian spirituality could be assimilated within imperial pan-Asianism. For once Manzhouguo had been established, the Japanese military actively courted these organisations, both inside and outside the borders of the puppet state. Their appeal to the Japanese lay in their ideal of a common Eastern civilisation, an ideal which seemed to unite Japanese and Chinese interests. The Asian Co-prosperity Sphere, formed by the Japanese in order to legitimise Japan's further territorial expansion within East Asia, continued this process of co-option. Although the Co-prosperity Sphere was claimed to be defending the spiritual life of Asian peoples, it also offered a ruthless programme of 'Oriental capitalist culture' and authoritarianism (Yabe, 1975). [1]

Attempts to combine pan-Asianism and Asian spirituality did not entirely collapse with the end of the Second World War. In India, in particular, this endeavour briefly retained political momentum. Following a number of 'All-Asia' conferences held in India during the 1930s, India's first Prime Minister, Jawaharlal Nehru, initiated a far larger and ambitious event that would 'weld the people and government of Asia together'. The Asian Relations Conference was held in New Delhi in 1947. Gandhi, Nehru and Sarojini Naidu all used the conference to voice Asia's uniquely spiritual and ethical message to the West. The idea of Asia that was offered remained suffused with themes that Tagore would have recognised and approved. It was, noted Werner Levi a few years later, 'the apex of Asian solidarity'. Yet, he adds, it was also 'the beginning of its decline' (Levi, 1952, p. 39). The colonial condition of most Asian states had long been the central cog in the engine propelling a sense of Asian mutual need. The Asian Relations Conference came at a time when nationalism had begun, not merely to dominate political thinking, but to marginalise trans-national ambitions. As Keenleyside reflects:

> With the achievement of independence by India and other Asian states shortly thereafter, the cornerstone on which the idea of Asian unity had been erected – solidarity in the struggle for freedom – was suddenly removed and, for the time being at least, the whole edifice of Pan-Asianism collapsed (1982, p. 224).

During the 1950s and 1960s, the theme of Asian spirituality appeared to be revived by a wider, emergent sense of the 'Third World' as, in general, a more ethical and less materialist entity than the 'First World'. 'Let a New Asia and a New Africa be Born' was the title of the opening address at the Bandung Conference in April 1955. Bandung brought together 29 newly independent or soon to be independent nations from the Afro-Asian world. The man who gave the opening address and President of the host nation of Indonesia, Achmed Sukarno, advised delegates that although they could 'wield little physical power', they could 'inject the voice of reason into world affairs. We can mobilise all the spiritual, all the moral, all the political strength of Asia on the side of peace' (Sukarno, 1970, p. 459).

Yet there is a gestural flavour to Sukarno's words. The argument that 'Third World' leaders want peace had become a political weapon, a symbolic gaining of a higher ethical ground that sidelined reflection on how statist modernisation was sustained through violence. By the early 1950s, nationalism and the diverse geo-political strategies of the Cold War, were turning visions of 'spiritual Asia' into sentimental rhetoric. Indeed, in the country once seen as the home of Asian spirituality – India – Asian identity was being increasingly ignored. National considerations and the rise of more immediate and pressing regional, South Asian and East Asian identities were leading towards Indians' disassociation from a wider sense of 'their continent'. By the end of the century Ravi Palat, writing in *The Hindu* in December 2000, felt able to be unequivocal about 'India's excision from dominant conceptions of Asia'. This process, he noted, has occurred 'both in the West and in much of Southeast and East Asia, as indicated by [East Asian focused] debates on "Asian values"'.

For Palat 'Asian values' must be placed in inverted comas. Like many other Asians (from whatever part of this disputed continent), he finds it a curious expression, not least because it appears to refer to such a limited part of Asia. Compared to Tagore's vision of Asia, the Asian-values debate is both geographically diminished and politically circumscribed. Indeed, it is sometimes associated with just one outcome, namely economic success and two countries, Singapore and Malaysia. Nevertheless, since its inception as a public discourse – which may be traced to the 1970s but is usually dated to the late 1980s and early 1990s – its themes have been taken up by political and economic leaders across East Asia.

The slacker West and Asian values

Hard-working Asians

Although what the central value is within Asian values has been the subject of dispute, a plausible case can be made for it being *work*, more specifically *hard work*. The history of the work ethic in Asia – that is, the history of the privileging of the work ethic as something needing to be endlessly strived for and/or, as something inherent in Asian culture – connects the influence of capitalism in Asia with the rise of the rhetoric of Asian values. However, although the capitalist contribution to Asian attitudes to work is often highlighted, the Asian work ethic also has a revealing relationship with communism. The idea that class enemies are parasites who live off the value produced by the labour of others had been cultivated by what was, indicatively, named the 'labour movement', in nineteenth-century Europe. It was a perspective that sustained a left-wing political culture where hard work and constant struggle were valued both as means to an end and as inherently beneficial. This muscular ethos was further developed by the vanguardist politics of the Bolsheviks: to be a revolutionary, to be a real communist, became associated with unstinting and self-sacrificing effort. Since left-wing anti-colonial activists saw a class relation between European colonies and the metropolitan powers, it was inevitable that the latter would come to be cast in the role of idle parasite, as *lazily* feasting off the labour of the exploited countries of the 'Third World'. In this way, the work ethic was mapped onto the geographical imagination of Asian communism. Conversely, the notion that Asia stood for a view of humanity that exceeded or transcended people's role as productive agents was increasingly interpreted as a reactionary folly.

In contemporary East Asia, the shared value communists and capitalists place upon hard work has smoothed China's transition from a communist to an entrepreneurial economy. This overlap also helps explain the mix of socialist and capitalist rhetoric that can often be heard from political leaders, both among the original 'Four Tigers' (Singapore, South Korea, Taiwan and Hong Kong) and the 'tiger cubs' (Malaysia, Thailand and Indonesia) of the 'East Asian economic miracle' (World Bank, 1993).

Drawing out the implications of the 'supply-side socialism' that characterises contemporary Singapore – one of the states most closely associated with Asian values – Chua (1999) offers the Asian attitude to work as the key ingredient that makes Asia both effective and distinctive in the world market. Thus the Asian relationship to work is seen as the central explanation of Asian economic success. Other supposed Asian values, such as strong family ties and collectivism, tend to be presented as fostering and sustaining this basic relationship. It is significant that, although strong family ties and collectivism can both be found across Asia, it is the supposed *absence of the work ethic* that differentiated Asians outside the fold of the Asian-values debate (especially South Asians) in the 1980s and 1990s, from those at its centre (East Asians). East Asians, the Malaysian intellectual, Noordin Sopiee, has argued, are characterised by their ability to 'work very hard' and a disposition to 'saving and thriftiness' (cited by Milner and Johnson, 2002). Indeed, the spirituality of Asia has, itself, been emptied of transcendental aspiration and put to work to suggest that the work ethic has a specific, East Asian, heritage. Thus, for example, Japanese Buddhism, and Confucianism in a number of East Asian countries, have been used to explain and illustrate a disposition towards asceticism, self-discipline and self-sacrifice. By contrast India, as Francis Fukuyama puts it, has the wrong kind of Asian religion: it suffers from the 'toper and inertia' (1992, p. 228) encouraged by Hindu mysticism. Hinduism, Fukuyama tells us, 'is in many respects the opposite of the spirit of capitalism' (1992, p. 228).

It is also revealing that the Malaysian Prime Minister, Dr Mahathir's (1970) vision of Asian values, was shaped by a desire to inculcate and discipline indigenous Malays with an attitude to work he associated with the country's Chinese minority. Asian values in Malaysia have been less about celebrating an achieved condition than inaugurating a cultural shift – in Mahathir's terms a 'revolution in thinking' – that would transform the practices of those groups who are deemed not to be hard workers. In fact, the ethnicised nature of the Asian-values perspective, more specifically the association of economic success and, hence, Asian values, with Confucian and Chinese values, forms a powerful and potentially destabilising current throughout East and Southeast Asia (Lim and Gosleng, 1983). '[T]here is indeed a broad empirical correspondence', explains Pinches: 'a high proportion of Asia's newly wealthy have Confucian or Chinese ancestries, and a high proportion of those who are not from such backgrounds do not possess new wealth' (1999, p. 18). Despite the fact that 'Chinese identity' is locally adapted and diverse, this ethnic concentration of wealth has helped ensure the continued politicisation of ethnicity in a region where the management of 'ethnic plurality' is often a determining factor in national stability.

The idle West

Asian-values perspectives emphasise social cohesion and community. However, societal progress is measured, overwhelmingly, in economic terms. In his widely read book *Can Asians Think?*, the Singaporean ambassador to the United Nations, Kishore Mahbubani, is unapologetic about the primacy of wealth creation as the focus and destiny of Asian culture. Answering 'yes' to the bizarre question he poses in his title, Mahbubani finds the conclusive evidence from a single source, 'the incredible economic performance of East Asian societies in the past few decades' (1998, p. 23).

As with nearly all proponents of Asian values, Kishore Mahbubani's idea of Asia relies on an interpretation of what is wrong with the West. Tagore's concern with soulless and mechanical Westernisation is replaced by a West of decadence and indulgence. It is a West that will be familiar to readers of Chapter 1. The debauched, idle and self-destructive West is not a new image, either in the West or Asia. However, its ubiquity and unrivalled deployment in the 1990s to shape what Asia is, more specifically to shape the Asian ideal, was unprecedented. The West's 'undoing' is not merely a favourite theme amongst advocates of Asian values but a *defining* theme: without 'Western decadence' the notion that real or good Asians are devoted to wealth creation would be incomprehensible and easily rendered as a shallow and materialistic subversion of Asian identity. Mahbubani provides a fairly typical account of Western decline:

> Only hubris can explain why so many Western societies are trying to defy the economic laws of gravity. Budgetary discipline is disappearing. Expensive social programs and pork-barrel projects multiply with little heed to costs. The West's low savings and investment rates lead to declining competitiveness vis-à-vis East Asia. The work ethic is eroding while politicians delude workers into believing that they can retain high wages despite becoming internationally uncompetitive. Leadership is lacking. Any politician who states hard truths is immediately voted out (1998, p. 97).

Mahbubani admits that 'there is no question that western societies remain in many ways more successful than their East Asian counterparts' (p. 25). However, it is revealing that his three examples of Western success are not economic indicators, but the standard of Western universities, think tanks and orchestras. Western success thus seems a pretty insubstantial affair, especially when set against both the priority Mahbubani elsewhere accords to wealth creation and what he claims Asians think of the West.

> Asians are shocked by the scale and depth of the social and economic problems that have afflicted many Western societies. In North America, societies are troubled by the relative breakdown of the family as an institution, the plague of drug addiction and its attendant problems, including crime, the persistence of ghettos and the perception that there has been a decline in ethical standards. U.S. government statistics tracking social trends for the period 1960–90 show that in those thirty years the rate of violent crime quadrupled, single-parent families almost tripled, the number of U.S. state and federal prisoners tripled. Asians are also perplexed by the seeming addiction of Europeans to their social safety net despite the clear evidence that these nets now hold down their societies and has created a sense of gloom about long-term economic prospects (p. 25).

The twin themes of the work-shy West and the violent, 'out of control' West can be found throughout Asian-values narratives. It is an interpretation of Western decay that carries a historical judgement. For it shows, as Singapore's Prime Minister, Goh Chok Tong, put it during his National Day speech on 21 August 1994, that 'societies can go wrong quickly'.

> US and British societies have changed profoundly in the last 30 years. Up to the early 60s they were disciplined, conservative, with the family very much the pillar of their societies. Since then both the US and Britain have seen a sharp rise in broken families, teenage mothers, illegitimate children, juvenile delinquency, vandalism and violent crime (cited by Sheridan, 1999, p. 72).

Traditionally, Asian Westernisers and Asian critics of Western soul-lessness saw themselves as under the thumb of the West, as reacting against its crushing force. In this context one can read a certain pleasure in-between Goh's and Mahbubani's lines: they are recording that the tables have been turned, that it is now 'we' who can patronise and lecture 'them'.

Yet however sweet and, given the historical record, temperately expressed, this revenge must seem, a number of persistent ironies sour its enjoyment. The Singaporean sociologist Soek-Fang Sim has high-lighted the suspiciously over-zealous way that anti-social behaviour is presented as Western. This kind of geographical despatching of the sins of modernity (which we also encountered in Chapter 2) never rings true. 'With the increasing realisation that the "West" is within and inevitable, that Singaporeans are indelibly Westernised', Sim (2001, p. 51) argues, this kind of rhetoric is required, 'not only to protect the Singapore nation from the dangerous West but also to protect Singapore from Singaporeans'. In other words, Goh's and Mahbubani's attitude towards the West represents an 'othering' of internal problems. It is a process of purification of the nation that sanctions and demands strict protection and self-discipline as well as the perpetuation of an image of the West as a spatially displaced 'folk-devil'.

Asia's 'new wealth'

A basic irony within Asian-values perspectives is that, by emersing Asia into the global market, they hasten the erosion of regional and local cultural distinctiveness and, hence, of Asian identity itself. This is, in part, seen in the way that economic success and 'new wealth' in Asia are tied to the consumption of things Western (films, clothes, food, music, and so on; see Robison and Goodman, 1996; Pinches, 1999). For advocates of Asian values, the 'value' of Asia can often appear to lie in little more than its ability to be a front-runner in a generic, worldwide process of economic liberalisation.

The erasure of Asia through economic success is widely claimed to be tempered by the fact that Asian values bring together economic goals with *traditional* family values and *traditional* networks. Such a combination of old and new is said to promise a different, less disruptive and less inhumane, route to modernisation (as compared, inevitably, with Western industrialisation). A related notion has it that business practices in East Asia are less brutal and instrumental than those in the West. In the words of business journalist Shui-shen Liu, the Chinese 'pay more attention to human relations than to "things"...In the West "things" are more important than human relations' (cited by Tai, 1989, p. 19). It may be admitted that a commitment to a holistic view of employment was apparent within many East Asian enterprises, at least before the late 1990s. Moreover, it appears that globalisation can be harnessed by certain familial networks that are adaptive to neo-liberal transnationalism (Chinese business networks, in particular, have been claimed to be both familial and adaptive to globalisation, as discussed by Castells, 1998).

However, the evidence that the commercialisation and industrialisation of East Asia is being sustained hand-in-hand with a family-friendly, community-supporting traditional culture is both thin and unpersuasive. When seen against the remorseless and rapid urbanisation, cultural deracination and industrialisation witnessed in Asia, these examples start to appear, not as exemplars of a wider paradigm, but as counter-currents of questionable importance. Family networks have been placed under considerable strain throughout the region. Patterns of social alienation and breakdown have emerged, patterns that are the inevitable consequence of a combination of increasing geographical mobility, mercurial employment patterns and the rise of consumerism. The uncertainty and familial isolation that is a widespread experience of those dependent upon jobs within the 'footloose' businesses that dominate the 'miracle' economics, combined with the destruction of traditional ways of life, particularly within the countryside, and the increasingly calamitous deterioration of the natural environment; all combine to query how much value the discourse of 'Asian values' places upon either Asia or Asians (Bello and Rosenfeld, 1991; Bello, 1995; Swift, 1995).

Even the most ardent supporters of a stern Asian work ethic can sometimes appear unconvinced. Investigating what he calls the 'ferocious' work ethic in South Korea, the Australian journalist Greg Sheridan usefully draws attention to the way ordinary Koreans sanction such sacrifices. Yet the contradictions of self-sacrifice also emerge from his interviews. Indeed, it is difficult not to wonder whether social self-denial has become an end in itself when one listens to the words of one Korean professional and mother: 'In order to achieve economic growth', she argues, 'you have to sacrifice the environment, plus our mental outlook and quality of life' (Sheridan, 1999, p. 221). She adds, as a merely wistful afterthought, 'I would like more leisure time and time with my child.'[2]

The impact of such values in Thailand is one of the subjects of Ekachai's (1993) *Behind the Smiles*. Ekachai's exposé portrays rural Thailand as a place of cultural decay and economic plunder. It is a process sanctioned by reference to tradition, deference and Asian values and the increasing use of family networks as a substitute welfare state. The family becomes an economic resource, to be abused and eroded in good times but relied on when the economy fails to provide. Talking in the wake of the economic collapse of 1997, the Thai Prime Minister, Chuan Leekpai, was clear about the economic function of Asian 'family values'. The unemployed created by the crisis, Chuan observed 'will have the option of going back to their extended family networks, to be back with their fathers, mothers and relatives' (cited by Sheridan, 1999, p. 179). Chaun cannot resist contrasting this situation with the West, where lack of family ties means that economic crisis results in the problems of homelessness and destitution. However, since few other sources of support are available in Thailand (as in the other 'miracle' economies), the 'option' Chaun describes is, in reality, compulsory. More fundamentally, it displays a naïve faith that, no matter what forces of geographical displacement and alienation are unleashed by a capitalist economy, the family will always be there when things go wrong, saving the state the cost of providing support for its citizens.

'Globalisation is Westernisation': Asian meltdown

It was in Thailand that the Asian economic crisis of 1997 began. The Thai national economy was suddenly exposed as heavily reliant on the fragile confidence of foreign speculation. 'At the root of the crisis', noted the economic journalist Bradford Delong (1998), 'was a sudden change of heart on the part of investors in the world economy's industrial core – in New York, Frankfurt, London and Tokyo'. The collapse of this confidence soon drew much of South East Asia into an economic and social crisis.

As the realities of Western domination were laid bare, the notion that the Asian 'miracle' was the product of Asian thrift and diligence began to seem like self-delusion. In an essay published in 1999, the Malaysian social scientist Khoo Boo Teik wrote:

> Now the miracle has turned to meltdown in the short period of one and half years, Asians have been scrambling to distinguish themselves from other Asians – not least in the eyes of a western-dominated international money market. Under the conditions which began in July 1997, the consensus of the Asian state elites over critical issues – so to speak, a surrogate measure of the workability of the principle of 'Asian consensus' – has been almost nowhere in sight. In economic and financial terms, Japan could not or would not help the rest of East Asia to implement an 'Asian' monetary fund in the face of western opposition (1999, p. 188).

A former minister in the Thai government, Dr Likhit Dhiravegin, came to a similar, if more trenchantly expressed position. 'Globalisation is not really globalisation', he noted post-crisis, adding,

> Globalisation is Westernisation. The International Monetary Fund, the World Trade Organisation etc – all this originated in the West. It's all modelled and patterned after the US and Europe (cited by Sheridan, 1999, p. 187).

The sudden collapse of faith in the East Asian model turned the 'lazy West' back into a disciplined and disciplinarian force. As Sparks (1998, p. 4) phrased it, the 'solution to the world's problems is no longer to make the West more like the East, but to make the East more like the West'.

In the aftermath of the crisis, the reaction amongst East Asian political leaders to explicit Western economic intervention was largely one of stoic resignation. The less easily caged Dr Mahathir tried to rally traditional anti-colonial rhetoric. He talked of the whole saga as a 'Western conspiracy' driven by 'descendants of the old white-supremacist colonists' and designed to 'shake up the economies of the Asian miracle nations' (cited by Milner, 2002). Yet, in the light of the mass deportations of Indonesians and Filipinos from Malaysia in 2002, Mahathir's commitment to Asian solidarity has itself been shown to be weak. More fundamentally, Mahathir's attempt to invoke the West as a foreign enemy is undermined by the fact that the very form of Asian capitalism which he encouraged and disseminated has seen the relentless Westernisation of Asia. It is true that this process has been diverse, that Western culture has been appropriated, and made local. Yet, the inflections of globalisation do not constitute resistance. The authority that Tagore sought to impart to the idea of Asia has melted away, to be replaced by a role for Asia as just another player in the circuit of global capital.

Conclusions

Asia has witnessed a shift from one vision of Western decadence to another. It has been a movement from the West seen as a soulless machine that produces an inhuman modernisation, to the West seen as lazy and lacking a competitive edge. The former interpretation of the West lies at the centre of narratives of Asian spirituality, whilst the latter is a common thread amongst those who espouse Asian values.

The shift, in the mid-to-late twentieth century, to notions of an Asian regional identity that are eagerly submissive to neo-liberal globalisation has subverted the appeal of Asian spirituality. Some will be tempted to describe this shift in terms of a decline in the ability of South Asia to determine the meaning of Asia and the rise of pragmatic, secular East Asia. However, since such an explanation would have the unhelpful effect of cementing stereotypes whose creation is part of our enquiry, it is better to approach these regional attributes as changeable and temporary. Moreover, it would be untrue to say that the ideal of Asian spirituality is entirely dead in Asia today. It is, rather, petrified: frozen into cultural capital, into a symbol of Asian ethnic specialness. It is sustained as a marketable cultural distinction, one that implies that, no matter how ferocious and flexible the labour market may be in East Asia, certain values, especially those associated with the family, will remain unchanged. Thus a non-instrumental essence of Asianess continues to be invoked, in large measure, because it consolidates the legitimacy of the dominant paradigm of economic growth. Perhaps, though, it is retained for another reason too. Asian spirituality clings to our imagination because it is an idea made necessary by the revolutions of modernity; it offers a necessary hope. For whilst Asian values and Western values now chorus that, in the words of Deng Xiaoping, 'to get rich is glorious', many continue to sense that materialistic, industrialised lives are not full lives; that there may be some other type of value in Asia.

The vision of Asia as containing the potential to transcend both the West and industrialised modernity, a vision associated with 'Asian spirituality', continues to be hard to entirely dispatch. It casts its shadow over the debate, especially whenever Asian 'family values' are relied on as the uncommercialised, bedrock of humane conduct that will help Asia get through its latest economic crisis. It also has a certain sickly presence in the conduct of Asian statism: the state that directs all, knows all, looks after the righteous and punishes the wrong-doers, takes on the role of an omnipresent and all-knowing deity. More concretely, it was political nous rather than woolly liberalism that seems to have spurred the Malaysian deputy Prime Minister, Anwar Ibrahim, to flesh out a conception of a more democratic and less soulless Asia – to be achieved by what he called an 'Asian Renaissance' – in the early 1990s (Ibrahim, 1996). Ibrahim's project explicitly cited Tagore as an inspiration. It also directly challenged Mahathir's 'Asian values', an act of insubordination that many consider to have provoked Ibrahim's persecution (and nine-year jail sentence). Ibrahim's contention that 'Asian man at heart is *persona religiosis*' (cited by Milner and Johnson, 2002), may appear anachronistic. Yet it reflects a persistent ideal.

Further reading
Pan-Asianism

Further historical background on the ambiguities of pan-Asianism can be found in:

Duara, P. (2001) 'The discourse of civilization and Pan-Asianism', *Journal of World History*, 12, 1, pp. 99–130.
Iida, Y. (1997) 'Fleeing the West, making Asia home: transpositions of otherness in Japanese Pan-Asianism, 1905–1930', *Alternatives*, 22, pp. 409–432.
  A recent overview of Japanese pan-Asian imperialism is provided by Louise Young in *Japan's Total Empire: Manchuria and the Culture of Wartime Imperialism* (1998, Berkeley, University of California Press).

Asian values

There is a growing critical literature on Asian values, some of the most useful sources are listed below. However, it is also helpful to refer to the works of those who have espoused Asian values, such as Mohamad Mahathir in *The Malay Dilemma* (1970, Singapore, Asia Pacific Press), *The Challenge* (1986, Petaling Jaya, Pelanduk Publications), *A New Deal for Asia* (1999, Pataling Jaya, Pelanduk Publications); Lee Kuan Yew in *From Third World to First* (2000, New York, HarperCollins), Kishore Mahbubani's *Can Asians Think? Understanding the Divide Between East and West* (1998, South Royalton, Vermont, Steerforth Press) and Anwar Ibrahim's *The Asian Renaissance* (1996, Singapore, Times Books International).

  Much of the academic commentary on Asian values maintains a critical perspective and tone. Amongst the more informative and distinctive contributions have been:

Barr, M. (2002) *Cultural Politics and Asian Values: The Tepid War*, London, Routledge.
—— (2000) *Lee Kuan Yew: The Beliefs Behind the Man*, Richmond, Curzon.

Bell, D., Brown, D., Jayasuriya, K. and Jones, D. (1995) *Towards Illiberal Democracy in Pacific Asia*, Basingstoke, New York, Macmillan/St. Martin's Press.

Chua, B. (1999) '"Asian-values" discourse and the resurrection of the social', *Positions: East Asia Cultures Critique*, 7, 2, pp. 571–592.

Kahn, J. (1997) 'Malaysian modern or anti-anti Asian values', *Thesis Eleven*, 50, pp. 15–33.

Khoo Boo Teik (1999) 'The value(s) of a miracle: Malaysian and Singaporean elite constructions of Asia', *Asian Studies Review*, 23, 2, pp.181–192.

Sheridan, G. (1999) *Asian Values, Western Dreams: Understanding the New Asia*, St Leonards, New South Wales, Allen & Unwin.

Chapter 6

Occidental Utopia: The Neo-Liberal West

Introduction

The idea of the West remains in motion. Despite the confidant predictions of its certain and imminent decline that have accompanied every stage of its modern life, the West today is a far more ubiquitous concept than it was one hundred years ago and, perhaps, at any point in the past. The challenge that presents itself is to divine the current trajectory of the idea of the West; to sketch a map of the West's present and future terrain.

In this chapter, I describe some trends within contemporary portrayals of the West. They are trends towards ideological narrowness. More specifically, I will be claiming that the idea of the West that is becoming *most* familiar to people around the world today is *more* ideologically limited than 'the Wests' of the past.

I shall be stressing the muscular self-confidence of the contemporary West: more specifically, the notion that the Western 'liberal democratic' blueprint represents the only viable choice for humanity. This combination of narrowness and confidence leads me to the political conclusion that neo-liberal visions of the West have, on balance, became more injurious than beneficial to democracy and should be distinguished from it. Indeed, I depict the assertion of Western triumph through neo-liberal capitalism as a *utopian* political discourse. This criticism is designed to defamiliarise the omnipresent logic of neo-liberal globalisation, making exotic what is often offered as pragmatic and inevitable.

Towards utopia

Benjamin Kidd had a model of Western civilisation premised on its military strength. Ramsay MacDonald's West was a set of legal and ethical practices designed to sustain a humane society but betrayed by the imperial powers. Trotsky's West was the home of the socialist imagination. Just as the geographical boundaries of where the West physically lies have changed, so too have the political implications of the West and Westernisation. All the visions of the West just mentioned contained a faith in Western Europe as the centre of world civilisation. Yet although they shared much, it remains the case that the West, even within the West (which has not proved the most fertile territory for critical insight into the topic), has been imagined in a variety of ways. Today, however, it is widely assumed, both in the West and across the globe, that the Western model has a more uniform meaning. It is seen as a socio-economic form that combines the free market and democratic institutions. This model is often called 'liberal democracy'.

The idea of liberal democracy has a complex history. Traditionally it has been theorised in terms of political pluralism and the limitation of state powers over individuals (Macpherson, 1977; Holden, 1988). This association has, in turn, been connected with a view of the authentic liberal state as benignly neutral or indifferent to the various choices made by its citizens (Rawls, 1971). However, it is indicative that whilst recent exponents of Western triumph litter their commentaries with the terminology of liberal democracy, they do not feel the need to make use of these theoretical traditions (Fukuyama, 1992; Mandelbaum, 2002). For this group the term 'liberal' is associated, very firmly, with a capitalist economy and society. Thus the phrase 'liberal democracy' is used to denote a capitalist economic foundation aligned to a democratically accountable political process. In order to flag-up the existence and importance of this terminological slippage it is appropriate to talk of this new model, not as 'liberal democracy', but as 'capitalist democracy' or 'neo-liberal democracy'.

The economic aspects of this model have emerged, not merely as a favoured pathway amongst international institutions (notably, the International Monetary Fund and the World Bank), but as the only option that is considered viable. It is interesting to note that many of those who oppose this consensus are politically conservative (Scruton, 2002) or position themselves as broadly pro-capitalist (Luttwak, 1999; Gray, 2002). Along with left-wing anti-capitalists, these critics object to the logic of 'one size fits all' that is associated with neo-liberal globalisation. In *Turbo Capitalism*, Edward Luttwak displays bewilderment at the evangelical nature of the new faith. 'At present, almost all elite Americans' as well as '[b]usiness people all over the world'

> are utterly convinced that they have discovered the winning formula for economic success – the *only* formula – good for every country, rich or

poor, good for all individuals willing and able to heed the message, and, of course, good for elite Americans: PRIVATIZATION+DEREGULATION+ GLOBALIZATION = TURBO-CAPITALISM = PROSPERITY (p. 25).

In order to grasp the novelty of this position it is necessary to have some knowledge of the fate of other narratives of the West in the years subsequent to the Second World War. The two that demand our attention are:

1. Social democracy; and
2. Global cultural Westernisation.

The first of these visions of the West is clearly at variance with the story of ascendant Western neo-liberal democracy. The second is designed to suggest that one of the immediate predecessors of contemporary triumphalism was the attempt, in the face of decolonisation, to cast Westernisation as an unstoppable and inevitable process of modernisation.

Social democracy: the unproclaimed West

At the start of the twentieth century the West was synonymous with Western Europe. The USA was understood as Western only in the sense that it represented an export or extension of the real West. The transition made by the USA, from a peripheral to a dominant status, was enabled by the rise and global deployment of its industrial and military power. It was also a consequence of the seemingly permanent image of decline that came to be attached to Western Europe subsequent to the 'fratricidal' war of 1914–1918.

'Europe is ruined', proclaimed Trotsky at the third congress of Comitern in 1921: 'the economic centre has moved over to America' (cited by Carr, 1966b, p. 341). Soviet politicians were the quickest to recognise that, as a headline in *Izvestiya* put it, also in 1921, the USA was 'The Hegemon of the World' (ibid., p. 517). By the end of the Second World War, Europe's position was weaker still. Sundered between two superpowers, the loss of empire now an inevitability, it appeared humiliated and shrunken: 'On the morrow of the Second World War', observed Toynbee, 'the dwarfing of Europe is an unmistakably accomplished fact' (1948, p. 125).

Western Europe remained firmly within the West. The increasingly taboo associations of racial affiliation that clung to the term ensured that it was in no danger of being kicked out of the club. But now it was Europe's turn to appear peripheral. Western Europe, even when united

in a European Economic Community and then a Union, had become
a minor player in shaping the meaning of the West. This marginality
was not a reflection of a lack of political innovation. In particular, the
politics of post-Second World War Western Europe are notable for the
broad and deep acceptance of a political form that had previously been
merely an oppositional tradition across much of Europe, namely social
democracy. Yet the diminution of Europe's ability to act as a central
symbol of the West ensured that the post-Second World War social
democratic political settlement, achieved in a number of Western
European nations, had a relatively short-lived influence on developing
notions of either Westernisation or globalisation. At the very moment
that issues of social justice had finally come to the fore in the old heartland of the West, these concerns were becoming increasingly marginal
to the idea of the West.

In her insightful studies of British politics in the late 1940s, Kirby
(2000, p. 398) has drawn attention to 'the mood of antagonism to
American-style capitalism which existed in Britain, almost unimaginable
today'. This political current was vulnerable to the confusion of social
democracy with Soviet communism. As Kirby shows, British Foreign
Office officials were particularly sensitive to this equation and strained
to avoid projecting a socialist image of Britain abroad. This ambition
was eased by the fact that the large-scale experiments with the 'mixed
economy' that characterised post-war European state policy (exemplified
by nationalisation programmes and the expansion of 'cradle to grave'
welfare provision in a number of Western European countries), were far
less ideologically driven than is sometimes imagined. They were introduced, in large part, as *practical* solutions for war-torn economies. Thus
the desire to actively *proclaim* democratic socialism as a world model
was muted by the sense that, even if it was politically desired, capitalism was simply not up to the job of rebuilding new, modern states.

The conviction, increasingly common from the 1960s onwards, that
socialism is ideological whilst capitalism is pragmatic and 'hard-nosed',
may give a somewhat counter-instinctual flavour to these remarks.
However, the utilitarianism of post-war socialism was clear enough to,
otherwise non-partisan, commentators in the late 1940s. 'Post-war
conditions in Western Europe are not so bad as to give the desperate
remedies prescribed by communism', Toynbee told his audience at
Chatham House in 1947,

> but Western Europe is at the same time not so prosperous as to be able to
> afford the undiluted regime of private enterprise that still prevails in

North America above the Rio Grande. In these circumstances, Great Britain and her West European neighbours are each trying to arrive at a working compromise – suited to their own economic conditions here and now, and subject to their own modification in either direction as these conditions may change for better or for worse – between unrestricted free enterprise and unlimited socialism (1948, p. 147).

Many European socialists considered that the post-war period presented them with a historic opportunity to bury capitalism for good. However, the political confidence displayed by socialists at this time was powered less by dreamy idealism than by the concrete fact that capitalism had did not appear a credible way of ensuring post-war reconstruction, or of creating the kind of society that European workers were now demanding. Indeed, such considerations were being articulated before the war and during it. G.D.H. Cole's little book *Europe, Russia, and the Future*, published in Britain in 1941, is essentially a commentary on the central question its author poses: 'Can Europe go back to capitalism?' (see also Cole, 1932; Wright, 1979). As a socialist, Cole's answer is predictable. Less so, his emphasis on the *impracticality* of capitalism. His answer is an unblinking, common sense, no. Capitalism is an ideology of the past:

> a restoration of the old State system still on capitalist foundations – is, I believe, now out of the question over any considerable area as a solution having in it any element of durable success (p. 9).

Cole wanted to identify Western socialism as democratic socialism and, hence, distinguish it from its Soviet form. The introduction of socialism 'does not mean', he wrote,

> that Western Socialism has to adopt as its faith the Communism of the Russians. There are ways of thought and living in Western Socialism, belonging to the common cultural tradition of the Western peoples, which make this impossible as well as undesirable (p. 33).

We hear here a defence of the Western socialist tradition. Yet what a timorous statement it is. Cole's advocacy of democratic socialism seems reducible to the fact that it 'suits us'. Cole's hesitancy to criticise the USSR reflected the Soviet role in the war. But it is still clear that, given that socialism in the USSR was being articulated as a new and universal civilisation, to identify Western socialism in the way Cole does, as a local form suited to local, Western European conditions, was to admit its marginality.

A contentment with, or resignation to, the parochial, came to characterise the Western social democratic tradition. This is not an indication of innate humility on the part of Western socialists. It reflects, rather, an awareness of Europe being exceeded, both by its former colonies and by the two superpowers. The popularisation of the notion that social democracy was merely 'in-between' communism and capitalism may also have played a part. For it implied that, however workable and sustainable social democracy might prove, it was marginal to the real political conflict of the Cold War era, between the USA and capitalism and the USSR and communism. Thus Myrdal's (1980, p. 84) depiction of the two superpowers 'gaming over a passive Europe' contains a political as well as a military implication: Europe had been assigned and had largely accepted a subordinate identity.

Westernisation: victory in defeat

The dates of national independence are a familiar and long role-call. In September 1945 Ho Chi Minh declared the independence of Vietnam. By the end of that decade India (1947), Burma (1948) and Indonesia (1950) had joined the list. Over the next twenty-five years, the British and French empires had gone. From the end of the Second World War, especially from 1948 onwards, global geo-politics was increasingly staged as a clash between the East (i.e., USSR+other communist countries) and the West (that is, USA+European heritage capitalist countries+Japan). This binary division provided the framework for the slightly more fluid model which emerged from the mid-1950s which had a Western part, a Soviet (or Sino-Soviet) part and a 'Third World' (or 'Afro-Asian') component.

The rise of national self-confidence in European colonies and ex-colonies appeared to augur a world preparing to escape European control. Inevitably, these events provoked a crisis of Western authority.[1] Yet, although highly developed at the more extreme ends of the political spectrum and within youth culture, any sense of Western decline was considerably tempered within mainstream intellectual circles by an appreciation of the global reach of Westernisation. Toynbee's prophesy of a Westernised world culture was proving to be an influential vision. Thus, although political turbulence and insurgency were acknowledged, a kind of quite triumphalism could also be voiced (for example, Kohn, 1957; McNeill, 1963; Ormsby-Gore, 1966); a harbinger of later neo-liberal proclamations that the West had won and that history was at an end.

The ability to pluck triumph from colonial retreat rested on the conviction that Westernisation had now acquired a life of its own; that it no longer needed hands-on control or encouragement. Although this perspective had been expounded before the collapse of European colonialism, it became more widely accepted as the new nations of Asia and Africa were formed. The belief that the process of nation-making, combined with the take-up of industrial and scientific methodologies and technologies across the world, signalled not merely a commitment to, but a profound internalisation of, Western values, turned colonial retreat into cultural victory. At its most confidant, this line of argument rendered the military assertiveness of the West in the past a symptom of weakness, an outcome of the need to physically dominate in the absence of the ability to dominate where it really matters, in the arena of ideas.

An illustration of this attitude may be found in the speech to the Parliament of South Africa delivered by the British Prime Minister, Harold Macmillan in 1960. In it he spoke of the 'winds of changes' sweeping Africa. It is less frequently recalled that he understood this blowing away of the past as a vindication of Western influence. More specifically, Macmillan called attention to the way the West had ignited national consciousness in non-Western societies, as seen in the rise of nationalism and in a willingness to acquire modern technology. His speech exemplifies how Westernisation and decolonisation could be *combined* by construing the former as the source of political and intellectual liberty that had led to the latter.

> Ever since the break-up of the Roman Empire, one of the constant facts of political life in Europe has been the emergence of independent nations... In the twentieth century, and especially since the end of the war, the process which gave birth to the nation-states of Europe have been repeated all over the world. We have seen the awakening of national consciousness in peoples who have for centuries lived in dependence on some other power. Fifteen years ago this movement speared through Asia. Many countries there, of different race and civilisations, pressed their claim to an independent national life. Today the same thing is happening in Africa. The most striking of all the impressions I have formed since I left London a month ago is of the strength of African national consciousness. In different places it may take different forms. But it is happening everywhere. The wind of change is blowing through the continent... this tide of national consciousness which is now rising in Africa is a fact for which you and we and the other nations of the Western world are ultimately responsible. For its causes are to be found in the achievements of Western civilisation in pushing forward

the frontiers of knowledge, applying science in the service of human needs, expanding food production, speeding and multiplying means of communication, and, above all, spreading education (1966, p. 512).

Macmillan assumes that the role of South Africa in this process is as a Western nation. It is an assumption that couples a desire to flatter his white audience with a 'common-sense' conviction that white people are Western people and white dominated societies are, *ipso facto*, Western. Yet it provides an awkward moment in what is supposed to be a magnanimous speech. For it implies that, no matter how hard the 'winds of change' may blow across Africa, *full* access to Western modernity will be out of the reach of most people.

Yet, what stands out most starkly from Macmillan's speech is the way that, by imagining the West to be the common heritage of all peoples, even those overseeing the collapse of empire could construe in their work a kind of victory.

Arnold Toynbee's interpretation of Westernisation carried a comparable claim. It was inflected by his, in part religious, belief in the desirability of a single world culture. For it was not simply a Western world culture that Toynbee forecast but a new synthesis, framed, imagined and disseminated by the West. It is a final testament to Western superiority and achievement, Toynbee (1948) explained, that it alone should be capable of forging a multicultural synthesis of world cultures. In fact, Toynbee's vision of transcendence through multicultural synthesis was not entirely novel. It echoes the advocacy of 'The cosmic Race' developed by the Mexican politician and social reformer José Vasconcelos (1997, first published 1925) over twenty years earlier. Nevertheless, the appeal of such ideas to Westerners is obvious; for they provide for them a happy conflation of anti-racism and cultural supremacism.

This formula was soon to occupy a central role in popular narratives of 'the victory' of the West. In *The Triumph of the West* (1985) by John Roberts, a book drawn from the 13-part BBC series of the same title, the real and final conquest of the West is seen to come in its disappearance, that is in the West's development from a local force with the power to dominate others into *the* global culture of the modern. Roberts's final two sentences explain:

> What seems to be clear is that the story of western civilisation is now the story of mankind, its influences so diffused that old positions and antitheses are now meaningless. 'The West' is hardly now a meaningful term, except for historians (p. 431).

This argument sidesteps self-congratulatory bombast for a more subtle, yet profoundly Eurocentric, commitment to world unity. It refutes crude attacks on the non-West and acknowledges anti-colonial critiques of Western racism and the post-colonial collapse of European imperial power. Yet it ultimately relies on the identification of the West as the cockpit of history, as the bestower of modernity, and consequently as the arbiter of modernity, consigning all other cultures to the status of ethnic heritage.

Neo-liberal democracy: Western triumph and Western blueprint

> An awkward feature of the American ideology of free enterprise – as well as of the Russian ideology of Communism – is precisely that it presents a social 'blue print' as a panacea for every conceivable social ill in every known set of social circumstances (Toynbee, 1948, p. 148).

We have seen already in this chapter a shift in the political centre of gravity of the West, a shift towards the USA and free market principles as models of the authentic West. This section offers a critical interrogation of this process. More specifically, it detects a utopian current within the neo-liberal Western new world order.

I am using 'utopian' as a term of criticism. Although it is often seen as the playpen of benign eccentrics, the pursuit of utopia has been dominated by totalitarians. Utopianism is driven by a simplistic vision of the perfect society. It is a society in which all social and economic mechanisms are in accordance with one vision. Thus, it has become common in studies of Soviet communism and Nazism to label these movements as utopian (for example, Heller and Nekrich, 1985; Burleigh and Wippermann, 1991). It may be objected here that both these ideologies were avowedly anti-utopian and, indeed, tended to stress the practicality and verifiability of their methods. Yet the fact that utopian politics does not usually label itself as such is no surprise. Through its associations with romanticism and anarchism, the term 'utopian' has become an exoticised tradition against which all other political forms like to define themselves. Utopianism is something 'proper politics' conceals; something that, once glimpsed, exposes claims of hard-nosed practicality as attempts to disguise tyranny.

Within neo-liberal politics, pragmatism is rhetorically to the fore. It is 'what works' that counts. The notion that neo-liberalism does, in fact, work has, in large part, been built on the ability to correlate its implementation in a range of countries with rising average (but, often,

not median) income, the reduction of unemployment and lower infla-
tion. However, its other consequences, such the erosion of economic
and social security for the majority population, and the enforcement of
a militantly profit-led attitude to the human and natural world, indicate that its long-term social costs can outweigh its short-term economic
benefits.

McReason or McMagic?

Perhaps the ultimate icon of neo-liberalism's global success are the
golden arches of the McDonalds food franchise chain. The two thinkers
most associated with a critical interrogation of 'McDonaldisation',
Barber (1996) and Ritzer (2000), have also provided some interesting
insights into the utopian logic of neo-liberalism. Barber's analysis is the
more uneven of the two,[2] but his portrait of 'McWorld's' vision of the
future is immediately recognisable.

> [It] paints the future in shimmering pastels, a busy portrait of onrushing
> economic, technological, and ecological forces that demand integration
> and uniformity and that mesmerize peoples everywhere with fast music,
> fast computers, and fast food – MTV, Macintosh and McDonald's –
> pressing nations into one homogenous theme park (1996, p. 4).

Within 'McWorld' freedom and democracy are aligned with con-
sumers' power to choose. However, as world markets are globalised,
homogenised and monopolised, consumer choice is not necessarily
expanded. Drawing on examples of the aggressive campaigns by
American food companies to weaken cultural attachments to 'local'
foods, Barber again employs satire of the utopian ambition of McWorld
to make his point,

> If only every Indonesian could switch from tea to Coke – and from sandals
> to Nikes and from rice to chicken McNuggets and from saris to Laura
> Ashley dresses and from oxen to Arnold Schwarzenegger videos and from
> Buddhism to consumerism – imagine what 'worlds of opportunities'
> would be thrown open to McWorld's bold corporate adventures; imagine
> what kind of homogenous and profitable McWorld-wide market those
> once distinctive regions would constitute (p. 70).

In *The McDonaldization of Society*, Ritzer (2000) empirically
expands Barber's depiction by detailing the routinisation and banalisa-
tion of diverse social roles that are characteristic of contemporary
capitalism (Ritzer uses such terms as 'McJobs', 'McIdentities',
'McMovieworld', 'McDoctors', 'McUniversities'). However, Ritzer is

also more theoretically explicit than Barber. His McDonaldisation thesis is offered as an update of Weber's idea that capitalism leads to the accelerating rationalisation and, hence, disenchantment of the world. 'McDonaldization is related to, if not inextricably intertwined with, disenchantment', says Ritzer, 'A world without magic and mystery is another irrational consequence of increasing rationalisation' (p. 133).

Yet is neo-liberalism really without magic? Developing Marx's concern with commodity fetishisation, a number of commentators have recently begun to explore the role, not simply of the irrational but, more provocatively, of the magical, in capitalism. In *Capital*, Marx talked metaphorically of the 'mystery of commodities, all the magic and necromancy that surrounds the products of labour as long as they take the form of commodities (1998, p. 110). The role of transformational rituals takes a more literal form within contemporary magico-Marxism.[3] Marx's 'entire theory relies heavily for its exposition on magical allusion', Taussig (1997, p. 139) tells us. Taussig adds darkly that Marx's 'text seems to welcome the mysteries and gleefully embrace them in that instant before they crush him'. The celebration and institutionalisation of ritual and talismanism in the process of capitalist financial speculation has also begun to attract attention (Comaroff and Comaroff, 2000). Drawing out the contrast between this new work and the Weberian assumption that capitalism leads to a disenchantment of the world, Harootunian (2002, p. 29) cites Marx to explain that:

> Capitalist modernity was enchanted from its beginnings and has continued to be so precisely because it is a world populated by 'objects of value' and 'objectified values'. And the subsequent history of capitalist modernization everywhere has been marked by ceaseless enchantment acting in concert with commodification and consumption to ensure the smooth reproduction of accumulation and the fiction of rationalizing means and ends...If an older liberalism in the age of the first coming [of capitalism] once appealed to culture and religion (as different sides of enchantment) in the hope of finding the reservoir of true (class based) value, the neoliberalism of today supplies enchantment with newer forms of magic to enable economies to perform and create objectified values.

Clearly we have contradictory interpretations here. Ritzer sees a world of rationalism and disenchantment whilst the analysts Harootunian draws on have reached the opposite conclusion. Both the 'disenchanters' and 'enchanters' are offering revealing arguments. However, we may also conclude that the Weberian and Marxist traditions they are drawing on are proving inadequate: they propel Ritzer into an a priori acceptance that neo-liberalism is a form of rationalism, and the magico-Marxists into the exoticising, anthropological language of ritual and sorcery. Here my suspicion that neo-liberalism contains a utopian dynamic may be helpful. It allows us to appreciate the current of irrationalism within neo-liberalism, more specifically, to see in it a desire to escape from logic and immerse oneself in faith. Yet it also connects neo-liberalism with a clear political tradition and form. Thus it allows us to place neo-liberalism alongside other political projects that have had similarly extraordinary ambitions.

Capitalist utopias

An unexpected source of doubts about 'global capitalism' has been the political theorist John Gray. Gray (2002, 2003) has moved from being a supporter to a critic of economic liberalism, a transition provoked by concerns about its universalist pretensions and democratic potential. One of Gray's favourite terms for the neo-liberal experiment is 'utopian'. Thus he aligns the 'global free market' with other extreme political movements, such as Bolshevism, noting:

> What these Utopias have in common is more fundamental than their dif-
> ferences. In their cult of reason and efficiency, their ignorance of history and
> their contempt for the ways of life they consign to poverty or extinction,
> they embody the same rationalist hubris and cultural imperialism that
> have marked the central traditions of Enlightenment thinking throughout
> its history (2002, p. 3).

Gray rightly identifies rationalist and unversalist hubris as part of the utopian imagination. However, utopianism has a more specific structure than Gray's general portrait allows. Utopias are traditionally based on fantasies of the past, the future and far away places. Utopia, then, is less about 'no place' (the Greek meaning of the term) but about real places and times misinterpreted and misunderstood. Utopia's have, then, a *mythological* structure; something that Gray's emphasis on utopian rationalism inevitably misses.

Myths of the past, the future and somewhere else, were constant reference points for the European utopian socialists of the nineteenth century. In England the egalitarian past was located in pre-Norman England. The future was represented as a moment of return to, and reaffirmation of, the values of that lost, Anglo-Saxon, community. By contrast, exotic destinations provided a present day – but conveniently geographically displaced – fulfilment of the utopian imagination. For nineteenth-century utopians, the idyllic, tribal societies of the tropics were a favourite model of 'primitive' or natural equality. *The utopian triptych of the past, future and exotic places, is equally apparent amongst neo-liberals.* The notion that a period once existed when laissez-faire went unfettered and was, hence, successful, performs the role of historical myth. Nineteenth-century Britain and USA are often offered as prime examples (including by many critics, see, for example, Keynes, 1926; Hobsbawn, 1968). In fact, the golden age of laissez-faire was always more of an ideal than a reality. As an ideology it certainly had a wide audience amongst the socially liberal middle class in Britain. However, the notion that it was put into practice, or that it was successful, is far more contentious (Taylor, 1972). The interventions of tradition, the state and of colonialism ensured that there was little opportunity for visions of a truly commercial society to ever be put to the test.

Early economic liberalism was premised on a set of cultural assumptions that are no longer widely held. In *The Wealth of Nations* Adam Smith (1910, p. 400; first published 1776) offers a well-known formula of liberal morality: 'By pursuing his own interest [the merchant] frequently promotes that of the society more effectually than when he really intends to promote it.' However, a couple of sentences earlier, Smith also notes that whilst the merchant may not intend 'to promote the public interest', he is 'led by an invisible hand to promote an end which was no part of his intention'. Smith's 'invisible hand' is a reference to the laws of supply and demand. But it also evokes another force, the divine and, hence, benign ordering of both nature and human affairs. Thus human greed would be fettered by non-economic instincts. As explained by Habakkuk, for Smith,

> there existed behind the apparent confusion of events an order which was maintained . . . by the operation of instincts planted in men by Providence. This providence was assumed to be benign and the order so established was favourable to the welfare of men (Habakkuk, 1971, p. 45).

Contemporary neo-liberals have a much higher level of faith in both the global capacities of the free market and in the inherent and self-sufficient wisdom of anti-protectionism than their putative forbears. This helps to explain why the politics of economic liberalism have shifted so markedly. The emancipatory and egalitarian agendas of eighteenth-century liberals bear little comparison with the lobbying for international, corporate freedoms that characterise the activities of contemporary champions of the market. The shift from a human welfare to a corporate agenda has also severed the traditional allegiance between liberalism and individualism. Neo-liberals pursue and defend the freedoms, not of individuals, but of an already enormously powerful business sector.

The exotic geographies of anarchist and romantic utopians tended to be based on fantasies of unspoilt, primitive communities. The utopian currents within neo-liberalism have produced a somewhat different set of aspirational 'dream destinations'. Supposedly 'free market' countries, entrepreneurial urban niches and Export Processing Zones perform, however, the same structural function: of providing places that seem to prove the possibility of neo-liberalism as a total social philosophy. In the first of these categories the USA continues to loom large. At a more local level, shopping malls and the virtual spaces of e-commerce appear to reflect the fulfilment of a consumerist society in which democracy is just another form of shopping (and vice versa). That the places of capitalist utopia are also places of Westernisation and Americanisation is in keeping with another characteristic impulse behind utopian thought, its desire for homogeneity. Utopian ambitions are marked by a desire to create one landscape, one solution, one final fix. They do not permit deviation from their ideal, except within their own terms. Heterogeneity is only permitted as a form of empty symbolism. The sensation of sameness that one finds within shopping malls, real or virtual, is not undermined in any way by the vast range of products that are being sold. For, when compared, for example, to the traditional British high street, the variety of social interactions and possibilities on offer in shopping malls is negligible. The experience of variety is reduced to a variety of things to buy, in the same way from the same sort of outlets. In this way, public space – with its accommodating and non-instrumental sense of human activity – is largely extinguished.

Export Processing Zones (EPZs) provide an even more ambitious model of an ideal neo-liberal society. They have been heralded as sites of exemplary economic practice. The key characteristics of EPZs are: exemption from duty and value added tax; unrestricted offshore borrowing; freedom from exchange controls; repatriation of dividends; work permits for managerial, technical and specialist staff; goods not produced for domestic consumption and, finally, exemption from various domestic heath and safety laws. EPZs are today offered as prototypes for the integration of the entire Third World into the orbit of Western wealth and finance. The World Export Processing Association (1999), which represents EPZs in over 40 countries, explains that it is their 'highly flexible operating environment' that makes them so attractive. No unions or labour regulations distort this pure space. Yet, the notion that EPZs exemplify undiluted neo-liberalism avoids certain details of their development and survival. EPZs are, in fact, the creatures and creations of the states that establish them. For example, they use the infrastructure their sponsor state's provide, their educated human resources, and their physical protection. Indeed, even the strongest claim EPZs have to an autonomous identity, their workforce flexibility, has clear limits.

Since it is through labour flexibility that they tend to cut costs, there exists within EPZs a self-destructive momentum to accelerate this process and, hence, to provide less and less integration between the company and its staff. This process is finite and, after a while, starts to produce less effective employees. It certainly provides no basis to imagine that EPZs are a successful model of neo-liberalism that can be extended ever further and deeper into the world economy.

Myths of the past, of the present and the future have always been at the heart of utopian politics. Rationalism and irrationalism are combined and cohered within such projects, as they create and enforce a blueprint for the earth. Neo-liberalism is part of this tradition. However, unlike other forms of utopianism, it has secured sole custody over the authority and the name of the West. Thus, the idea of the West has been narrowed into a very particular project. It is a process that, as I explain in the conclusion to this chapter, makes the West vulnerable at the very moment of its triumph.

However, there remains one more aspect of neo-liberalism's utopian character that must be addressed. One of the contrary aspects of utopianism is that, although it wishes to defer political gratification to an idealised vision of the future, it also wishes to be above criticism in the present. Thus, even though it placed social perfection on a receding horizon, the Soviet state forbade internal political criticism. The communist path was claimed to be unsurpassable. Here the quiet note of resignation that often accompanies utopian thought can be discerned. Having itemised what a perfect society consists of, and having placed ticks all down that list, utopianism is driven to a rather weary message: 'this is as good as it gets'. Soviet ideologists were implying that history had come to an end. But it is neo-liberals who have had the audacity to make this position explicit.

As good as it gets: Fukuyama's weary utopianism

It might seem perverse to offer Fukuyama's (1992) *The End of History and the Last Man* as a utopian text. Fukuyama is careful not to merely celebrate the achievement of 'liberal democracy'. He is restlessly aware that people will seek to oppose its certainties and confines. However, the *End of History* also offers the most sophisticated argument we have for neo-liberal democracy as a political achievement. Fukuyama asserts that 'liberal democracy' has delivered an unsurpassable framework for the recognition and fulfilment of human needs, not just for those in the West but for everyone. It is this belief that establishes a persistent utopian trend within his work.

Fukuyama argues that 'history has come to an end if the present form of social and political organization is *completely satisfying* to human beings in their most essential characteristics' (p. 136). He sees the origins of this process in modern citizenship and its confirmation in the present day: 'there are no serious ideological competitors left to liberal democracy' (p. 211). Yet, although 'liberal democracy' is the key political term of *The End of History* its meaning remains elusive. Fukuyama roots political liberalism in the universalist philosophies of the Enlightenment, most notably in Hegel's universal history. However, it is then offered as the worldview of the contemporary West with little regard for the historical specificity of the forms of liberal and civic thought of the eighteenth and early nineteenth centuries. In fact, what animates contemporary 'liberal' endeavour is better termed 'neo-liberalism'. 'Neo-liberalism' registers both the re-imagining of market forces as a total philosophy and the dawning of a capitalist era in which corporate institutions have a global reach and a power over individual freedoms that would have been hard to imagine two hundred years ago.

Part of Fukuyama's dexterity is the occasional, fleeting, way he incorporates a more inclusive interpretation of the category 'liberal democracy'. Fukuyama briefly alludes to the fact that 'liberal democracy' accommodates a variety of traditions, including 'social democracy' (the example given is Scandinavia) and 'statist regimes' (the countries mentioned here are Mexico and India). These political forms and these geographical examples have a peripheral and minor place in *The End of History*. This is not because they are claimed to be less democratic but because they are seen to be insufficiently capitalist. For the most part 'the broad tent of liberal democracy' (p. 294) is shrunk to fit only one occupant, namely 'Anglo-Saxon' free market democracy. The success of the 'oldest and most durable liberal societies – those in the Anglo-Saxon tradition' (p. 145) is offered as resting on *one* type of economics, the 'liberal principles in economics – the 'free market' – [which] have spread, and have succeeded' (p. xiii). Thus Fukuyama's history is also a geography: it is 'Anglo-Saxon' society, more specifically US society, that is offered as the culmination of 'the struggle for recognition'.

Given the considerable and continuing levels of state intervention and public spending in 'Anglo-Saxon' countries, including within the USA, Fukuyama's belief in the ascendancy of the 'free market' is one of the aspects of his thesis that appears most idealised. In Britain and the USA, the social and physical infrastructure of society is not left to the free-market. Unsurprisingly, Fukuyama makes no mention of those studies of the modern capitalist state which have demonstrated the inevitability of state intervention and 'welfare'. Offe (1984, 1985) has provided some of the most penetrating of these investigations. Offe stresses that the administrative and financial assistance that contemporary capitalism requires from international and national forms of governance make any claims for the autonomous success of free markets both suspect and unverifiable. He also shows that the increasing commodification of the social and natural world and the related expansion of the ideologies and practices of consumerism, are dependent upon the development of an educated, socio-economically mobile and ideologically enculturated population. In order to create such an educated, self-motivated society a state sector is required capable of providing educational, health and other social interventions beyond the means and organisational capacity of the business community. This welfare sector is integral to capitalism but structurally at a remove from the ethics and praxis of the free market. It is, Offe (1984, p. 48) explains, 'foreign to capital', yet capital is dependent upon it. 'The embarrassing secret of the welfare state', Offe (1984, p. 153) continues, 'is that while ... capitalism cannot exist with, neither can it exist without, the welfare state'.

Conclusions: the vulnerability of the neo-liberal blueprint

The identification of the idea of the West with capitalism is neither surprising nor particularly new. From 1917 to 1991 the West's West was shaped in opposition to communism, more specifically the authoritarian communism of the Soviet Union. However, it remains the case that the idea of the West, both before 1917 and for many years after, was more politically plural than the West we are offered today. Over the past thirty years, the neo-liberal appropriation of the idea of the West has introduced an intellectual narrowness to the concept. It has become a very particular model, associated with specific economic practices (such as privatisation, and labour and capital market flexibility) that are globally and militarily enforced.

What Coronil (2000, p. 354) has called 'the dissolution of the "West" into the market' can easily be read as a sign of its success. When a pattern of domination becomes so extensive as to be accepted as part of everyday life, something curious happens. It disappears. More precisely, it becomes a natural, common sense, aspect of existence and, as such, unworthy of notice or comment. However, I want to conclude this chapter by offering another scenario. For the association of the West with 'the market' may also be seen as a process that makes the West *vulnerable*. It can do this in two ways:

1. by associating the West with a rigid formula for success in a volatile global economic and political system; and
2. by weakening the association between the West, democracy and political pluralism.

The periodic crises of capitalism over the last century have proved its adaptability. Within Western Europe and North America, economic slumps have not led to anti-capitalist revolution, largely because Western workers have believed in the possibility of reform. In his *A History of Soviet Russia*, E.H. Carr makes a telling point about the Western history of non-revolution:

> Lenin never really understood why 'reformism', which meant nothing in Russia, was a persistent and successful rival to the teaching of revolution in western Europe, why illegal action, which was accepted as a matter of course by Russian workers, aroused strong prejudices in the west (1958a, p. 185).

What Lenin did not appreciate, Carr tells us, is that many – perhaps, most – Western workers had faith in the flexibility of their own societies. I mention Carr's appraisal because it indicates that a key aspect of the past success of Western society was its room for manoeuvre. Economic crisis and political unrest have been accommodated by minor or major reforms. The substantial re-ordering of the roles and responsibilities of state and business in the post-Second World War period, in order to create the 'welfare state', is, perhaps, the principal example of this adaptability.

Adaptability is a resource subverted by blueprint politics. Utopianism is rigid and doctrinaire and, hence, its history is littered with failures. It must be admitted that neo-liberalism is not simply and purely utopian. But it contains that political trace. It has acquired utopian characteristics and has developed a utopian tendency. With this tendency comes a vulnerability to collapse. For if reform does not seem possible, then the kind of attachments and loyalties that so perplexed Lenin, will wither. The believe that distinct political programmes and aspirations not only exist but are viable choices has meant that, in the past, the West has been able to retain a broad political constituency and culture. If such choices cannot be accommodated within the 'Western model', then the resolution of crises becomes far more difficult.

The weight of emphasis within the new, neo-liberal model of the West is upon the West as an economic system. It may be objected that the West is also associated with democracy. Moreover, that not only has Westernisation become synonymous with democratisation but that this process is inseparable from the liberties that arise from a free market economy. The plausibility of this argument has suffered in recent years as a consequence of the development of one-party tendencies in capitalist Russia and free market economics in authoritarian Asian societies, most notably in China. On the other hand, democracy can, at least, be correlated to the spread of capitalism in Eastern Europe and Latin America. In sum, it seems that whilst neo-liberalism does not need democracy, neither is it necessarily hostile to it. The question that remains, though, is what the *kind* of democracy is enabled by neo-liberalism? Clearly, if neo-liberalism was an actively pro-democratic force its application should be able to be correlated with the drive for greater popular participation and control. Moreover, we would expect to find that neo-liberalism's ideological heartlands, the USA and Britain, had experienced an upsurge in democratic control. In fact, both societies have seen a crisis in popular participation in democracy and, at least in the case of Britain, have fewer institutions under democratic control today than prior to the ascendancy of neo-liberalism. There has been no democratising project to accompany liberalisation. This pattern is indicative of the political character of contemporary Westernisation: it *pursues* liberalisation but merely acknowledges democracy. The former is the active partner, the passion, the latter a hollow duty. Thus we are left with democracy as neo-liberals would like it, not market forces as democrats would like them. I return to this unsatisfactory state of affairs in my 'Conclusion'.

Further reading

Western social democracy

Some of the most useful assessments of social democratic regimes in post-Second World War Europe derive from national histories. For example, the tensions and limitations of social democracy in Britain emerge clearly from Kenneth Morgan's *Labour in Power 1945–1951* (1984, Oxford, Clarendon Press). The specific issue of the British Government's management of the image of British social democracy in the USA is addressed in Caroline Anstey's essay 'The projection of British socialism: Foreign Office publicity and American opinion, 1945–50', *Journal of Contemporary History* (1984, 19, 3, pp. xxx) and Dianne Kirby's 'Divinely sanctioned: The Anglo-American Cold War alliance and the defence of Western civilization and Christianity, 1945–48', *Journal of Contemporary History* (2000, 35, 3, pp. 385–412).

Western neo-liberal democracy

Francis Fukuyama's *The End Of History And The Last Man* (1992, London, Hamish Hamilton) remains an essential text for those who wish to explore the optimism of neo-liberal democracy. Also to be recommended is Michael Mandelbaum's *The Ideas that Conquered the World: Peace, Democracy, and Free Markets in the Twenty-first Century* (2002, New York, Public Affairs). Although sometimes mistakenly aligned with this group of thinkers, Samuel Huntingdon asserts the impossibility of thorough global Westernisation. His *The Clash of Civilisations and the Remaking of the World Order* (1997, London: Simon & Schuster) is a fascinating if anachronistic challenge to the idea of globalisation.

There are many excellent and accessible critical accounts of the neo-liberal blueprint:

Barber, B. (1996) *Jihad vs. McWorld: How Globalism and Tribalism are Reshaping the World*, New York, Ballantine Books.

Frank, T. (2001) *One Market Under God: Extreme Capitalism, Market Populism and the End of Economic Democracy*, London, Secker & Warburg.

Gibney, M. (ed.) (2003) *Globalizing Rights: The Oxford Amnesty Lectures 1999*, Oxford, Oxford University Press.

Gray, J. (2002) *False Dawn: The Delusions of Global Capitalism*, London, Granta.

Hutton, W. (2002) *The World We're In*, London, Little, Brown.

Klein, N. (2002) *Fences and Windows: Dispatches from the Frontlines of the Globalization Debate*, London, Flamingo.

Luttwak, E. (1999) *Turbo Capitalism: Winners and Losers in the Global Economy*, London, Orion Business Books.

Scruton, R. (2002) *The West and the Rest: Globalization and the Terrorist Threat*, London, Continuum.

Chapter 7

Western Dystopia: Radical Islamism and Anti-Westernism

Introduction

When Frantz Fanon's *L'An Cinq de la Révolution Algérienne* appeared in 1959 it seemed to be part of an unstoppable tide of anti-colonial socialist liberation. Translated as *Studies in a Dying Colonialism*, the publisher's blurb on the first English edition (1965) proclaims that this is a work that 'has much to say to a world dominated by revolutionary movements in the underdeveloped countries'. Introducing the book, Adolfo Gilly reminds us that 'Revolution is mankind's way of life today. This is the age of revoution; the "age of indifference" is gone forever' (p. 1).

Few would have predicted, in either 1959 or 1965, that our 'age of revolution' would see the retreat of internationalist socialism within 'underdeveloped countries'. Or that some of the most resilient forms of ideological anti-colonialism would come to be rooted, not in projects of secular insurrection, but in religious movements that have managed to harness the rhetoric and anger of left-wing revolt and shape them to their own ends.

This chapter has two aims: (1) to illustrate how anti-Westernism has been recuperated by radical Islamism; and (2) to exemplify how radical Islamism constructs a dystopian model of the West.

To do this I employ a limited but focused methodology. I shall be looking at two examples of occidentalist literature, one from Iran (Jalal Al-e Ahmad's *Plagued by the West*) and one from Pakistan (Maryam Jameelah's *Western Civilization Condemned By Itself*). These are not recent works. Both were initially written in the 1960s. Yet they provide important insights into contemporary debates and concerns. More specifically, they have been chosen because they represent different traditions of anti-Westernism. Through them we can witness the absorption of political by religious anti-Westernism. Al-e Ahmad's book, which is the earlier and more famous of the two, provides an example of political anti-Westernism. By contrast, Jameelah's work exemplifies radical Islamist clichés of Western dystopia, clichés that are used to evoke an Islamic social utopia.

Given the tendency within much post-September 11 Western commentary to conflate radical Islamism with both terrorism and an all-consuming hatred of the West, it is necessary to note that I make no such equation here. The West is a key geo-political category for the radical Islamists I discuss (as it is for Al-e Ahmad). But it is corrupt Islamic societies that draw their most heated condemnations. Al-Qa'idah'-style violence against Western targets represents an extreme tangent from the main body of radical Islamism.[1] If the Islamisation of anti-Westernism is important it is not because it led to September 11 but because it has come to dominate the political landscape and lexicon of militant resistance across the Islamic world.

The clash of utopias?

In identifying anti-Westernism within a *utopian* radical Islamism, I am conscious of a misleading conclusion that might be drawn from a skim of Chapters 6 and 7: namely, that neo-liberalism and radical Islamism are mirror images of each other.

The 'narrowing of the west' does have a relationship with the 'narrowing of anti-Westernism'. It is a relationship that has witnessed the development of utopian tendencies in both Western and Islamic societies. However, these are not equivalent movements. At the start of the twenty-first century, and on a global scale, anti-Westernism is a defensive current. Its power and influence are small when set beside the omnipresent economic and military might of the West.

It is useful to be reminded that anti-Western utopianism has a long and diverse history. Needless to say, few of these traditions actually claimed to be utopian. Yet, as we saw in the last chapter, utopianism is not something usually openly declared. Four of the most important forms are:

1. *Communist utopia*   From the late 1920s the communist regime of the Soviet Union became wedded to anti-Western positions which helped define a utopian model of Soviet society's potential and achievements.
2. *Primitivist utopia*   Primitivism conflates modernity with Western modernity. Thus in escaping and rejecting modernity it is,

inevitably, anti-Western. Primitivism may be discerned in many parts of the world, examples including radical environmental movements and some forms of social ultra-conservatism.

3. *Indigenist utopia*   Here an idealised non-Western ethnic community is imagined in order to encourage a return to cultural and economic independence. This form has sometimes overlapped with primitivism. However, it is important to keep the two conceptually separate, not least because primitivism, unlike indigenism, is shackled to the West (through its desire to be its 'other') and to anti-modernism.

4. *Transnational cultural utopianism*   Derives from cultural traditions that are international and transethnic. The principal examples of cultural utopianism are continental affiliations (for example, pan-Asianism and pan-Africanism) and religious movements (notably radical Islamism).

The utopian impulse is not *intrinsic* to communism, indigenism or transnational cultural solidarity. Nor does the use of a stereotyped, negative image of the West necessarily involve a corresponding fantasy of non-Western perfection. Utopianism develops from the narrowing of the political and intellectual horizons of these currents. In large part, they become utopian because they exist in a defensive relationship with the West. Deploying dystopian images of a Western world which is imagined to be encircling and all-powerful, they become imprisoned by in a discourse of permanent resistance. Thus, each of these currents has often seen critique of the West mutating into a fundamentalist rejection of all things Western. It is a manoeuvre that again highlights the difference between the Western neo-liberal blueprint and these 'alternative' positions. Neo-liberals are so confident in the power and ascendancy of their vision that all other stances are interpreted as anachronistic, as non- or anti-modern. Since the end of the Cold War, there is no single or core dystopia that neo-liberalism is defined in relation to, only a set of errant faiths, none of which appear successful in generating economic growth and, therefore, none of which are taken seriously as rivals. I shall return to the consequences of neo-liberalism's global power for Islamism at the end of this chapter.

The Islamisation of anti-Westernism

I am using the, admittedly clumsy, phrase – 'the Islamisation of anti-Westernism' – to denote how radical Islamism has been able to absorb, yet also discipline and subvert, anti-Western sentiment. It has become a master narrative of anti-Westernism, yet one that is incapable of giving voice either to the strength or the range of anti- and non-Western feeling.

The political uses of being 'Plagued by the West'

Plagued by the West is a short book that circulated in samizdat form in the 1960s and 1970s during the reign of Muhammad Reza Shah Pahlavi. It is a work that has also been translated and published in English as *Occidentotis* (1984), although its Persian title, *Gharbzadegi*, is more literally translated as 'Weststruckness'.

Jalal Al-e Ahmad (1923–1969) wrote *Plagued by the West* in the early 1960s (the translation I will using here is of the second edition, written in 1963). At the beginning of the 1979 revolution in Iran, after years of widespread but covert distribution, it 'flooded almost every bookshop and bookstand in Iran' (Yarshater, 1982, p. ix). Al-e Ahmad subsequently received official sanction from a variety of quarters. Sadeq Qutbzada, who later became Foreign Minister, noted in 1979 that he was one of the 'models in the struggle of intellectuals to negate the influence of [westernism]' (cited by Sprachman, 1982, p. xiii). Sayyid Ali Khamenei, the religious leader of Iran since 1989, said of Al-e Ahmad that he 'stood at the summit of the literature of resistance' (cited by Dabashi, 1993, p. 94).

In his wide-ranging study of the intellectual roots of the Iranian revolution, Hamid Dabashi (1993) makes the case that Al-e Ahmad's writings were 'more instrumental than those of any other single individual in pointing elements of a mobilizing ideological language towards a revolutionary discourse' (p. 41). Of *Plagued by the West* (Dabashi translates the title as *Westoxication*), Dabashi says the following:

> [It is] perhaps the single most important essay published in modern Iranian history. In creating a wide range of positive and negative reactions, in constituting the very vocabulary of Iranian social criticism in the two decades preceding the Revolution, and in formulating the most essential 'anti-western' disposition of the Islamic revolutionary discourse, no other single text comes even close to *Westoxication* (p. 74).

However, the acceptance of *Plagued by the West* by Islamist revolutionaries reflects the *absorption* of established anti-Shah and anti-Western traditions rather than an active, or straightforward, commitment to Al-e Ahmad's argument. Although Al-e Ahmad was committed to notions of organic tradition and religious and national continuity, *Plagued by the West* remains militantly pro-democratic.

Indeed, politically, it has more in common with the progressive, Islamic modernism of the exiled scholar Ali Shariati than with Khomeini's blueprints for earthly perfection. Another connection with Shariati may also be noted. For, whilst studying in Paris in the early 1960s, Shariati became influenced by the anti-colonial agenda associated with Frantz Fanon. As a result he commenced (but never completed) a Persian translation of *A Dying Colonialism*. In some ways *Plagued by the West* prefigures this orientation. For like Fanon in *Black Skin, White Masks* (1986, first published 1952) or Albert Memmi in *The Colonizer and the Colonized* (1965, first published 1957), Al-e Ahmad draws attention to the existential and psychological damage of 'westitis'. Moreover, as the passages cited later illustrate, Al-e Ahmad's style is informal and anti-authoritarian. Reflecting the author's Marxist leanings (from 1943 to 1948 Al-e Ahmad was a leading member of the pro-Soviet Tudeh Party) it is suffused with the populist, critical tone that had come to be the preferred voice of the international countercultural and leftist milieu.

This commitment needs to be set against the ersatz spectacle of Iranian national antiquity developed by the Shah, a project that demoted Islam to a mere episode within the Iranian national story. The Shah had acquired absolute authority following his ascension to power after a CIA-backed coup in 1953. From the early 1960s, the monarchy pushed forward a centralised and authoritarian Westernisation of the country. Westernisation came to be associated with corruption, political oppression and the destruction of rural life. As summarised by Keddie (1983, p. 588):

> People were torn from their ancestral ways, the gap between the rich and the poor grew, corruption was rampant and well known, and the secret police, with its arbitrary arrests and use of torture, turned Iranians of all levels against the regime. And the presence and heavy influence of foreigners provided major, further aggravation.

Whether the Westernising reign of the Shah was a more or less brutal regime than the Islamist one installed from 1979 remains a point of controversy. What is far harder to dispute is that the Shah's regime was highly repressive, that it came to power and remained there largely because of the assistance of the USA and other Western powers, and that anti-Westernism in Iran emerged against a background of tyranny carried out in the name of Western modernisation. For Al-e Ahmad,

> A west-stricken man who is a member of the ruling establishment of the country has no place to stand. He is like a dust particle floating in space,

or a straw floating on water. He has severed his ties with the essence of society, culture, and custom. He is not a bond between antiquity and modernity. He is not a dividing line between the old and the new. He is something unrelated to the past and someone with no understanding of the future. He is not a point of the line, but an imaginary point on a plane or in space – just like that dust particle. Of course, you are probably asking: then, how has he risen to a position of leadership among the people? He has done so through the pre-determined decree of the machine and the prerequisites of politics which cannot but conform to the politics of the great nations. In this part of the world, especially in oil-rich countries, it is customary for that which is lighter to float to the surface. The wave of events in this type of oil depository only brings the chaff to the surface. It does not have enough power to touch the bottom of the sea and extract the gems lying there. We in our west-stricken state with all of its concomitant problems are dealing with lightweight drifters who float on the wave of events. The ordinary man on the street is not at fault here; his voice is not heard, his record is clean. He will go in any direction you point him; that is, he will assume any shape you train him to (1982, p. 67).

Al-e Ahmad's images of Western influence are nearly always of disease. Hence the terms 'west-stricken' and 'westitis'. In *Plagued by the West* he sets out 'to discover the characteristics of this illness and its cause or causes and, if possible, find a cure' (p. 3). This language of illness reflects an emerging consensus within anti-colonial and anti-racist work, namely that colonialism led to *individual, inner contamination*. Yet it also functioned as a prescription of national salvation through the purification of Iranian culture.

Al-e Ahmad stresses the long tradition of Islamic and Iranian interest in the West. 'It appears from history that we have always been watching the West', he tells us, adding, '[w]e used the term 'western' before foreigners called us 'eastern' (p. 11). At the time Al-e Ahmad was writing, the idea of the West in the West had become defined in opposition to communism and the Soviet Union. However, Al-e Ahmad adopts the less politically exclusive definition common across Asia throughout much of the twentieth century. It is a definition that stresses the industrial nature of the West.

> In place of the 'West', we can say almost all of Europe and Soviet Union and all of North America. Or let us say all of the advanced countries which, with the aid of machines, are capable of converting raw materials into something more complex and marketing it in the form of manufactured goods (p. 3).

Al-e Ahmad's concern with mechanisation recalls Tagore's critique of the alienated nature of Western modernity. Indeed, he devotes a chapter to the subject, titled 'A bit about "Machinitis"'. Here he identifies machine-based societies with the politics of homogeneity, rigidity and authoritarianism. He extends this critique even further by associating fascism with 'machine-based' societies and attacking the hollowness of Western claims on democracy.

> The political parties in a western democratic society are pulpits used to relive the feelings of depression of those unstable and neurotic people whose regimented daily lives (their rising on time, getting to work, and not missing the subway) rob them of any opportunity to demonstrate their own free will (p. 100).

Plagued by the West draws on established traditions, both from within and outside the West, for representing the ills of Western modernity. The book brings together leftist, post-colonial and somewhat inchoate, but clearly religiously driven, representations of the disease of 'Westitis', in order to provide an original account of how Iranian culture is being subverted.

In seeking to appreciate how such a work could have been incorporated into radical Islamism, it is necessary to look at the Iranian revolution as both a political *and* a religious event.

Ayatollah Khomeini referred to Iran's poor as the 'pillar of the revolution'. He looked to them, like Al-e Ahmad, as the source and soul of pure non-Westernism. Identifying this 'leftist' current, Moin (1994) explains that 'the languages of class struggle appeared in a religious guise' (p. 91). Choueiri (1997, p. 66) offers the broader thesis that 'Marxism itself can be seen as the immediate progenitor of Islamic radicalism', both inside and outside Iran. However, there is another kind of absorption going on in Moin's and Choueiri's analysis, an absorption of religious commitment into the 'familiar' – that is European – rhetoric of rationalisation and politicisation. In fact, the 1979 revolution in Iran was an anti-colonial, revolutionary *and* theocratic seizure of state power that finds no obvious parallels in the history of Western social upheaval. It is unfortunate that some Western Marxists have naively imagined that Khomeinism can be characterised as an example of a generic 'Third World populist resistance', with the title 'Imam' just 'the Shii-Iranian version of the Latin American El Lider, El Conductor, Jege Maximo (Chief Boss), and O Paid do Povo (Father of the Poor)' (Abrahamian, 1993, p. 38). Such a misreading exposes an inability to take religion seriously. Rather than assuming that religion was a mask for a 'familiar' left-wing message, it is more accurate to say that, in Iran, a revolutionary 'Third Worldist' emphasis on anti-imperialism and populist egalitarianism was actively *assimilated* into a discourse of religious authority.

Khomeini's search for the 'perfect man' combined religious and political utopianism. 'Islamic government', instructed Khomeini in 1988,

> which stems from the absolute guardianship of the Prophet Muhammad, is one of the primary injunctions in Islam, taking precedence over all subsidiary precepts, even praying, fasting, and performing the Hajj (cited by Moin, 1994, p. 93).

Although Iran was to maintain many of the reforms associated with Western modernisation – including a degree of democracy – in the first few years of the revolution Khomeini presided over an increasingly violent and authoritarian regime. By contrast with Al-e Ahmad, whose stereotyping of the West contributed to a reflexive interrogation of the uses and abuses of authority in Iran, 'Khomeinism' became politically dependent upon the demonisation of the West and Westernised Muslim states as repositories of evil in order to *avoid* addressing the problems of Iranian society. One of Khomeini's last acts (February 1989) recalls the ersatz spectacles of the Shah, in as much as it was a totalitarian perform-ance designed to distract and confuse. I am referring to the 'death sentence' passed on Salman Rushdie, the British author of the supposedly anti-Islamic text, *The Satanic Verses*. A reading of *Plagued by the West*, allows us to see this act as a degradation of the anti-Western imagination. Once aligned with a spirit of critical and anti-authoritarian questioning, the anti-Western position had been hollowed out into a politics of posture and utopian cliché.

Western dystopia and Islamist utopia

The West is central to radical Islamism. Indeed, it has become conven-tional to define radical Islam by reference to the West. For example, Youssef Choueiri defines 'radical Islamism' as 'a politico-cultural movement that postulates a qualitative contradiction between Western civilization and the religion of Islam' (1997, p. 123).

However, there exists a danger in any definition that opens the door to the misconception that Islamism is a reactive off-shoot of Western power and Western ideas. Disputing what he sees as the imperial arrogance of those who construe Islamism as a local echo inside a broader, overarching European world story, Sayyid (1997, p. 155) offers a different starting point: 'The emergence of Islamism', he contends, 'is based on the erosion of eurocentrism'. In other words, it is the weakening of the Western influence in a post-colonial era, rather than its all-defining presence, that has provided the opportunity for Islamism. Sayyid supports this contention in a number of ways but places his empirical emphasis on the relative scarcity of references to the West in the theocratic vision of Khomeini. Sayyid argues that Khomeini made few allusions to Western political theory because, quite simply, that is not what concerned him. Thus Sayyid is saying that we need to take Khomeini's stated ambitions of developing an Islamic theocracy on their own terms and let go of the Eurocentric impulse to imagine that everyone is, really, talking and thinking about 'us' (i.e. Westerners).

Sayyid's position is a valuable corrective. Yet, although we should insist that radical Islamism be understood in its own terms, it is also necessary to understand how radical Islamism has developed an idea of the West and defined itself in relationship to it. The need for the Iranian revolutionaries to absorb anti-Western work, such as *Plagued by the West*, reflected a need to 'other the West' in order to give shape and force to Islamic reform and revival.

The 'othering' of the West can be seen as central to radical Islamism without falling into the trap of seeing Islamism as derivative of the West. As we saw in Chapter 5, the argument that 'Asian spirituality' and 'Asian values' are merely inverted and mutated Western values – that Asian identity is a by-product of the West – is not just simplistic but historically misleading. It erases the way the West has been actively constructed by Asians. A similar argument may be offered for the Islamist construction of the West. Indeed, the radical Islamist vision of the West has shown itself to be both dynamic and influential. A range of negative and positive stereotypes have arisen (or been recycled) that fuse tradition and innovation. For the most part, the creative energy that animates radical Islamism has been harnessed to an authoritarian agenda, an agenda which has employed clichés of Western doom in the service of an attack on the diversity of Islam. In this way, the construction of the Western enemy has been employed to suppress the political and religious traditions of Islamic societies.

Religious texts are, perhaps by definition, inclined to utopianism. Religion offers a transcendental code of morality and salvation that makes it a fertile territory for that brand of militant enthusiasm associated with utopianism. Nevertheless, religious *extremism* has an important additional relationship to the utopian project. For rather than placing utopianism at the level of mystical aspiration, it demands the subordination of earthly life to a very particular, narrowly conceived blueprint of the perfect society. It is a position that tends to lead to calls for the establishment of theocratic government and the destruction of secular society. Radical Islamism, Christian fundamentalism and militant Hinduism represent the three most active forms of religious extremism today. Of these, it is radical Islamism that has had most opportunity to translate its priorities into practice. This has occurred in many different ways.[2] The intellectual lineage of radical Islam is complex. However, before moving on to Jameelah's contribution, it is necessary to outline an important influence upon her position, the anti-Western radicalism of Sayyid Qutb.

Sayyid Qutb (1906–1966) was tortured and hanged in 1966 for his outspoken opposition to the Egyptian state. His hostility to government[3] and his religious authoritarianism are clearly apparent in his seminal statement, *Milestones* (1990; first published 1964). For Qutb, Islam

> proclaims the universal freedom of every person and community from ser-
> vitude to every other individual or society, the end of man's arrogance and
> selfishness, the establishment of the sovereignty of Allah and His Lordship
> throughout the world and the rule of the Divine *Shari'ah* in human
> affairs ... When Islam calls for peace, its objective is not a superficial peace
> which requires only that the part of the earth where the followers of Islam
> are residing remain secure. The peace of Islam means that *din* [ie. the law
> of the society] be purified for Allah, that all people should obey Allah
> alone, and every system that permits some people to rule over others be
> abolished (pp. 50–51).

Qutb's position emerged as a reaction to a perceived 'deIslamisation' of traditionally Islamic societies. The 'Muslim community has been extinct for a few centuries', says Qutb, and now 'must be restored to its original form' (p. 7). Writing in the 1950s and 1960s, Qutb's conclusion that Arab states were becoming less Islamic was not inaccurate. During these decades the ideologies of pan-Arabism, socialism, nationalism, and the mixture they formed in Nasserism in Qutb's own country, appeared to be displacing Islam. The 'post-Islamic era' was proclaimed in certain quarters and feared in others. For Qutb, Islam was being subverted in Egypt and across the Islamic world by the forces of West-ernisation. His reaction was to assert Islamic intellectual and political independence. Ideas or practices understood as *foreign* to Islam, such as socialism, democracy or capitalism, were, for Qutb, *ipso facto*, illegitimate. Qutb's emphasis on independence is identified clearly in Moussalli's study of his theology:

with politics, as with philosophy, and wanting terms and notions to be indigenous to the Muslims, Qutb underlines the necessity that institutions and forms of government be the result of evolution from within, and not imposed from without. Qutb's purpose here is not only to reject terms and idioms but, more importantly, the West (1992, p. 167).

Charles Tripp, a scholar of contemporary Egyptian society, concludes that in Qubt's Islam:

> There can be no room, indeed no grounds, for discord or disagreement. Faith and reason, individual and community, human freedom and servitude to God would all work in concord towards the same harmonious end. Qutb had thereby reconciled a vision of Utopia in which the human and the divine are reconciled: not only would conflict cease between individuals, but also humanity could rest secure in the knowledge that the path they had chosen was that favoured by God (1994, p. 174).

The vanguardist and anti-nationalist message contained in *Milestones* is designed to convince and stir potential activists. The book argues for a revolutionary cadre of Muslims prepared to create and fight for a pure vision of a totally Islamic society. The following passage explains this attitude, providing a clear sense of Qutb's concerns about the extent of Western encirclement as well as his desire for a decontamination from 'paganism' (*jahiliyya*, referring to the beliefs of pre-Islamic times).

> Today too we are surrounded by *jahiliyya*. Its nature is the same as during the first period of Islam, and it is perhaps a little more deeply entrenched. Our whole environment, people's beliefs and ideas, habits and art, rules and laws, is *jahiliyya*, even to the extent that what we consider to be Islamic culture, Islamic sources, Islamic philosophy and Islamic thought are constructs of *jahiliyya*! This is why the true Islamic values never enter out heart (p. 15).

Having sketched Qutb's radical Islamism, we are in a better position to read the 1095 pages of Maryam Jameelah's *Western Civilization Condemned By Itself: A Comprehensive Study of Moral Retrogression and its Consequences*. This two volume work was first published, in English, in Lahore, Pakistan, in 1970 (though I shall be referring to the revised edition published in 1979). Its target audience, as explained in the book's dedication, is educated Muslims around the world, especially those 'misled by the delusion that the adoption of Western culture is the only route to progress in human welfare' (p. v).

Jameelah was born Margaret Marcus and is a Jewish-American convert to Islam. Although a far less influential figure than Al-e Ahmad,

Jameelah has made a distinctive contribution. Indeed, in their book *Makers of Contemporary Islam*, Esposito and Voll (2001, p. 67) devote a chapter to Jameelah, and suggest that she 'has played a pioneering role as an activist Muslim intellectual'. Although she often appears not to be aligned with any particular Islamist faction, there is much of the enthusiasm of the convert in Jameelah's zeal to appear fully and unhesitatingly Islamic. Her Islam is militantly conservative. Her chosen commentaries tend to come from radical Islamists, such as Qutb, of whom she notes that he did 'more than any other individual to preserve the faith of Islam in the hearts of the Egyptians' (p. 1089). She also gives fulsome support to both Khomeinism and Jama'at-e-Islami in Pakistan.

Western Civilization Condemned By Itself consists of 31 abridged versions of essays by Western intellectuals and scientists interlaced with the work of Western poets and often lengthy commentaries by the author and other Islamic scholars. The articles range from ancient Greece (excerpt from *The Republic*) to the late twentieth century. The majority of the Western pieces derive either from social critics (such as Oscar Lewis, Irving Goffman and Trevor Huddleston) or from key public thinkers and ideologists (for example, Darwin, Marx, Freud, Hitler, Krushchev and de Beauvoir).

With a few notable exceptions, the twentieth-century writers Jameelah abridges are socialists or left liberals. Their forced coalition with her theocratic agenda has the interesting effect of exposing the social conservatism of socialist thought: the hankering for organic community and authentic relationships that characterises so much radical social criticism in the West. Indeed, it is upon this territory that Western and Islamic radicalism appear to meet. The slogan 'modern life is rubbish' is one I am familiar with from the situationists, an anarchist avant-garde group. For Jameelah too, modern life is rubbish. For both radicals and conservatives, the modern Western world is a threatening, engulfing force. This may help to explain why Jameelah's anti-Western evidence will have a double life for some Western readers: it appears both accurate and muddled, insightful and wide of the mark.

The notion that, as the title of Maryam Jameelah's work suggests, many Westerners now *admit* to the decadent nature of their society, is central to her argument. Indeed, it is something of a *leit-motif* within non-Western criticism of the West. Certainly, the same theme is apparent within the 'Asian values' debate. It is also at work within *Plagued by the West*: Al-e Ahmad claims it was Camus who first made him understand and wish to resist the mechanical nature of Western civilisation. Jameelah's book represents, perhaps, the most exhaustive treatment of this form of anti-Westernism. Yet as an intellectual contribution it does not compare well with *Plagued by the West*. In Jameelah's hands the conviction that the inadequacy of Western civil- isation is supported by Western self-criticism becomes a hostage to fortune. It is clumsily allied to the utopian position that internal criticism either does not exist in authentic Islamic countries (in the 1979 edition, only Saudi Arabia and Iran meet Jameelah's criteria for Islamic status) or is inherently invalid in such societies. In either case, Jameelah's endeavours throw up more questions about her vision of Islam than they do about the West. Islamic government is represented as an utterly pure condition: it is narrated as fantasy, a social form without tension, change or public debate.

Like *Plagued by the West*, Jameelah's book was written in the face of a perceived onslaught by the West. Jameelah casts Westernisation as a danger to the survival of Islam. It is a force that requires defensive and urgent action. It should not be forgotten that neither Al-e Ahmad's nor Jameelah's contributions are leisurely studies of the West as a distant object of enquiry. Both these authors feel they are writing under con- ditions of occupation, in the midst of occidental power. At the same time, both focus their sharpest criticisms on Westernisation as a *corrupting* process; something that 'we' (non-Westerners) allow to happen; that 'we' do to 'ourselves'. Both authors specify 'petro-dollars in the oil-rich countries' (Jameelah, 1979a, p. 353) as being a particular source and site of degradation. Indeed, Jameelah echoes Al-e Ahmad in her disap- pointment with 'modern Arabs', who 'due to the influence of western culture have become very materialistic' (p. 353). 'The history of the Muslim majority countries', Jameelah has written elsewhere, 'no longer has any vital connection to Islam but is merely an extension of the West and its total domination' (Jameelah, 1982, p. 215).

Western Civilization Condemned By Itself offers Western dystopia in two forms:

1. *decadent ideologies of the West* (especially secularism, materialism, consumerism, racism and feminism);
2. *decadent social roles and identities in the West* (especially of the young and women).

Decadent ideologies of the West

The allusion to 'moral retrogression' in the title of Jameelah's book implies an account of social change. In this, however, the title misleads.

For Jameelah's historical portrayal suggests that the West has witnessed merely the repackaging of 'retrogressive' currents that are *primordial and inherent*. Thus the West emerges as naturally decadent. Indeed, Jameelah's attempt to represent the West as a fixed social form leads her to trace its dystopian characteristics to the supposed foundations of Western society, in classical Greece. 'The society of ancient Greece was the earliest in history to detach its institutions, customs, arts and sciences from religion', she notes, adding 'This secular ideal has remained the dominant theme of Western civilization to this day' (1979a, p. 3).

This chronology creates a unique role for the Middle Ages:

> the civilization of the Middle Ages could be classed 'Western' only on the basis of its geographical location. The civilization of the Middle Ages was in every respect hostile and contradictory to that of modern times. This is why no period of European history has been more unfairly maligned (1979a, p. 49).

Despite this moral mediaeval blip, the culture of the West soon returned to its established secular and materialist pattern. These propensities are used to explain the emergence and similarity of capitalism and communism. Prefacing an excerpt from *The Communist Manifesto*, Jameelah explains:

> Although the Western democracies like America, England and France reject the totalitarian system of Government devised by the Communists, their intellectual leaders believe as firmly as do the intelligentsia of the Socialist nations, the Marxist fallacy that an improvement in economic conditions will automatically result in the moral and spiritual progress of mankind, although all evidence is contrary to this blind assumption. Marxism is responsible to a very great extent for Western civilisation as it is today. It has found as enthusiastic acceptance in America as in the Soviet Union, the only difference being that the latter is honest in the pursuit of its goal while the former is hypocritical (1979a, p. 230).

Jameelah's binding of Marxism and capitalism together as expressions of materialism reflects her wider political disdain for both ideologies as Western exports. The reduction of life to consumption and commodification under capitalism, and the reduction of life to production and labour under communism, are viewed by Jameelah as two sides of the same alien coin. Although this analysis contains genuine insight, the crude strokes with which it is drawn (for example, the contention that Marxism has had as an 'enthusiastic reception' in the USA as in the USSR) ensure that it appears as a caricature, a dystopia that will convince only those predisposed to believe the worst about the West.

Appearing in stark contrast to the soulless, meaningless, Western world of socialism and capitalism, Islam is represented by Jameelah as a paradise of philanthropy. Islam, she explains, allows a society in which material needs and material questions become irrelevant, for it enables a culture of religiously motivated altruism and self-sacrifice. In other words, material needs and questions can be answered, not by creating a society that is materialistic, but by the obligations of religious duty. The payment of the Zakat (a charitable levy), the prohibition of both usury and alcohol and distributive inheritance laws are offered as practical examples of this process. Yet these illustrations remain thinly sketched. They are essentially marginalia; overshadowed by Jameelah's vast and deep nostalgia for a bygone era in which:

> Acting through simplicity, the Muslim people understood each other. The wealthy neighbour was the friend of his poor neighbour; he knew him and his children personally... His children, despite the comfort they enjoyed, were like all children of the tribe or village, playing the same games, eating similar food and wearing the same kind of clothes (Azzrm, cited by Jameelah, 1979a, p. 277).

Jameelah's bucolic visions also suggest the essentially rural nature of the perfect Islamic society towards which she is drawn. Indeed, the sins of 'retrogression' she finds in the West are nearly all typically urban. The ideal of simple, agrarian communities is a theme shared with much primitivist and indigenist commentary and points to a certain overlap between radical Islamism and these traditions.

However, with respect to another of the ideologies of the West that Jameelah identifies, racism, she is far closer to the anti-Westernism of Soviet communism. Racial discrimination is seen as endemic within and typical of the West. Thus the 'atrocities committed by the Nazi regime... were no freak accident. Rather they represent the logical culmination of modern Western civilization' (1979b, p. 1003). The section of Jameelah's book headed 'Western Civilization in Practice' commences with four pieces: 'Children of the Kibbutz' (Melford Spiro), 'The Biography of the Last Wild Indian in North America' (Theodora Kroeber), 'A Record of Negro Childhood and Youth in Urban America' (Richard Wright) and 'Apartheid in South Africa' (Trevor Huddleston). Combined with racist essays by Darwin and Hitler and an account of Nazi concentration camps, the overall effect is to highlight racism as both an invention of the West and an inherent part of its social structure. By contrast not only is Islam seen as non-racist but as offering emancipation from racism and nationalism. Jameelah asks a revealingly phrased question in regard to the spread of Islam in Africa: 'What is the result of the civilizing mission of Islam among the primitive peoples subjected to its influence?' (1979a, p. 381). Her answer is a society without colour prejudice.

Decadent social roles and identities in the West

Five of the essays Jameelah abridges concern the problem of delinquent youth and of generational conflict. One of these deals with 'Life in an Old-Age Home' (Dorothy Rabinowitz and Yedida Nielsen). The others concern the disrespectful and alienated nature of Western adolescents. This focus reflects, in part, the fact that, as a work first compiled in the 1960s, Jameelah is reacting to the eruption of Western youth culture. Yet although there is a clear sense that this is a contemporary phenom-enon, youth anomie is, nevertheless, treated as a discharge from a long diseased body, a manifestation of something basically wrong with Western modernity. The 'worship of youth and contempt for the aged is inherent in the very essence of the modern way of life' (1979b, p. 593) explains Jameelah. The image of Western youth that emerges is of a generation of pathetic pseudo-rebels, frightened, aggressive and, above all, cocooned. Jameelah uses extensive quotations from American youth to make her point; including the worldview of the following 'adolescent boy':

> I don't want to see the raws of life. I don't like to see poor people, the beggars, the cripples and like that. They make me feel uncomfortable. But television is so different! . . . when there's torture or killing or poverty, you don't feel the pain. Then when the programme is finished, you can get a glass of milk and a sandwich from the refrigerator (1979b, pp. 778–779).

Jameelah explains that:

> The Western youth rejects religion and morality because his society has long since ceased to bother about these values . . . Such experiences create a impression on their minds that the older generations are insensitive to the challenges of the time and consequently, unreasonable. That is why the slogan of the West youth is: 'Do not trust anyone above the age of 30!.'

The resulting 'utter disrespect for the authority of parents and teachers' (1979a, p. 137) is contrasted to a set of images of traditional, uncor-rupted Islam. Jameelah draws on portraits of life in what she calls 'medieval times' to provide a model of quiet discipline and devotional activity as typical of authentic Islamic behaviour amongst young men.

It is a version of events that sustains her anti-imperialist theory of first sin, in which the fall from grace occurs at the moment Western power connives its way into the garden: 'The system of education which prevailed in the Muslim world before the advent of European imperialism and the imposition of Western education, was diametrically opposed to the dehumanised schools of today' (Nasr, cited by Jameelah, 1979a, p. 142).

The other social role that concerns Jameelah is gender relations. Two abridged essays concern this topic directly ('A Plea for the Emancipation of Women' by Simone de Beauvoir and 'Excepts from the Autobiography of a Modern "Emancipated" Woman', by Lucy Freeman). However, it is a key theme in a number of the essays Jameelah includes (such as in the commentaries surrounding 'Family Disintegration under the Blows of Materialism' by Oscar Lewis, and 'Arguments in Favour of Mass Birth Control' by William Vogt). Jameelah judges women's liberation as *the central claim* to social progress made by Western civilisation. Despite her strictures against materialist explanations of moral progress or decay, Jameelah often employs them, such as in the passage below, where she connects the rise of feminism to the need of industrial societies to have a large pool of labour unfettered by family ties and domestic concerns.

> The feminist movement was a direct result of the Industrial Revolution when factories began to employ women on a large scale. These women were exploited mercilessly and assigned to the least desirable tasks at the lowest possible pay. Simultaneously all semblance of home life and family ties began to disappear. In the factory the humiliation of the woman became complete (1979a, p. 177).

The most telling examples of feminism, argues, Jameelah, have arisen from the Soviet Union, where such ideas have been 'translated into the fullest practice' (p. 191). Jameelah makes extensive use of images of female manual labourers in the USSR to provide what she evidently regards as a grotesque tableau of masculinisation. More typical of her data from the capitalist West are representations of sexual promiscuity and moral incontinence. In either case, 'Women's "liberation" and the disintegration and break-up of the family go hand in hand, afflicting its victims with acute loneliness, social isolation and alienation' (1979b, p. 687). Uniquely, these dytopian images are not framed or balanced by nostalgic visions of female fulfilment in traditional Islamic society (though see Jameelah, 1976). The effect is to create a silence around Islamic female identity, a silence that only

accentuates the fact that all of Jameelah's many Islamic authorities and
inspirations are men.

Conclusions: Islamism and neo-liberal globalisation

This chapter has painted a portrait of anti-Westernism becoming
absorbed and narrowed by religious radicalism. In Chapter 6, we saw
the politics of the West also becoming narrower. What are we to make
of this similarity? Any plausible answer to this question has to take into
account that, in terms of power and influence, the West and radical
Islam are not comparable. Neo-liberal utopianism in the West has a
global impact on an entirely different scale to that of radical Islamism.
Radical Islamism is not a merely reactive, anti-Western phenomenon.
But it has come into existence and definition in the context of Western
dominance. What this situation portends, I would suggest, is that radical
Islamism will tend to adopt techniques of symbolic resistance towards
the West whilst avoiding, or being unable to confront, the deeper, more
powerful currents of neo-liberal globalisation.

The tendency of religious fundamentalist movements to focus on
issues of *individual* morality and, effectively, to close down debate
on questions of *public* policy by placing them in the hands of politico-
religious authorities, means that clear and constructive engagement with
neo-liberalism becomes very difficult. Indeed, much contemporary
Islamist resistance to the West appears to have little to say on many of
the great social and economic issues of our era (such as technological
change and the environment). Moreover, within a context in which
neo-liberalism is the hegemonic ideology of globalisation and in which
the public sphere is suppressed, Western commodity culture becomes
hard to oppose. In other words, by focusing people's attentions onto
their domestic lives, and away from political debate, religious revivalist
moments place them in exactly the situation where the comforts and
pleasures of Western-style consumerism appear most alluring. Highlighting the way Islamic Shari'a law acts to focus attention on issues of
family duty and subverts the public sphere, Oliver (1994) and Ruthven
(2000) have made the same point, although in more predictive terms:

> the practical effects of Islamisation entails, not a confrontation with the
> West, but rather a cultural retreat into the mosque and private family
> space. Because the Shari'a protects the family—the only institution to
> which it grants real autonomy—the culture of Islam is likely to become
> increasingly passive, privatized, and consumer-orientated (Ruthven, 2000,
> p. 139).

Despite its recent and spectacular rise to visibility in the eyes of the West, radical Islamism may be helping to ensure the triumph of its supposed rival.

Further reading

Islamist visions of the West

Primary sources remain the best starting point. Although the translation of important works into English remains haphazard, it includes some essential texts such as: Sayyid Qutb's *Milestones* (1990, Burr Ridge, American Trust Publications); Ali Shariati's *Marxism and Other Western Fallacies: An Islamic Critique* (1980, Berkeley, Mirzan); and Ruhallah Khomeini (Ayatollah Khomeini) in *Islam and Revolution* (1981, Berkeley, Mirzan). Aside from *Western Civilization Condemned By Itself*, Maryam Jameelah has written a number of other works in English that critique the West, including *Islam and Western Society* (1982, New Delhi, Adam Publishers); *Islam and Modernism* (1971, Lahore, Muhammad Yusaf Khan); and *Westernization versus Muslims* (1978, Lahore, Muhammad Yusaf Khan).

Within the secondary literature a provocative and useful starting point is Bobby Sayyid's *A Fundamental Fear: Eurocentrism and the Emergence of Islamism* (1997, London, Zed Books). This is a short and clear text that sets out to challenge the Eurocentric assumptions of many Western commentators on Islamism. For background reading on the rise of Islamism see also:

Abu-Rabi, I. (1996) *Intellectual Origins of Islamic Resurgence in the Modern Arab World*, Albany, State University of New York Press.

Al-Azmeh, A. (1991) 'The discourse of cultural authenticity: Islamist revivalism and Enlightenment universalism', in Deutsch, E. (ed.) *Culture and Modernity: East-West Perspectives*, Honolulu, University of Hawaii Press.

Choueiri, Y. (1997) *Islamic Fundamentalism: Revised Edition*, London, Pinter.

Dabashi, H. (1993) *The Theology of Discontent: The Ideological Foundation of the Islamic Revolution in Iran*, New York, New York University Press.

Rahnema, A. (ed.) (1994) *Pioneers of Islamic Revival*, London, Zed.

In the main, commentaries on the terrorist attacks of 'September 11' on the US have been disappointing and are best avoided. One of the more informative has been Malise Ruthven's *A Fury for God: The Islamist Attack on America* (2002, London, Granta Books).

Arab and Iranian occidentalism: critical voices

Jalal Al-e Ahmad's *Plagued by the West (Gharbzadegi)* (1982, Delmar, Caravan Books) remains a lively, polemical introduction to 'non-fundamentalist' and 'left-Islamic' Iranian visions of the West. A very different starting point is the scholarly history of Mohamad Tavakoli-Targhi. The themes of 'Persianate Europology' and 'the crafting of national memory' in nineteenth-century and early twentieth-century Iran are addressed by Tavakoli-Targhi in *Refashioning*

Iran: Orientalism, Occidentalism and Historiography (2001, Basingstoke, Palgrave).

Turning to Arab occidentalism, an interesting set of contemporary accounts can be found in a special issue on 'L'Occident au miroir de l'Orient' of the magazine of Paris-based Institute du Monde Arabe, *Qantara* (issue 42) in 2002.

Said's *Orientalism* (1978) helped instigate the debate on occidentalism in Arabic. The most substantial work to date has been the Egyptian philosopher Hassan Hanafi's *Muquaddima fi 'ilm al-istighrab* [Introduction to the Science of Occidentalism] (1991, Cairo, Madbuli). Hanafi views occidentalism as a new science of liberation. In *Islam in the Modern World: Tradition, Revolution, and Culture* he explains that 'Occidentalism is a discipline constituted in Third World countries in order to complete the process of decolonization' (1995, Cairo, Anglo-Egyptian Bookshop, p. 354). Hanafi's aim is to study and, hence, objectify the West in order to enable a clearer sense of an independent Islamic (more specifically, Arab Muslim) sense of 'self'. However, the *Muquaddima* has been sharply attacked by some Arab critics for its dualistic, one-dimensional and essentialised vision of the West. Drawing these critical voices together Yudian Wahyudi accuses Hanafi of accepting orientalist dualism, of Arab ethnocentrism and of ignoring the basic fact that,

> making Western thought an object of study, as does the *Muquaddima*, does not amount to establishing a new science, since university and public libraries are full of studies of Western schools of thought. In this regard, Occidentalism ... constitutes more of a type of ideologically based preaching than a 'science' (Wahyudi, 2003, p. 242).

Unfortunately, this important debate has yet to penetrate English-speaking academia. Two informative sources are Wahyudi's essay 'Arab responses to Hanafi's *Muquaddima fi'ilm al-Istighrab' The Muslim World* (2003, 93, 2, pp. 233–248) and Esposito and Voll's chapter on Hanafi in *Makers of Contemporary Islam* (2001, New York, Oxford University Press).

Conclusion

The West is not a Western invention. At least, not simply or merely. It was developed and imagined in important, new and influential ways in the non-West. This argument implies a re-orientation of the way the modern world is imagined. It challenges the tautological use of such phrases as 'Western modernity' and 'Western civilisation'. It also suggests that the common image of Western action and non-Western re-action was always inaccurate: that 'the West' has been employed, and deployed as an idea to develop and secure a variety of geo-political projects across the globe.

Once these processes are explored it becomes impossible, indeed meaningless, to strike poses of condemning or celebrating either the Western or non-Western world. The notion that the West is something of which non-Westerners are ignorant is absurd. Yet so too are efforts to portray the West as some monolithic, malign force, which has been resisted by a ceaselessly radical non-Western politics of liberation.

The West has proved a malleable idea in the past and its future does not lie in any one set of hands. Its fluidity ensures that it is likely to retain its currency, at least for the next half century. The continuing awkwardness of racial categories (like 'white') will sustain the appeal of terminology (like 'Western') that carries only indirect inferences of ethnicity. Moreover, people around the world have acquired the habit of using the West to define their own identities. Labels such as 'Westerniser', 'Asian spirituality', 'Asian values' and 'radical Islamist' provide illustrations of this process. Each has both created and depended upon the idea of the West. The West has been model and anti-model, but also a site of innovation and transcendence.

The West has long been associated with modernity. A claiming of progress, of the future, for the West and only for the West, has accompanied the concept in a variety of settings and political guises. Today this claim remains as ubiquitous and as dangerous as at any point in the past. For the association between neo-liberal democracy and the West, which I sketched in Chapter 6, means that being pro-Western today implies an acceptance of a narrow ideological agenda. The West has become shackled to a very particular socio-economic blueprint for the world. Within the context of an ascendant 'turbo-capitalism', it is difficult to articulate the principles of democracy and justice as Western. Of course, the association between the West and the politics of greed and self-interest is far from new. However, this negative connotation was once balanced by the conviction that Western technological advances were both unique and a basic requirement of social progress. Tagore may have opposed Western soullessness but, like the great majority of those who have been critical of the West, he welcomed Western science and technology as valuable and potentially liberating.

However, at the start of the twenty-first century, it is East Asia, not Britain, that is the workshop of the world. Even specialist manufacture and research is far from being a Western preserve. The tautological use of phrases such as 'Western technology' and 'Western science' has become anachronistic. Westerners can no longer plausibly imagine technology and science to be their gift to the world. Western 'industrial societies' have been transformed into post-industrial societies, where service-sector employment is dominant. This new role may or may not be economically sustainable. However, what is not questionable is that it undermines the image of the West as a repository of those things needed for social progress. The West has thus been deprived of its trump card. In this context the question 'what does the West have to offer?' becomes harder to answer, for Westerners and non-Westerners alike.

The realities of Western power mean that it is foolish to imagine that the West can be re-invented by merely emphasising its various alternative heritages. I cannot conclude this book, then, with a bold vision of a new West. Indeed, it is more helpful to question the mutually defining relationship between 'the West and the rest', a relationship that has come to colonise the political imagination, excluding many communities whose attachment to vast entities, like the West or Asia or Africa, is weak or non-existent. Rather than trying to re-invent the idea of the West, a more modest and appropriate project is to draw out the most humane and hopeful traditions encountered in this book. Amongst these I would privilege democracy and self-determination, both because they have been recurrent concerns voiced across the world and because they are themes that bring together Western and non-Western aspirations of progress. The right of free communities to establish and control their own circumstances is a conviction found throughout the political philosophy of Tagore. We also find it clearly expressed within social democracy. Its traces may also be detected, between the lines, in the ideals of the Westernisers discussed in Chapter 3, as well as in pan-Asianism, Asian values and radical Islam.

The ability of global commercial interests to weaken attachment to 'local' culture and create a market for globalised media, food, music and so on, bypasses and undermines the practice of self-determination and democratic control. In as far as these global forces are presented as inevitable and, hence, as outside of democratic systems, they are essentially authoritarian. The logic of neo-liberal globalisation reduces political choice to a hollow performance. One can be either for or against the global market. To take the latter path guarantees impoverishment and isolation. To take the former is to disappear into the market and extinguish political choice. Hence, the pervading sense that political debate is disappearing, to be replaced by spectacles of political entertainment.

Can we imagine mechanisms of global governance that ferment democracy and extend political choice? I do not see why not. I would also suggest that these mechanisms are already at hand. The World Trade Organisation, the World Bank, and the United Nations, are institutions with developing and, hence, changeable ideologies. They represent the only existing, practical mechanisms for achieving radical reform. It is empirically inaccurate and a counsel of inaction to construe them (along with democracy itself) to be solely or inherently capitalist and Western. The challenge is to view them, not as ideologies, but as structures that can accommodate new ways of ordering global governance. If international bodies are to adopt a democratic agenda then the financial and other forms of assistance they offer must be cut free from the dogma of economic liberalisation. To imagine such mechanisms as actively democratic is to imagine that their primary aim could be to support the choices of self-determining communities.

Self-determination should not be confused with protectionism. Neither anti-protectionism or protectionism are coherent or sufficient as economic and social philosophies. The question of self-determination concerns but is not determined by economic priorities. It recognises that a community may not wish to sacrifice quality of life for economic growth. Such a choice cannot be taken freely – indeed, cannot be taken at all – if not supported by democratically oriented international political and economic structures. This orientation does not lead towards the extremism and contradictions latent within multicultural relativism.

Multicultural relativism refers to the notion that communities are autonomous cultural entities and no one group has the right to tell any other what is wrong or right. Again, there is a problem of coherence in this approach, since it demands the imposition of a moral framework and standards of cultural authenticity. In fact, an international politics of democracy and self-determination does not need to enter the quagmire of extreme relativism. An insistence that self-determination only makes sense within the context of free communities exercising democratic choice is neither a relativist nor a universalist stance, but a workable mixture of both. Using international institutions to enable democratic control will, inevitably, make global administration a more complex task. However, if democracy is an aim of our politics, then we must be prepared to accept that, economically, politically and culturally organisational complexity is inevitable and necessary.

The idea of the 'non-West' arises from the experience of vulnerability; an experience that, as we have seen, has driven non-Westerners to create and shape various stereotypes of the West, both positive and negative. An appreciation of what it is like to witness massive, imposed change, is not widespread within Britain or the USA. Feeling inviolable is something that wealthy Anglo-American commentators often take for granted. Perhaps it is because the USA and Britain have not experienced invasion or social upheaval for very many years; perhaps it is because these are countries that appear to influence others rather than be influenced by them. Whatever the explanation, in both nations there is scant regard for the fact that much of humanity has not felt an equivalent sense of control over its own destiny, not in the last century and not in this. The USA and Britain have developed a brash public culture that appears to defer to 'risk takers' and transgression. Yet those who have known the real risks and the real transgressions of our era continue to be dismissed as not yet up to speed with the West.

One can only hope, of course, that this sense of stability and security will be sustained. But if that is to happen we must also imagine that a sense of control be extended to others: that the creative power to choose a path through modernity be recognised, not as the West's sole property, but as something profuse.

Notes

1 From White to Western: 'Racial Decline' and the Rise of the Idea of the West in Britain, 1890–1930

1. The period 1890–1930 contained the rise and fall of the literature of white crisis, as well as the rise of the idea of the West. However, the years at either end of this span have no special significance. In support of this periodisation we may refer to GoGwilt's (1995, p. 221) conclusion that 'the idea of "Western" history ... [emerged] between the 1880s and the 1920s', as well as to Rich's (1994, p. 90) assessment that 'In the course of the 1890s ... writers began expressing pessimism over the future of the white race', and that 'a new climate of opinion [on the legitimacy of 'race patriotism'] among the ruling class' became apparent 'in the 1930s' (p. 98).

2. My focus on Britain should not be taken to indicate that a literature of white crisis was uniquely British. In particular, a similar genre developed in France and the USA. Pearson's racial pessimism had been preceded in France by Gobineau (1915, first published 1853–1855) and was echoed in the late nineteenth century by Faguet (1895). The regeneration of whiteness is the main theme of *L'Avenir de la race blanche* (Novicow, 1897) and *Le destin des races blanches* (Decugis, 1936). This theme was given an anti-feminist twist by Henry Champly in works translated as *The Road to Shanghai: White Slave Traffic in Asia* (1934) and *White Women, Coloured Men* (1936). A large and diverse body of white crisis literature was produced in the USA, the principal examples of which are Stoddard (1922, 1925) and Grant (1917, originally published 1916).

3. The waning of Anglo-Saxonism may also be discerned in Pearson's work. Indeed, like most of the authors discussed here, Pearson appears to have little interest in the Anglo-Saxon, as either a racial or national group. The decline of this identity reflected the exhaustion of the imperial fervour of the 1880s and 1890s. This process may, in turn, have encouraged the celebration of whiteness precisely because, as a supra-national identity, it was less intimately bound to the increasingly uncertain fortunes of the British empire (see also Rich, 1986).

4. Pearson's emphasis on the inevitably degrading relationship between social welfare and racial character re-affirmed Darwin's position as stated in *The*

Descent of Man (1901, first published 1871; see also Lankester, 1880). In a passage that indicates how open Darwin was to the eugenic interpretation of evolutionary theory, he notes that modern social assistance allows 'the weak members of civilised societies to propagate their own kind... accepting in the case of man himself, hardly any one is so ignorant as to allow his worst animals to breed' (p. 206). The literature of white crisis encompassed this eugenic tendency. Yet is not reducible to it. The debate on whiteness registered concerns that went far beyond the creed of national 'better breeding'. Indeed, although the institutional and ideological organisation of the eugenics movement was oriented towards national categories (more specifically, the British or English race), its work may be better understood if placed within a broader discussion concerning the imperial and racial character of Britons (and/or Englishmen and women) as white people (cf. Searle, 1976; see Stone, 2001, for discussion). It is whites and whiteness that provide the shared focus of the commentators considered here, some of whom were influenced by eugenics, but few of whom can be said to articulate a simply or purely eugenic form of social theory.

5. A related irony concerns the fact that, despite its disgust for the white masses, this is a literature that is coming to terms with the latter's claim on whiteness. At no point do any of the author's discussed here doubt that the European heritage working class is white. The tradition of defining whiteness as a bourgeois possession and of seeing the urban working class (more specifically, the so-called 'residuum') as unworthy of the same racial status, may certainly be detected, particularly within the more bellicose commentators such as Curle and Inge. However, by the end of the nineteenth century such exclusivity was being effectively challenged by national and imperial forms of social inclusivity, forms that made white identity increasingly available to the working classes (see Bonnett, 1998; Hyslop, 1999). Lord Curzon's often attributed remark, made when watching English soldiers washing during the Battle of the Somme – 'I never knew the working classes had such white skins' – signals the survival of somewhat older attitudes amongst the British upper classes. It is the *anachronistic* quality of the remark that is of interest here: by the 1910s the public articulation of the idea that the working class was less than white had become noteworthy, indeed eccentric. As this implies, the contradictory and self-defeating nature of the literature under consideration here derives, in large measure, from the difficulties that a class inclusive view of whiteness present to those who wish to employ racism as a form of social elitism.

6. A concern with the low birth rate of the middle classes has been claimed to be the primary motive behind the eugenics movement (MacKenzie, 1976; Searle, 1976). As Stone has recently explained, this position has been used by contemporary historians to justify a view of British eugenics as a class, rather than a race-based ideology. Whilst agreeing with Stone that 'there is plenty of evidence to the contrary' (p. 418) this chapter is suggestive of the

mutually subversive tension between these concerns. For discussion of the relationship between these concerns and socialism, see Whetham and Whetham (1911) and Webb (1907); see also Winter (1974) and Paul (1984).

7. These considerations imply that the 'discovery' of working-class ill health at the turn of the nineteenth century developed from a discourse of white decline, rather than the other way round. The supposed poor physical state of army volunteers for the Boer War, particularly those from the cities, encouraged and enabled the articulation of concerns about the degeneracy of 'the race' and its urban context (see, for example, White, 1899, 1901; Shee, 1903). However, the 'evidence' of ill-health reflected less an empirical reality (since it was both misread and considerably exaggerated; see Soloway, 1982, for discussion) than a class investment in representing the proletarian as a degenerate group.

8. It might be expected that those contributors to the white crisis literature, such as Inge and Stoddard, most concerned to assert the importance of racial divisions within whiteness, would find the terms 'the West' and 'Western' too loose and homogenising. However, it is revealing that, as with Money, Stoddard's (1922), otherwise constant, anxieties about the racial and class composition of whiteness fade into the background when he adopts the terminology of 'western civilisation' (p. 6). This process is allied with an appropriation of the tradition of casting Christianity as Western and Islam as Eastern and the, also well-established, extension of this practice to allow 'East' to mean Asia. Thus, Inge's (1922) extreme sensitivity to the divisions within whiteness is allowed occasionally to be salved by knowledge of 'the unending dual between East and West' (p. 211). The same process may be seen at work in the, less militantly supremacist, contributions of Putman Weale (1910), whose depiction of 'the conflict between East and West' as 'the oldest of problems' (p. 3) belies his highly contemporary usage of both terms. For, despite these claims on historical depth, all these authors use the idea of the West, not as a religious term, nor even as one defined in relation to the East but, rather, as a cultural entity variously synonymous with military might, industrialism, progress and the modern.

9. GoGwilt claims Benjamin Kidd to be the first English-language author to employ a recognisably contemporary idea of the West. Kidd's reference in *Social Evolution* (1894) to 'our Western civilization' is the 'first clear instance' of the use of the term 'Western' as a discrete society with its own history, notes GoGwilt (1995, p. 54) and, as such, 'an idiosyncratic formulation'.

10. The difficulty of combing the two discourses is also apparent within Hubbard's *The Fate of Empires* (1913), a book which provided a somewhat uneasy definition of race as 'the sum of the, as yet, unborn generations' (p. 33) in order to marry a theory of 'future oriented' societies with the dictates of the conventional 'white crisis' debate.

11. The Unity History School lectures were published in the nine volumes of The Unity Series (Marvin, 1915, 1916, 1920, 1921, 1922b, 1923, 1925, 1932; Marvin and Clutton-Brock, 1928).

12. That the mystification of race allows the re-introduction of the language of white identity and white supremacy is apparent from Spengler's *The Hour of Decision* (1934).

13. The association between being Western and a cosmopolitan, global and, hence, relativist, worldview sustained the deracinating, deracialising aspects of the idea of the West. Indeed, Toynbee himself may be taken as an archetype of the cosmopolitan Westerner. Multilingual, urbane, a prophet of our 'post-Modern Age' (1954, p. 338), apparently able to intellectually bestride not merely his own but all the other cultures of the world, Toynbee appeared all-knowing. In this way he not only explained but personified the West. Taking this line of thinking a little further – and in order to consider the way the 'real west' has come to be represented as possessing 'urban, bourgeois, cosmopolitan values' – we may usefully turn to Nadel-Klein's (1995) portrait of the way rural life in the West is depicted as a kind of interior non-West. She details a tendency to symbolise the 'truly Western' person as 'one [who] must think, live and act independently of local custom and kinship, free from the parochial constraints of any particular community' (p. 111). The deployment of the urban cosmopolis as the real West, Nadel-Klein implies, demands its association with middle class sophistication. Thus the working class 'city type' that so frightened earlier commentators disappears (even further) from view.

14. The racialisation of affluence in the context of neo-liberal globalisation is also the focus of Chua's (2003) recent exposition *World on Fire: How Exporting Free Market Democracy Breeds Ethnic Hatred and Global Instability*.

2   Communists Like Us: The Idea of the West in the Soviet Union

My title is both an allusion to the ethnocentricity of Bolshevik communism and to one of the better-known attempts to breath new life into the communist project, Guattari and Negri's (1990) short book *Communists Like Us: New Spaces of Liberty, New Lines of Alliance*. Whilst stripping away the authoritarian and repressive attributes of communist social planning and making a plausible case for a re-invigorated libertarian communism, *Communists Like Us* is typical of contemporary revolutionary thinking in its failure to address the ethnic and racial dynamism of the Bolshevik project. It is an absence that undermines the credibility of Guattari and Negri's claims to have synthesised liberty and communism (see also Hardt and Negri, 2000).

1. I have developed this argument in more detail elsewhere, see Bonnett, 2002.

2. The term 'Soviet' refers both to the Russian Soviet Federative Socialist Republic and to the USSR. The latter was formed in 1922 with the union of the Russian Soviet Federative Socialist Republic, Ukraine, Belorussia, and the Transcaucasian Federation.

3. For example: Conquest, 1970, 1986; Carrere d'Encausse, 1993; Lieven, 1995; see also Tucker, 1990; Rywkin, 1994; Suny, 1995; Dawisha and Parrot, 1997; Slezkine, 2000.

4. 'Russian' is a contested and multifaceted term which can refer to an ethnic and/or national group, a language and its users, a territory and a state. Moreover, 'the Russian people' are comprised of diverse ethnic groups, some of the main territorial distinctions being recognised in the form of autonomous areas and regions within the Russian Republic. In the nineteenth century, the category 'all-Russian' (or 'Rossian') was applied to diverse 'European' nationalities within the Russian Empire, although not to the peoples of the newly colonised peripheral regions (Tishkov, 1992). The diversity of the Russian people and the distinction between the state-centred category of 'Rossian' and the ethnic- and language-based idea of 'Russian' complicates notions of 'Russian dominance' within the Empire or, indeed, the Soviet Union.

5. The notion that Nazism was anti-Western was developed by Aurel Kolnai in *The War Against the West* (1938) and Leonard Woolf in *Barbarians at the Gate* (1939). It was a popular as well as an intellectual position: Keith (1946) noted 'the assertion so often made in our Press and in our pulpits: "We are fighting this war to save civilisation" – sometimes specified as "Western civilisation"; at others as "Christian civilisation"' (p. 92). The difficulty of accepting fascism and Nazism as Western was confronted by Toynbee in volume six of *A Study of History*, published in 1939: 'Italy and Germany are no alien appendages to the Western body social; they are bone of its bone and flesh of its flesh; and it follows that the social revolution which has taken place yesterday in Italy and Germany under our eyes may overtake us in France or England or the Netherlands or Scandinavia tomorrow' (p. 57; also Toynbee, 1953: 'tyranny...has raised its head among our Western selves' p. 7). Hitler himself seems to have concurred. In 1935 he challenged Spengler by proclaiming, 'We live in the firm conviction that in our time will be fulfilled not the decline but the renaissance of the West. That Germany may make an imperishable contribution to this work is our prond hope and our unshakeable belief' (cited by Rader, 1939, p. 282).

6. Chamberlin (1944, p. 63) concluded that 'whether or not Stalin is to be regarded as a full-fledged Asiatic ruler' he was certainly a 'despot' in the Oriental mould (see also Wittfogel, 1957).

7. Even the most respected and careful of commentators apparently feel free to racially 'other' communist tyranny. For example, although Sakwa's (1990) *Gorbachev and his Reforms* is a detailed and useful book, we need to

wonder what the author means when he says that 'Gorbachev was the first thoroughly European leader that the Soviet Union has had' (p. 327), or that 'perestroika...[is] the triumph of suppressed elements of European civilisation in the Soviet Union' (p. 397).

8. The political commentary of Danilevskii, especially his book *La Russie et l'Europe* (1890, originally published 1869), is indicative of the way a range of Russian ideas about the West preceded Western accounts. Thus, for example, Danilevskii developed a model of the life cycle of civilisations, and argued that the West had entered its decadent stage; both ideas later to be re-invented by Spengler (MacMaster, 1954).

9. However, Conquest notes that, for Russians, Asia starts north of the Caucasus. For, whereas 'it is now common in Britain and elsewhere to regard the watershed of the Caucasus as marking the frontier of Europe, the Russian preference is still to take the line of the Kuma-Manych Depression as the physical boundary between the continents' (Conquest, 1970, p. 13).

10. Dostoevsky provided a typically reflexive and ironic critique of the Westernisers' Eurocentrism: 'In Europe we are hangers-on and slaves, but in Asia we are masters. In Europe we are Tatars, but in Asia we too are Europeans' (cited by Bassin, 1998, p. 75).

11. During the first two decades of the century, a distinction, albeit a loosening one, was maintained in Russia between 'the West' and the USA. The former term was used as a synonym for Western Europe. As this suggests, the notion that there existed a 'Western world' was rarely employed. The focus on Western Europe was a testament to the privileging of this region within Russian debate as the home and true centre of Westernism. Crucially, the USA was understood to be thoroughly Westernised; a free market export – albeit for the Bolsheviks, an impressively efficient and industrialised one – of the West.

12. The clunky, Moscow-authorised translation of the full quote has a slightly different emphasis:

> our task is to study the state capitalism of the Germans, to spare no effort in copying it and not shrink from adopting dictatorial methods to hasten the copying of it. Our task is to hasten this copying even more than Peter hastened the copying of Western culture by barbarian Russian, and we must not hesitate to use barbarous methods in fighting barbarism (Lenin, 1965, p. 340).

13. How assimilated these regions were to Bolshevism is another, although related, question: elections to the Constituent Assembly in 1917 show that the Bolsheviks 'got 50–56 per cent of the votes in central Russia with 16 per cent in the Volga region, 12 per cent in Ural and only 10 per cent in Siberia and Ukraine' (Kryukov, 1996, p. 372).

14. Lysenko became a hero of Socialist Labour in 1945 and was the director of the Academy of Sciences Institute of Genetics between 1940 and 1965.

15. Although Stalin was always explicit on the matter: 'Central Russia, that hearth of world revolution', he noted in 1920 (cited by Conquest, 1970, p. 124), 'cannot hold out long without the assistance of the border regions, which abound in raw materials, fuel and foodstuffs'. In fact, although Lenin's hostility to Russian chauvinism is legendary, a slippage from 'proletarian' to 'Russian' can also be found in his commentaries on the national question. 'What is important for the proletarian?' he asked in 1922, 'For the proletarian it is not only important, it is absolutely essential that he should be assured that the non-Russians place the greatest possible trust in the proletarian class struggle' (Lenin and Trotsky, 1975, p. 135).

16. Despite the strength of this current, opinion poles gathered in March 2001 show a majority of Russians (over 50%) wish to join the European Union (EU). Reporting this data, *The Economist* (2001) observes that the EU has yet to formulate a rationale for its (partly ethnic) instinct that Turkey and Russia should be kept out: 'The problem ... would be to find an objective reason for keeping Russia (or any other future applicant) out ... [The EU] cannot say (to Turkey): "We won't let you in because you are mainly Muslims", or (to Russia): "We won't let you in because we don't trust you".'

3   Good-bye Asia: The Westernisers' West, Fukuzawa and Gökalp

1. The rise of Japan was symbolised by Japan's alliance with Britain and defeat of Russia in the Russo–Japanese War of 1904–1905. The idea that Turkey could become the 'Japan of the near East' became an aspiration of the reformist Young Turks movement (Union and Progress Party, cited by Ahmad, 1993, p. 39).

2. The racial and breeding connotations of hybridity are critiqued historically by Young (1995). Bhabha (1994), who is often associated with the term's contemporary currency, tries to distance himself from such interpretations by insisting 'that colonial authority is not a *problem* of genealogy or identity between two *different* cultures which can then be resolved as an issue of cultural relativism. Hybridity is a problematic of colonial representation and individuation that reverses the effects of the colonialist disavowal, so that other "denied" knowledges enter upon the dominant discourse and estrange the basis of its authority – its rules of recognition' (p. 114). However, this deconstructive emphasis does not resolve the problem of either the political or the logical momentum of hybridity theory, which privileges the original, defining power of the West.

3. An emphasis on an *appropriation* of orientalism is seen in the work of Tong (2000, p. 18), who traces the way orientalism has been 'dislocated from the west, [and] resituated in China'. This focus still suggests that orientalism is essentially Western and that debate should focus on self-orientalising

Chinese intellectuals who see 'the West as "self"' (p. 18; see also Soguk, 1993). However, an interest in the appropriation of orientalism has the advantage of stripping discussion of the idea of a moralistic language of corruption and purity. Lee's remarks are illustrative of this tone of opprobrium:

> Said's (1978, p. 208) contention that 'Orientalism is fundamentally a political doctrine willed over the Orient because the Orient was weaker than the West' illustrates the tragedy of postcolonialism: that the illusion of independence masks the deeply embedded Occidentalism of the Orient. It is through this Occidentalism that the Orient has remade itself in the very images shaped and willed by the Orientalists (Lee, 1994, p. 24).

4. For an account of earlier Japanese intellectuals suspicions of the West see Chang (1970).
5. For discussion of Fukuzawa's complex relationship with the Meiji Restoration (1868–1912) see Daikichi, 1985; Pyle, 1969; Blacker, 1969, and Inkster, 1988.
6. Sakamoto (2001, p. 149) stresses Fukuzawa's 'Western racialist-Orientalist images' of China. However, in *Japan's Orient*, Tanaka (1993) details that the 'shift' from China to the West as the dominant influence on Japanese culture

> did not entail the simple replacement of China by the West ... The difference between the use of China and the use of the West was that the previous world was one in which all life was construed as being part of a fixed realm ... The West brought a different perspective, the probable future; knowledge was infinite (p. 32–33).

7. Thus Gökalp paved the way for the language reforms introduced after his death, such as the adoption of the Latin alphabet (1 November 1928) and the use of the Turkish language in the Islamic call to prayer (3 February 1932). The radicalism of the former reform is made clear by Ahmad (1993, p. 80), who notes that 'Overnight, virtually the entire nation was made illiterate.'
8. cf. Heyd, 1950 and Parla, 1985; see Davison, 1995 for discussion.

4   Soulless Occident/Spiritual Asia: Tagore's West

1. Communist criticism was also important in fermenting opposition to stereotypes of 'Asian spirituality' in India. In 1954, the Bengali revolutionary Roy (1950, p. vii) denounced criticism of Western materialism as 'heady wine'. An opponent of Tagore's vision of Asia, in his prison writings Roy noted that '[t]he "decline" of the West', was

> in reality only the decline of capitalism, the crises of Western civilization means only disintegration of the bourgeois social order. In that context,

India's 'spiritual mission' appears to be a mission with a mundane purpose, namely, to salvage a social system based upon the love of lucre... The claim that the Indian people as a whole are morally less corrupt, emotionally pure, idealistically less worldly, in short, spiritually more elevated than the bulk of the Western society, is based upon a wanton disregard for reality (pp. 190–191).

2. It was an interest both religious and aesthetic in character. Both currents were to the fore in the work of the Theosophical Society, established in 1875 in New York by Madame Blavatsky and Colonel Olcott. The Society promoted a creative, rather mercurial, blend of esoteric philosophy, Buddhism, Hinduism and evolutionism. However, Theosophy was far from being simply a Western project. It gained well over one hundred branches in India and provided an important stimulant to Hindu and Buddhist revival and self-awareness.

5 From Soulless to Slacker: The Idea of the West from Pan-Asianism to Asian Values

1. The redemptive societies may have been brought under the wing of the Japanese colonial authorities but they retained their 'egalitarian utopianism' (Duara, 2001, p. 125). Their adherence to spiritual and benevolent activities made them a potentially subversive partner. Indeed, their collaboration was limited: 'In the rural and peripheral areas', Duara explains, 'wherever the societies saw the Japanese-backed regime as inimical to their ideals and goals – whether towards their transcendent vision or towards their conception of an ideal community – the opposition to the regime was quite sustained' (p. 125). Thus, the redemptive societies represented another path for pan-Asian spirituality, one that appears closer to the kind of route Tagore wished to go down.

2. As Kahn (1997) and others have emphasised, that Asian values have come 'to resonate very strongly among a much wider circle of ordinary Malaysians' (p. 29) and other Asians indicates that this particular vision of Asia cannot be dismissed as an elite concoction. Yet, however popular, the problem remains that Asian values contain not only an undigested mix of neo-liberalism and traditionalism but little political or social substance to actually sustain a sense of regional solidarity and identity. The speed with which the rhetoric of 'Asian values' rose and fell makes it seem like a typical product of the restless and fast-moving culture of contemporary, post-modern capitalism. Within this context, the very shallowness of 'Asian values', its inability to appear as anything more than a regional inflection of global capitalist culture, is part of its appeal. Ironically , whilst the discourse of Asian values is associated with the promotion of hard work, as an ideology it can often appear lazily convenient and superficial. The theory of Asian values, as Kahn has observed, is 'remarkably thin, highly repetitive' (p. 19).

6 Occidental Utopia: The Neo-liberal West

1. A revival of white crisis literature was also witnessed in the 1960s, although shorn of white supremacism. Such works as Irvine's *The Rise of the Coloured Races* (1972), Melady's *The Revolution of Color* (1966) and Segal's *The Race War: The World-wide Conflict of Races* (1967) are revealing not simply because they seek to dissect the causes of white crisis (see also Plummer, 1996), but because of the weight they place on the political meaning of *demographic* change. Thus, for example, the ascendancy of the non-West discussed by Irvine is proven by reference to population 'explosions'. He tells us that in 'the face of unprecedented and overwhelming' relative increases in the size of the 'coloured' peoples, the orthodoxies of international relations will soon be surpassed: 'all calculations – including those based on the lessons of the past – will appear inconsequential' (p. 602). Melady repeats the common-sense demographic argument of the day: 'the rise to power of the people of color is intimately related to the worldwide population explosion' (p. 40).

2. In *McWorld vs. Jihad* Barber positions 'Jihad' as an atavistic reaction to neo-liberalism, a 'rabid response to colonialism and imperialism' (p. 11). Unfortunately, Barber's analysis becomes muddled when he tries to elucidate 'Jihad'. His decision to offer Catalonian nationalism and Occitan regionalism as examples of 'Jihad' is extraordinary. It suggests a difficulty in grasping that it is the largely undifferentiated linguistic and national geography of the USA that is exceptional, not the myriad small nations and tongues of other continents. Barber's conflation of anti-Westernism with parochialism and tribalism, and his representation of Islamism as the archetype of these forces, is also mistaken. Islamism is a pan-ethnic and internationalist (indeed, anti-nationalist) current. As Arjomand (1994, p. 673) explains, 'Islamic activists oppose the universalism of the secular state with a universalism of their own.'

3. The term 'magico-Marxism' was developed through neo-situationist interventions in the 1990s. The occasional journal, *Trangressions: A Journal of Urban Exploration*, provided a home for this novel tendency. The position advanced by a number of its contributors was, not simply that capitalism is ritualistic and akin to magic, but that: (a) exposing or imaginatively concocting occult practices amongst the ruling class is a form of political strategy; and (b) that revolutionary activity requires a disorienting engagement with popular heritage and everyday life (Blissett, 1996; Jorn, 1998).

7 Western Dystopia: Radical Islamism and Anti-Westernism

1. The term '*al-Qa'idah*' ('the base') referred initially to bin Laden's organisation of Arab resistance fighters in the war against the communist government of Afghanistan. It has since been used, often rather loosely, as a label attached to both those with direct experience of bin Laden's wider network of

supporters and what appear to be disparate and amorphous groups in a number of countries made up of militants sympathetic to bin Laden's strain of violent activism.

2. The four principal ways radical Islam has been translated into practice are as follows:

　1. By the strengthening or introduction of conservative interpretations of Islamic law in nations or national regions (as in Sudan, Libya, northern Pakistan and northern Nigeria).

　2. By means of the development of radical but nationally based Islamist movements. The oldest of these is the Muslim Brotherhood, founded by Hasan al-Banna in 1928 in Egypt. Such groups include both moderate, democratically oriented movements such as the Lebanese Resistance Battalions (AMAL), militarised groups engaged in territorial conflicts (such as The Party of God (Hizbullah) in Lebanon), and terrorist extremists (such as the Organisation for Holy War in Egypt and the Armed Islamic Group in Algeria).

　3. Radical Islamism has been put into practice through radical Islamist revolution, as in Iran in 1979. The most novel and experimental of these regimes was the Taliban ('student') government of Afghanistan (Kabul fell to the Taliban in 1996). This regime also exemplifies, in extreme form, the parochialism and sectarianism that has so often accompanied radical religious government (exemplified in Taliban-controlled Afghanistan by the persecution of shii minority Muslims, as well as other Muslims with non-majority tribal affiliations).

　4. Through the development of international radical Islamist organisation. Again these range from the moderate to extremist. In the latter category is the World Islamic Front for the Jihad Against Jews and Crusaders founded in 2000. Led by Osama bin Laden, the name of this group exemplifies: (a) the religious terminology of some radical Islamists (terms such as 'the West' and 'Westernisation' often being less common than 'Crusaders' and 'non-believers'); (b) the centrality of Palestine and the Israel–US relationship to the radical Islamist worldview (more specifically, the ethnic cleansing of the Palestinians from Palestine and the subsequent Israeli occupation and settlement of their remnant state, is offered as the paradigm of Judeo-Christian (more specifically, Israeli and US) attitudes to Islam); and (c) the emphasis on worldwide struggle.

3. When Western critics see similarities between non-Western sources and familiar Western ideologies they tend to imagine that the latter produced the former. Post-September 11 literature has been particularly prone to this convenient conceit. The supposed 'anarchism' of Qutb is a case in point. It is highlighted by Ruthven (2002, p. 91) who writes in *A Fury for God: The Islamist Attack on America*, that Qutb's views on the abolishment of earthly

authority '[owe] more to radical European ideas going back to the Jacobins' than to Islam. In *Al Qaeda and What it Means to be Modern* (2003, p. 24) John Gray makes the same equation, finding Qutb 'indebted to European anarchism'. However, it is noticeable that Qutb's indebtedness to European anarchism is asserted but not evidenced. In fact, another way of looking at this relationship exists. Anti-authoritarianism and anti-centralism are global phenomenon. They have strong and varied roots, especially in peasant cultures. Anarchism is a European category for this current. Thus although Qutb's anti-government views might be described as anarchist it does not follow he derived them from Europe. A similar point may be made about Western writers who claim al-Qa'idah as nihilist.

References

Abrahamian, E. (1993) *Khomeinism: Essays on the Islamic Republic*, Berkeley, University of California Press.

Ahmad, F. (1993) *The Making of Modern Turkey*, London, Routledge.

al-'Azm, S. (1981) 'Orientalism and orientalism in reverse', *Khamsin: Journal of Revolutionary Socialists of the Middle East*, 8, pp. 5–26.

Al-e Ahmad, J. (1982) *Plagued by the West (Gharbzadegi)*, Delmar, Caravan Books.

—— (1984) *Occidentotis: A Plaque from the West*, Berkeley, Mirzan Press.

Al-Ali, N. (2000) 'Women's activism and occidentalism in contemporary Egypt', *Civil Society: Democratization in the Arab World*, 9, at http://www.ibnkhaldun.org/newsletter/2000/april/essay, accessed 20 September 2002.

Aizawa, S. (1986) 'New theses', in B. Wakabayashi (ed.) *Anti-foreignism and Western Learning in Early-modern Japan*, Cambridge, Council on East Asian Studies, Harvard University.

Alliluyeva, S. (1968) *20 Letters to a Friend*, London, World Books.

Armstrong, C. (1927) *The Survival of the Unfittest*, London, C. W. Daniel.

Arjomand, S. (1994) 'Fundamentalism, religious nationalism, or populism', *Contemporary Sociology*, 23, 5, pp. 671–675.

Back, L. (1995) *New Ethnicities and Urban Youth Cultures*, London, University College London Press.

Bahry, D. (2002) 'Ethnicity and equality in post-communist economic transition: evidence from Russia's republics', *Europe-Asia Studies*, 54, 5, pp. 673–699.

Barber, B. (1996) *Jihad vs. McWorld: How Globalism and Tribalism are Reshaping the World*, New York, Ballantine Books.

Barkan, E. (1992) *The Retreat of Scientific Racism: Changing Concepts of Race in Britain and the United States Between the World Wars*, Cambridge, Cambridge University Press.

Baritz, L. (1961) 'The idea of the west', *The American Historical Review*, 66, 3, pp. 618–640.

Baron, S. (1975) *The Russian Jew Under Tsars and Soviets*, New York, Macmillan.

Bassin, M. (1991) 'Russia between Europe and Asia: the ideological construction of geographical space', *Slavic Review*, 50, 1, pp. 1–17.

—— (1998) 'Asia', in N. Rzhevsky (ed.) *The Cambridge Companion to Modern Russian Culture*, Cambridge, Cambridge University Press.

Barzun, J. (2001) *From Dawn to Decadence*, London, HarperCollins.
Beck, U. (1994) 'The reinvention of politics: Towards a theory of reflexive modernisation', in U. Beck, A. Giddens and S. Lash (eds) *Reflexive Modernization: Politics, Tradition and Aesthetics in the Modern Social Order*, Oxford, Polity.
Becker, S. (1991) 'Russia between East and West: the intelligentsia, Russian national identity, and the Asian borderlands', *Central Asian Review*, 10, 4, pp. 47–64.
Bellah, R. (1958) 'Religious aspects of modernization in Turkey and Japan', *American Journal of Sociology*, 64, 1, pp. 1–5.
Bello, W. (1995) 'Strip-mining the future', *New Internationalist*, January, pp. 20–21.
—— and Rosenfeld, S. (1991) *Dragons in Distress: Asia's Miracle Economies in Crisis*, London, Penguin.
Berkes, N. (1954) 'Ziya Gökalp: his contribution to Turkish nationalism', *Middle East Journal*, 8, 4, pp. 375–390.
Beus, J. (1953) *The Future of the West*, New York, Harper.
Bhabha, H. (1994) *The Location of Culture*, London, Routledge.
Bharucha, R. (2001) 'Under the sign of 'Asia': rethinking 'creative unity' beyond the 'rebirth of traditional arts', *Inter-Asia Cultural Studies*, 2, 1, pp. 151–156.
Blacker, C. (1969) *The Japanese Enlightenment: A Study of the Writings of Fukuzawa Yukichi*, Cambridge, Cambridge University Press.
Blissett, L. (1996) 'Ralph Rumney's revenge and other scams', *Transgressions: A Journal of Urban Exploration*, 2, 3, pp. 13–19.
Bonnett, A. (1998) 'How the British working class became white: the symbolic (re)formation of racialized capitalism', *Journal of Historical Sociology*, 11, 3, pp. 316–340.
—— (2000) *White Identities: Historical and International Perspectives*, Harlow, Prentice-Hall.
—— (2002) 'Communists like us: ethnicized modernity and the idea of "the West" in the Soviet Union', *Ethnicities*, 2, 4, pp. 435–467.
—— (2003) 'Geography as the world discipline: connecting the academic and popular geographical imagination', *Area*, 35, pp. 55–63.
Bradford Delong, J. (1998) 'Corral the Biannual crises', *Los Angeles Times*, 28 January.
Brower, D. and Lazzerini, E. (eds) (1997) *Russia's Orient: Imperial Borderlands and Peoples, 1700–1917*, Bloomington, Indiana University Press.
Brown, P. (2003) *The Rise of Western Christendom: Triumph and Diversity, A.D. 200–1000: Second Edition*, Oxford, Blackwell.
Buchanan, P. (2003) *The Death of the West: How Dying Populations and Immigrant Invasions Imperil Our Country and Civilization*, New York, Thomas Dunne Books.
Burleigh, M. and Wipperman, M. (1991) *The Racial State: Germany 1933–1945*, Cambridge, Cambridge University Press.
Burnham, J. (1964) *Suicide of the West*, New York, Knopf.
Canefe, N. (2002) 'Turkish nationalism and ethno-symbolic analysis: the rules of exception', *Nations and Nationalism*, 8, 2, pp. 133–155.

Cantlie, J. (1906) *Physical Efficiency: A Review of the Deleterious Effects of Town Life upon the Population of Britain, with Suggestions for their Arrest*, London, G.P. Putnam's Sons.

Carr, E. (1958) *A History of Soviet Russia: Socialism in One Country 1924–1926: Volume One*, London, Macmillan.

—— (1966a) *The Bolshevik Revolution 1917–1923: Volume One*, Harmondsworth, Penguin.

—— (1966b) *The Bolshevik Revolution 1917–1923: Volume Three*, Harmondsworth, Penguin.

Carrere d'Encausse, H. (1993) *The End of the Soviet Empire: The Triumph of the Nations*, New York, Basic Books.

Carrier, J. (1995) (ed.) *Occidentalism: Images of the West*, Oxford, Oxford University Press.

Castells, M. (1998) *End of Millennium*, Oxford, Blackwell.

Chakarabarti, M. (1990) *Rabindranath Tagore: Diverse Dimensions*, Atlantic Publishers, New Delhi.

Chakrabarty, D. (2000) *Provincialising Europe: Postcolonial Thought and Historical Difference*, Princeton, Princeton University Press.

Chamberlain, J. and Gilman, S. (eds) (1985) *Degeneration: The Dark Side of Progress*, New York, Colombia University Press.

Chamberlin, W. (1940) *The World's Iron Age*, New York, Macmillan.

—— (1944) *The Russian Enigma*, New York, Charles Scribner's Sons.

—— (1987a) *Russian Revolution: Volume One: 1917–1918: From the Overthrow of the Tsar to the Assumption of Power by the Bolsheviks*, Princeton, Princeton University Press.

—— (1987b) *Russian Revolution: Volume Two: 1918–1921: From the Civil War to the Consolidation of Power*, Princeton, Princeton University Press.

Champly, H. (1934) *The Road to Shanghai: White Slave Traffic in Asia*, London, John Long.

—— (1936) *White Women, Coloured Men*, London, John Long.

Chang, R. (1970) *From Prejudice to Tolerance: A Study of the Japanese Image of the West 1826–1864*, Tokyo, Sophia University Press.

Chatterjee, B. (1996) *Rabindranath Tagore and Modern Sensibility*, Oxford University Press, Delhi.

Chatterjee, P. (1986) *Nationalist Thought and the Colonial World: A Derivative Discourse*, London, Zed Books.

Chen, X. (1995) *Occidentalism: A Theory of Counter-Discourse in Post-Mao China*, New York, Oxford University Press.

Ching, L. (1998) 'Yellow skins, white masks: race, class, and identification in Japanese colonial discourse', in K. Chen (ed.) *Trajectories: Inter-Asian Cultural Studies*, London, Routledge.

Choueiri, Y. (1997) *Islamic Fundamentalism: Revised Edition*, London, Pinter.

Chua, A. (2003) *World on Fire: How Exporting Free Market Democracy Breeds Ethnic Hatred and Global Instability*, London, William Heinemnn.

Chua, B. (1999) 'Asian-values' discourse and the resurrection of the social, *Positions: East Asia Cultures Critique*, 7, 2, pp. 571–592.

Clarke, J. (1997) *Oriental Enlightenment: The Encounter Between Asian and Western Thought*, London, Routledge.

Coker, C. (1998) *Twilight of the West*, Boulder, Westview Press.

182 *References*

Cole, G. (1932) *The Intelligent Man's Guide Through World Chaos*, London, Victor Gollancz.
—— (1941) *Europe, Russia, and the Future*, London, Victor Gollancz.
Colussi, L. (ed.) (1991) *Universality of Tagore: Souvenir of a Symposium*, Nitika/Don Bosco and Firma KLM Private Limited, Calcutta.
Comaroff and Comaroff (2000) 'Millennial capitalism: First thoughts on a second coming', *Public Culture*, 12, 2, pp. 291–343.
Conquest, R. (1970) *The Nation Killers: The Soviet Deportation of Nationalities*, London, Macmillan.
—— (ed.) (1986) *The Last Empire: Nationality And The Soviet Future*, Stanford, Hoover Institution Press.
Corbett, P. (1945) 'Next steps after the Charter', *Commentary*, 1, 1, pp. 27–28.
Coronil, F. (1996) 'Beyond occidentalism: toward nonimperial geohistorical categories', *Cultural Anthropology*, 11, 1, pp. 51–87.
—— (2000) 'Towards a critique of globalcentrism: speculations on capitalism's nature', *Public Culture*, 12, 2, pp. 351–374.
Cowen, J. (1909) *Joseph Cowen's Speeches: Near Eastern Question*, Newcastle upon Tyne, Andrew Reid and Company.
Creighton, M. (1995) 'Imaging the other in Japanese advertising campaigns', in J. Carrier (ed.) *Occidentalism: Images of the West*, Oxford, Oxford University Press.
Crook, D. (1984) *Benjamin Kidd: Portrait of a Social Darwinist*, Cambridge, Cambridge University Press.
Curle, J. (1926) *To-day and To-morrow: The Testing Period of the White Race*, London, Methuen.
D'Agostino, A. (1988) *Soviet Succession Struggles: Kremlinology and the Russian Question from Lenin to Gorbachev*, Boston, Allen & Unwin.
Dabashi, H. (1993) *The Theology of Discontent: The Ideological Foundation of the Islamic Revolution in Iran*, New York, New York University Press.
Daikichi, I. (1985) *The Culture of the Meiji Period*, Princeton, Princeton University Press.
Danilevskii, N. (1890) *La Russie et l' Europe: Coup d' oeil sur les rapports politiques entre le monde slave et le monde germano-roman*, Bucarest, Bureaux de la Liberté Roumaine.
Darwin, C. (1901) *The Descent of Man and Selection in Relation to Sex*, London, John Murray.
Davison, A. (1995) 'Secularization and modernization in Turkey: the ideas of Ziya Gökalp', *Economy and Society*, 24, 2, pp. 189–224.
Dawisha, K. and Parrott, B. (1994) *Russia and the New States of Eurasia: The Politics of Upheaval*, Cambridge, Cambridge University Press.
—— (eds) (1997) *The End of Empire? The Transformation of the USSR in Comparative Perspective*, New York, M.E. Sharpe.
Decugis, H. (1936) *Le destin des races blanches*, Paris, Librarie de France.
Delanty, G. (1995) *Inventing Europe: Idea, Identity, Reality*, Basingstoke, Macmillan.
Diuk, N. and Karatnycky, A. (1993) *New Nations Rising: The Fall of the Soviets and the Challenge of Independence*, New York, John Wiley.

Duara, P. (1997) 'Transnationalism and the predicament of sovereignty: China, 1900–1945', *The American Historical Review*, 102, 4, pp. 1030–1051.
—— (2001) 'The discourse of civilization and Pan-Asianism', *Journal of World History*, 12, 1, pp. 99–130.
—— (2003) *Sovereignty and Authenticity: Manchukuo and the East Asian Modern*, Rowman and Littlefield.
The Economist, 'The limits of Europe', 19 May 2001.
Ekachai, S. (1993) *Behind the Smiles: Voices of Thailand*, Bangkok, Thai Development Support Committee.
Esposito, J. and Voll, J. (2001) *Makers of Contemporary Islam*, New York, Oxford University Press.
Faguet, M. 1895 'La prochain moyen age', *Le Journal des Débats*, 25 July.
Fanon, F. (1959) *L'An Cinq de la Révolution Algérienne*, Paris, François Maspéro.
—— (1965) *Studies in a Dying Colonialism*, New York, Monthly Review Press.
—— (1986) *Black Skin, White Masks*, London, Pluto.
Federici, S. (ed.) (1995) 'The God that never failed: the origins and crises of Western civilization', *Enduring Western Civilization: The Construction of the Concept of Western Civilization and its 'Others'*, Westport, Connecticut, Praeger.
Frankenberg, R. (ed.) (1997) *Displacing Whiteness*, Durham, Duke University Press.
Freeman, A. (1921) *Social Decay and Regeneration*, London, Constable and Company.
—— (1923) 'The Sub-Man', *Eugenics Review*, 15, 2, pp. 383–392.
Fowkes, B. (1997) *The Disintegration of the Soviet Union: A Study in the Rise and Triumph of Nationalism*, Basingstoke, Macmillan.
Fukuyama, F. (1992) *The End of History And The Last Man London*, Hamish Hamilton.
—— (2001) 'The west has won', *The Guardian*, 11 October.
Fukuzawa, Y. (1934) *The Autobiography of Fukuzawa Yukichi*, Tokyo, Hokuseido Press.
—— (1958) 'Seiyo Jijo' [Conditions in the West], in *Fukuzawa Yukichi Zenshu*, 1, Tokyo, Iwanami Shoten.
—— (1959) 'Sekai Kunizukushi' [World Geography], in *Fukuzawa Yukichi Zenshu*, 2, Tokyo, Iwanami Shoten.
—— (1969) *An Encouragement of Learning*, Tokyo, Sophia University Press.
—— (1973) *An Outline of a Theory of Civilization*, Tokyo, Sophia University Press.
—— (1985) *Fukuzawa Yukichi on Education*, Tokyo, University of Tokyo Press.
—— (1988) *Fukuzawa Yukichi on Japanese Women*, Tokyo, University of Tokyo Press.
—— (1997) 'Good-bye Asia (Datsu-a) 1885', in D. Lu (ed.) *Japan: A Documentary History: The Late Tokugawa Period to the Present*, Armonk, M.E. Sharpe.
Füredi, F. (1998) *The Silent War: Imperialism and the Changing Perception of Race*, London, Pluto.
Galton, F. (1883) *Inquiries into Human Faculty and its Development*, London, Macmillan.

Giddings, F. (1898) Review of 'National Life and Character: A Forecast. By Charles H. Pearson' *Political Science Quarterly* 10, 1, pp. 160–162.

Gilly, A. (1965) 'Introduction', in F. Fanon *Studies in a Dying Colonialism*, New York, Monthly Review Press.

Glacken, C. (1976) *Traces on the Rhodian Shore: Nature and Culture in Western Thought from Ancient Times to the End of the Eighteenth Century*, Berkeley, University of California Press.

Gleason, G. (1990) 'Leninist nationality policy: its source and style', in H. Huttenbach (ed.) *Soviet Nationality Policies: Ruling Ethnic Groups in the USSR*, London, Mansell.

Gobineau, A. (1915) *The Inequality of the Races*, New York, G.P. Putnam's Sons.

Goddard, E. and Gibbons, P. (1926) *Civilisation or Civilisations: An Essay in the Spenglerian Philosophy of History*, London, Constable.

GoGwilt, C. (1995) *The Invention of the West: Joseph Conrad and the Double-Mapping of Europe and Empire*, Stanford, Stanford University Press.

Gökalp, Z. (1981) *Turkish Nationalism and Western Civilization*, Greenwood Press, London.

Gollancz, V. (1946) *Our Threatened Values*, London, Victor Gollancz.

Gorbachev, M. (1987) *Perestroika: New Thinking for our Country and the World*, London, Collins.

Gramsci, A. (1971) *Selections from the Prison Notebooks of Antonio Gramsci*, London, Lawrence and Wishart.

Grant, M. (1917) *The Passing of the Great Race: or the Racial Basis of European History*, London, G. Bell and Sons.

—— (1925) 'Introduction', in L. Stoddard *The Rising Tide of Color Against White World-Supremacy*, New York, Charles Scribner's Sons.

Gray, J. (2002) *False dawn: The Delusions of Global Capitalism*, London, Granta.

—— (2003) *Al Qaeda and What it Means to be Modern*, London, Faber & Faber.

Greenslade, W. (1992) 'Fitness and the fin de siècle', in J. Stokes (ed.) *Fin de Siècle/Fin du Globe: Fears and Fantasies of the Late Nineteenth Century*, London, Macmillan.

Gregory, J. (1925) *The Menace of Colour*, London, Seeley Service.

Gress, D. (1998) *From Plato to NATO: The Idea of the West and its Opponents*, New York, Free Press.

Guattari, F. and Negri, T. (1990) *Communists Like Us: New Spaces of Liberty, New Lines of Alliance*, New York, Semiotext(e).

Guterl, M. (1999) 'The new race consciousness: race, nation and empire in American culture, 1910–1925', *Journal of World History*, 10, 2, pp. 307–352.

Habakkuk, H. (1971) 'Population, commerce and economic ideas', in A. Goodwin (ed.) *The New Cambridge Modern History VIII: The American and French Revolutions, 1763–93*, Cambridge University Press, Cambridge.

Haggard, R. (1905) *The Poor and the Land*, London, Longmans, Green and Co.

Haldane, J. (1938) *Heredity and Politics*, New York, W.W. Norton.

Hanchard, M. (1999) 'Afro-modernity: temporality, politics, and the African Diaspora', *Public Culture*, 11, 1, pp. 245–268.

Hanson, V. (2001) *Why the West Won: Carnage and Culture from Salamis to Vietnam*, London, Faber & Faber.

—— (2002) 'Occidentalism: the false west', *National Review*, May 10, at www.nationalreview.com/hanson/hanson051002.asp, accessed 21 November 2002

Hardt, M. and Negri, A. (2000) *Empire*, Cambridge, Harvard University Press.

Harootunian, H. (2000) *Overcome by Modernity: History, Culture and Community in Interwar Japan*, Princeton, Princeton University Press.

—— (2002) 'Quartering the millennium', *Radical Philosophy*, 116, pp. 21–29.

Hauner, M. (1990) *What is Asia to Us? Russia's Asian Heartland Yesterday and Today*, Boston, Unwin Hyman.

Hay, S. (1970) *Asian Ideas of East and West: Tagore and his Critics in Japan, China, and India*, Cambridge, Harvard University Press.

Hegel, G. (1991) *The Philosophy of History*, Amherst, Prometheus Books.

Heller, M. and Nekrich, A. (1985) *Utopia in Power*, London, Hutchinson.

Herman, A. (1997) *The Idea of Decline in Western History*, New York, Free Press.

Heyd, U. (1950) *Foundations of Turkish Nationalism: the Life and Teachings of Ziya Gökalp*, Luzac and Company/Harvill Press, London.

Hirsch, F. (2000) 'Towards an empire of nations: border-making and the formation of Soviet national identities', *The Russian Review*, 59, pp. 201–226.

Hirth, F. (1966) *China and the Roman Orient: Researches into their Ancient and Mediaeval Relations as Represented in Old Chinese Records*, New York, Paragon Book Reprint Corp.

Hobhouse, L. (1915) 'Science and philosophy as unifying forces', in F. Marvin (ed.) *The Unity of Western Civilization*, London, Oxford University Press.

Hobsbawn, E. (1968) *Industry and Empire*, New York, Pantheon Books.

Hobson, J. (1972) *The Crisis of Liberalism*, Sussex, Harvester Press.

Hogben, L. (1931) *Genetic Principles in Medicine and Social Sciences*, London, Williams and Norgate.

Holden, B. (1988) *Understanding Liberal Democracy*, Oxford, Philip Allan.

Horne, G. (2004) *Race War! White Supremacy and the Japanese Attack on the British Empire*, New York, New York University Press.

Hubbard, A. (1913) *The Fate of Empires: Being an Inquiry into the Stability of Civilisation*, London, Longmans, Green and Company.

Huntingdon, S. (1997) *The Clash of Civilisations and the Remaking of the World Order*, London, Simon & Schuster.

Hutchinson, R. (2001) 'Occidentalism and the critique of Meiji: the West in the returnee stories of Nagai Kafu', *Japan Forum*, 13, 2, pp. 195–213.

Huxley, J. and Haddon A. (1939) *We Europeans, A Survey of 'Racial' Problems*, London, Jonathan Cape.

Hyslop, J. (1999) 'The imperial working class makes itself "white": white labourism in Britain, Australia, and South Africa before the First World War', *Journal of Historical Sociology*, 12, 4, pp. 398–421.

Iida, Y. (1997) 'Fleeing the West, making Asia home: transpositions of otherness in Japanese Pan-Asianism, 1905–1930', *Alternatives*, 22, pp. 409–432.

Inge, W. (1919) *Outspoken Essays*, London, Longmans, Green and Company.

—— (1922) *Outspoken Essays (Second Series)*, London, Longmans, Green and Company.

—— (1933) *England: New and Revised Edition*, London, Ernest Benn.

Inkster, I. (1988) 'The other side of Meiji: conflict and conflict management', in G. McCormack and Y. Sugimoto (eds) *The Japanese Trajectory: Modernization and Beyond*, Cambridge, Cambridge University Press.

Ibrahim, A. (1996) *The Asian Renaissance*, Singapore, Times Books International.

Iqbal, M. (1955) *Poems from Iqbal*, London, John Murray.

Ireland, A. (1921) *Democracy and the Human Equation*, New York, E.P. Dutton.

Irvine, K. (1972) *The Rise of the Coloured Races*, London, George Allen & Unwin.

Jameelah, M. (1976) *Islam and the Muslim Woman Today*, Lahore, Mohammad Yusuf Khan and Sons.

—— (1979a) *Western Civilization Condemned By Itself: A Comprehensive Study of Moral Retrogression and its Consequences. Vol. I*, Lahore, Mohammad Yusuf Khan and Sons.

—— (1979b) *Western Civilization Condemned By Itself: A Comprehensive Study of Moral Retrogression and its Consequences. Vol. II*, Lahore, Mohammad Yusuf Khan and Sons.

—— (1982) *Memoirs of Childhood (1945–1962): The Story of One Western Convert's Quest for the Truth*, Lahore, Mohammad Yusuf Khan and Sons.

Joravsky, D. (1986) *The Lysenko Affair*, Chicago, University of Chicago Press.

Jorn, A. (1998) 'Critique of economic policy', *Transgressions: A Journal of Urban Exploration*, 4, pp. 13–35.

Kadioglu, A. (1996) 'The paradox of Turkish nationalism and the construction of official identity', *Middle Eastern Studies*, 32, 2, pp. 1–11.

Kahn, J. (1997) 'Malaysian modern or anti-anti Asian values', *Thesis Eleven*, 50, pp. 15–33.

Keddie, N. (1983) 'Iranian revolutions in comparative perspective', *The American Historical Review*, 83, 3, pp. 579–598.

Keene, D. (1969) *The Japanese Discovery of Europe, 1720–1830: Revised Edition*, Stanford, Stanford University Press.

Keenleyside, T. (1982) 'Nationalist Indian attitudes towards Asia: A troublesome legacy for post-independence Indian foreign policy', *Pacific Affairs*, 55, 2, pp. 210–230.

Keith, A. (1946) *Essays on Human Evolution*, London, Watts.

Kelman, J. (ed.) (1979) *Anti-semitism in the Soviet Union: Its Roots and Consequences*, Jerusalem, Centre for Research and Documentation of East-European Jewry.

Keynes, J. (1926) *The End of Laissez-faire*, London, The Hogarth Press.

Khoo Boo Teik (1999) 'The value(s) of a miracle: Malaysian and Singaporean elite constructions of Asia', *Asian Studies Review*, 23, 2, pp. 181–192.

Kidd, B. (1894) *Social Evolution*, London, Macmillan.

—— (1902) *Principles of Western Civilisation: Being the First Volume of a System of Evolutionary Philosophy*, London, Macmillan.

Kirby, D. (2000) 'Divinely sanctioned: The Anglo-American Cold War alliance and the defence of Western civilization and Christianity, 1945–48', *Journal of Contemporary History*, 35, 3, pp. 385–412.

Kirmaci, A. (1982) 'Nationalism-racism-Turanism in Turkey (a criticism)', in K. Karpat (ed.) *Political and Social thought in the Contemporary Middle East: Revised and Enlarged Edition*, New York, Praeger.

Kohn, H. (1957) *Is the Liberal West in Decline?*, London, Pall Mall.

Kolnai, A. (1938) *The War Against the West*, London, Victor, Gollancz.

Korhonen, P. (2002) 'Asia's Chinese name', *Inter-Asia Cultural Studies*, 3, 2, pp. 253–270.

Kotkin, S. (1995) *Magnetic Mountain: Stalinism as a Civilization*, Berkeley, University of California Press.

Krementsov, N. (1997) *Stalinist Science*, Princeton, Princeton University Press.

Krivorotov, V. (1990) 'Russkiy put', *Znamya*, 60, 8, pp. 140–164.

Kryukov, M. (1996) 'Self-determination from Marx to Mao', *Ethnic and Racial Studies*, 19, 2, pp. 352–378.

Lago, M. (1972) *Imperfect Encounter: Letters of William Rothenstein and Rabindranath Tagore 1911–1941*, Cambridge, Harvard University Press.

Lankester, E. (1880) *Degeneration: A Chapter in Darwinism*, London, Macmillan.

Lash, S. (1999) *Another Modernity, A Different Rationality*, Oxford, Blackwell.

Ledger, S. and Luckhurst, R. (eds) (2000) *The Fin de Siècle: A Reader in Cultural History c. 1880–1900*, Oxford, Oxford University Press.

Lee, C. (1994) 'Trend report', *Current Sociology*, 42, 2, pp. v–66

Lenin, V. (1935) *Selected Works, Volume 5*, London, Lawrence and Wishart.

—— (1962) *Collected Works, Volume 10, November 1905–June 1906*, Moscow, Progress Publications.

—— (1964a) *Collected Works, Volume 24, April–June 1917*, Moscow, Progress Publications.

—— (1964b) *Collected Works, Volume 23, August 1916–March 1917*, Moscow, Progress Publications.

—— (1965) *Collected Works, Volume 27, February–July 1918*, Moscow, Progress Publications.

—— and Trotsky, L. (1975) *Lenin's Fight Against Stalinism*, New York, Pathfinder.

Levi, W. (1952) *Free India in Asia*, Minneapolis, University of Minnesota Press.

Lewis, M. and Wigen, K. (1997) *The Myth of Continents: A Critique of Metageography*, Berkeley, University of California Press.

Lieven, D. (1995) 'The Russian empire and the Soviet Union as imperial polities', *Journal of Contemporary History*, 30, pp. 605–636.

Lim, L. and Gosleng, P. (eds) (1983) *The Chinese in Southeast Asia: Ethnicity and Economic Activity*, Singapore, Maruzen Asia.

Little, J. (1907) *The Doom of Western Civilization*, London, W.H. and L. Collingridge.

Luttwak, E. (1999) *Turbo Capitalism: Winners and Losers in the Global Economy*, London, Orion Business Books.

Lyall, A. (1910) 'Introduction', in V. Chirol *Indian Unrest*, London, Macmillan.

Macaulay, T. (1970) *Prose and Poetry*, Cambridge, Harvard University Press.

MacDonald, J. [R.] (1901) 'The propaganda of civilization', *International Journal of Ethics*, 11, 4, pp. 455–468.

MacKenzie, D. (1976) 'Eugenics in Britain', *Social Studies of Science*, 6, 3/4, pp. 499–532.

MacMaster, R. (1954) 'Danilevsky and Spengler: A new interpretation', *The Journal of Modern History*, 26, pp. 154–561.

Macmillan, H. (1966) 'Triumph of Europe: political', in L. Stavrianos (ed.) *The Epic of Modern Man: A Collection of Readings*, Eaglewood Cliffs, New Jersey, Prentice-Hall.

Macpherson, C. (1977) *The Life and Times of Liberal Democracy*, Oxford, Oxford University Press.

Mahbubani, K. (1998) *Can Asians Think? Understanding the Divide Between East and West*, South Royalton, Vermont, Steerforth Press.

Mandelbaum, M. (2002) *The Ideas that Conquered the World: Peace, Democracy, and Free Markets in the Twenty-first Century*, New York, Public-Affairs.

Mandelstam, O. (1974) *Osip Mandelstam: Selected Poems*, London, Atheneum.

Margalit, A. and Buruma, I. (2002) 'Occidentalism', *The New York Times Review of Books*, January 17, at www.nybooks.com/articles/15100, accessed 20 September 2002.

Martin, T. (1996) *An Affirmative Action Empire: Ethnicity and the Soviet State, 1923–1938*, PhD dissertation, University of Chicago.

Marvin, F. (ed.) (1915) *The Unity of Western Civilization* [The Unity Series I], London, Oxford University Press.

—— (ed.) (1916) *Progress and History* [The Unity Series II], London, Oxford University Press.

—— (ed.) (1920) *Recent Developments in European Thought* [The Unity Series III], London, Oxford University Press.

—— (ed.) (1921) *The Evolution of World-peace* [The Unity Series IV], London, Oxford University Press.

—— (ed.) (1922a) 'Introductory: An educational problem' in F. Marvin (ed.) *Western Races and the World* [The Unity Series V], London, Oxford University Press.

—— (ed.) (1922b) *Western Races and the World* [The Unity Series V], London, Oxford University Press.

—— (ed.) (1923) *Science and Civilization* [The Unity Series VI], London, Oxford University Press.

—— (ed.) (1925) *England and the World* [The Unity Series VII], London, Oxford University Press.

—— (ed.) (1932) *The New World-Order* [The Unity Series IX], London, Oxford University Press.

—— and Clutton-Brock, A. (eds) (1928) *Art and Civilization* [The Unity Series VIII], London, Oxford University Press.

Marx, K. (1969) *Karl Marx On Colonialism And Modernization*, New York, Anchor Books.

—— (1992) *Surveys from Exile: Political Writings: Volume 2*, London, Penguin.

—— (1998) 'Capital: Volume 1', in *Essential Classics in Politics: Marx and Engels* (CD Rom), London, ElecBook, The Electric Book Company (eb 0002).

Masterman, C. (ed.) (1901) *The Heart of Empire: Discussions of Problems of Modern City Life in England*, London, Unwin.

McNeill, W. (1963) *The Rise of the West: A History of the Human Community* Chicago, University of Chicago Press.

Melady, T. (1966) *The Revolution of Color*, New York, Hawthorn Books.

Memmi, A. (1965) *The Colonizer and the Colonized*, New York, Orion Press.

Miller, J. (ed.) (1984) *Jews In Soviet Culture*, New Brunswick, Transaction.

Milner, A. (2002) 'Asia' consciousness and Asian values' at http://www.anu.edu.au/asianstudies/cons_vals.html, accessed 28 August 02.

—— and Johnson, D. (2002) 'The idea of Asia', at http://www.anu.edu.au/asianstudies/ideas.html, accessed 28 August 02.

Milosz, C. (1985) *The Captive Mind*, Harmondsworth, Penguin Books.

Moin, B. (1994) 'Khomeini's search for perfection: theory and reality', in A. Rahnema (ed.) *Pioneers of Islamic Revival*, London, Zed.

Money, L. (1925) *The Peril of the White*, London, W. Collins.

Montesquieu, C.L. de (1973) *Persian Letters*, Harmondsworth, Penguin.

Moussalli, A. (1992) *Radical Islamic Fundamentalism: The Ideological and Political Discourse of Sayyid Qutb*, Beirut, American University of Beirut.

Myrdal, A. (1980) 'The superpowers' game over Europe', in E. Thompson and D. Smith (eds) *Protest and Survive*, Harmondsworth, Penguin Books.

Myres, J. (1915) 'Unity in prehistoric times', in F. Marvin (ed.) *The Unity of Western Civilization*, London, Oxford University Press.

Nadel-Klein, J. (1995) 'Occidentalism as a cottage industry: representing the autochthonous 'other' in British and Irish rural studies', in J. Carrier (ed.) *Occidentalism: Images of the West*, Oxford, Clarendon Press.

Nandy, A. (1994) *The Illegitimacy of Nationalism: Rabindranath Tagore and the Politics of Self*, Delhi, Oxford University Press.

Neumann, I. (1996) *Russia and the Idea of Europe: A Study in Identity and International Relations*, London, Routledge.

—— (1999) *Uses of the Other: 'The East' in European Identity Formation*, Minneapolis, University of Minnesota Press.

Ning, W. (1997) 'Orientalism versus occidentalism?', *New Literary History*, 28, pp. 57–67.

Nordau, M. (1993) *Degeneration*, Lincoln, University of Nebraska Press.

Novicow, J. (1897) *L'Avenir de la race blanche*, Paris, Felix Alcan.

Novikov, A. (1991) 'Ya – rusofob' *Vek XX I mir*, 33, 7, pp. 12–14.

Offe, C. (1984) *Contradictions of the Welfare State*, Hutchinson, London.

—— (1985) *Disorganized Capitalism*, Polity Press, Cambridge.

Okakura, K. (2000) *The Ideals of the East, with Special Reference to the Art of Japan*, ICG Muse, New York and Tokyo.

Oliver, R. (1994) *The Failure of Political Islam*, Cambridge, Harvard University Press.

Ormsby-Gore, D. (1966) *Must the West Decline?*, New York, Columbia University Press.

Palat, R. (2000) 'India and Asia', *The Hindu*, Monday, 4 December, at http://www.hinduonnet.com/thehindu/2000/12/04/stories/05042524.htm, accessed 28 August 02.

—— (2002) 'Is India part of Asia?', *Environment and Planning D: Society and Space*, 20, pp. 669–691.

Parla, T. (1985) *The Social and Political Thought of Ziya Gökalp, 1876–1924*, Leiden, E.J. Brill.

Pannikar, K. (1953) *Asia and Western Dominance: A Survey of the Vasco da Gama Epoch of Asian History, 1498–1945*, London, Allen & Unwin.

Paul, D. (1984) 'Eugenics and the left', *Journal of the History of Ideas*, 45, 4, pp. 567–590.

Pearson, C. (1894) *National Life and Character: A Forecast*, London, Macmillan.

Pearson, K. (1897) *The Chances of Death and Other Studies in Evolution*, London, E. Arnold.

Pinches, M. (1999) 'Cultural relations, class and the new rich of Asia', in M. Pinches (ed.) *Culture and Privilege in Capitalist Asia*, London, Routledge.

Plummer, B. (1996) *Rising Wind: Black Americans and US Foreign Affairs, 1935–1960*, Chapel Hill, University of North Carolina Press.

Porter, B. (1968) *Critics of Empire: British Radical Attitudes to Colonialism in Africa 1895–1914*, London, Macmillan.

Pozdnyakov, E. (1991) 'The Soviet Union: the problem of coming back to European civilisation', *Paradigms*, 5, 1/2, pp. 45–57.

Putnam Weale, B. (1910) *The Conflict of Colour*, London, Macmillan.

Pyle, K. (1969) *The New Generation in Meiji Japan: Problems of Cultural Identity, 1885–1895*, Stanford, Stanford University Press.

Qutb, S. (1990) *Milestones*, Burr Ridge, American Trust Publications.

Rader, M. (1939) *No Compromise: The Conflict Between Two Worlds*, London, Victor Gollancz.

Rawls, J. (1971) *A Theory of Justice*, Oxford, Oxford University Press.

Rentoul, R. (1906) *Race Culture; or Race Suicide? (A Plea for the Unborn)*, London, Walter Scott Publishing.

Reymond, L. (1945) *Nivedita, fille de l'Inde*, Victor Attinger, Paris.

Riasanovsky, N. (1967) 'The emergence of Eurasianism', *California Slavic Studies*, 4, pp. 39–72.

Rich, P. (1986) *Race and Empire in British Politics*, Cambridge, Cambridge University Press.

—— (1994) *Prospero's Return? Historical Essays on Race, Culture and British Society*, London, Hansib Publishing.

Ritzer, G. (2000) *The McDonaldization of Society: New Century Edition*, Thousand Oaks, Pine Forge Press.

Roberts, J. (1985) *The Triumph of the West*, London, British Broadcasting Corporation.

Robison, R. and Goodman, D. (eds) (1996) *The New Rich in Asia: Mobile Phones, McDonalds and Middle-Class Revolution*, London, Routledge.

Roman, M. (2002) 'Making Caucasians black: Moscow since the fall of communism and the racialization of non-Russians', *Journal of Communist Studies and Transition Politics*, 18, 2, pp. 1–27.

Roy, M. (1950) *India's Message: Fragments of a Prisoner's Diary, Volume 2*, Renaissance Publishers, Calcutta.

Ruthven, M. (2000) *Islam: A Very Short Introduction*, Oxford, Oxford University Press.

—— (2002) *A Fury for God: the Islamist Attack on America*, London, Granta Books.

Rywkin, M. (1994) *Moscow's Last Empire*, New York, M.E. Sharpe.

Said, E. (1978) *Orientalism: Western Representations of the Orient*, Harmondsworth, Penguin.

Sakamoto, R. (1996) 'Japan, hybridity and the creation of colonialist discourse', *Theory, Culture and Society*, 13, 3, pp. 113–128.

—— (2001) 'Dream of a modern subject: Maruyama Masao, Fukuzawa Yukichi, and "Asia" as the limits of ideology critique', *Japanese Studies* 21, 2, pp. 137–153.

Sakwa, R. (1990) *Gorbachev and his Reforms 1985–1990*, New York, Philip Allan.

—— (1999) (ed.) *The Rise and Fall of the Soviet Union, 1917–1991*, London, Routledge.

Sayyid, B. (1997) *A Fundamental Fear: Eurocentrism and the Emergence of Islamism*, London, Zed Books.

Scruton, R. (2002) *The West and the Rest: Globalization and the Terrorist Threat*, London, Continuum.

Searle, G. (1976) *Eugenics and Politics in Britain 1900–1914*, Leyden, Noordhoff International Publishing.

Segal, R. (1967) *The Race War: The World-wide Conflict of Races*, Harmondsworth, Penguin.

Sen, N. (1966) 'The "foreign reincarnation" of Rabindranath Tagore', *Journal of Asian Studies*, 25, 2, pp. 275–286.

Shafarevich, I. (1989) 'Rusofobia', *Nash sovremennik*, 57, 6, pp. 167–192.

Sharma, T. (ed.) (1987) *Essays on Rabindranath Tagore*, Ghaziabad, Vimal Prakashan.

Shee, G. (1903) 'The deterioration in national physique', *Nineteenth Century*, 53, 798–801.

Sheridan, G. (1999) *Asian Values, Western Dreams: Understanding the New Asia*, St Leonards, New South Wales, Allen & Unwin.

Siddiqi, M. (1956) *The Image of the West in Iqbal*, Lahore, Bazm-I-Iqbal.

Sim, S. (2001) 'Asian values, authoritarianism and capitalism in Singapore', *Javnost: The Public*, 8, 2, pp. 45–66.

Simon, G. (1991) *Nationalism and Policy Towards the Nationalities in the Soviet Union*, Boulder, Westview Press.

Slezkine, Y. (1996) 'The USSR as a communal apartment, or how a socialist state promoted ethnic particularism', in G. Eley and R. Suny (eds) *Becoming National: A Reader*, New York, Oxford University Press.

—— (2000) 'Imperialism as the highest stage of socialism', *The Russian Review*, 59, pp. 227–234.

Smith, A. (1910) *The Wealth of Nations in Two Volumes: Volume One*, London, J.M. Dent.

Smith, G., Law, V., Wilson, A., Bohr, A. and Allworth, E. (1998) *Nation-building in the Post-Soviet Borderlands: The Politics of National Identities*, Cambridge, Cambridge University Press.

Soguk, N. (1993) 'Reflections on the "Orientalized Orientals"', *Alternatives*, 18, pp. 361–384.

Soloway, R. (1982) 'Counting the degenerates: the statistics of race deterioration in Edwardian England', *Journal of Contemporary History*, 17, pp. 137–164.

Song, X. (2000) 'Post-Mao new poetry and "occidentalism"', *East Asia*, 18, 1, pp. 82–109.

Sparks, C. (1998) 'The eye of the storm', *International Socialism*, 78, pp. 3–37.

Spencer, J. (1995) 'Occidentalism in the East: the uses of the West in the politics and anthropology of South Asia', in J. Carrier (ed.) *Occidentalism: Images of the West*, Oxford, Oxford University Press.

Spengler, O. (1918) *Der Untergang des Abendlandes, Gestalt und Wirklichkeit*, Munich, C.H. Beck'sche Verlagsbuchhandlung.

—— (1922) *Der Untergang des Abendlandes, Welhistorische Perspecktiven*, Munich, C.H. Beck'sche Verlagsbuchhandlung.

—— (1926) *The Decline of the West: Volume One: Form and Actuality*, New York, Alfred A. Knopf.

—— (1928) *The Decline of the West: Volume Two: Perspectives of World-History*, New York, Alfred A. Knopf.

—— (1934) *The Hour of Decision*, New York, Alfred A. Knopf.

—— (2001) 'The burden of English', in G. Castle (ed.) *Postcolonial Discourses: An Anthology*, Oxford, Blackwell.

Spivak, G. (2002) 'Resident alien', in D. Goldberg and A. Quayson (eds) *Relocating Postcolonialism*, Oxford, Blackwell.

Sprachman, P. (1982) 'Translator's note', in J. Al-e Ahmad *Plagued by the West (Gharbzadegi)*, Delmar, Caravan Books.

Stalin, J. (1954) *Works: Volume 10: August–December 1927*, Moscow, Foreign Languages Publishing House.

—— (1955) *Works: Volume 13: July 1930–January 1934*, Moscow, Foreign Languages Publishing House.

—— (1999) 'Speech at the reception in the Kremlin in honour of the commanders of the Red Army troops, 24 May 1945', in R. Sakwa (ed.) *The Rise and Fall of the Soviet Union, 1917–1991*, London, Routledge, pp. 287–288.

Stephan, J. (1982) 'Asia in the Soviet conception', in D. Zagoria (ed.) *Soviet Policy in East Asia*, New Haven, Yale University Press.

Stoddard, L. (1922) *The Revolt Against Civilization: The Menace of the Under-Man*, London, Chapman & Hall.

—— (1925) *The Rising Tide of Color Against White World-Supremacy* New York, Charles Scribner's Sons.

Stone, D. (2001) 'Race in British eugenics', *European History Quarterly*, 31, 3, pp. 397–425.

Sukarno, A. (1970) 'Let a new Asia and Africa be born', in L. Castle and H. Feith (eds) *Indonesian Political Thinking 1945–1965*, Ithaca, Cornell University Press.

Sun, Ge. (2000a) How does Asia mean? (part II), *Inter-Asia Cultural Studies*, 1, 2, pp. 319–341.

Sun, G. (2000b) How does Asia mean? (part I), *Inter-Asia Cultural Studies*, 1, 1, pp. 13–47.

Suny, R. (1993) *The Revenge of the Past: Nationalism, Revolution and the Collapse of the Soviet Union*, Stanford, Standford University Press.

—— (1995) 'Ambiguous categories: states, empires and nations', *Post-Soviet Affairs*, 11, 2, pp. 185–196.

Swift, R. (1995) 'Unmasking the miracle', *New Internationalist*, January, pp. 4–8.

Tagore, R. (1921) *Greater India*, Madras, S. Ganesan.

—— (1922) *Creative Unity*, London, Macmillan.

—— (1924) 'City and village', Visva-Bharati Quarterly, 2, 3, pp. 215–227.

—— (1966) 'The sunset of the century', in W. de Bary (ed.) *Sources of Indian Tradition: Volume II*, New York, Columbia University Press.

—— (1991) *Nationalism*, London, Macmillan.

Taguieff, P-A. (1995) *Les fins de l'antiracisme*, Paris, Editions Michalon.

Tang, X. (1996) *Global Space and the Nationalist Discourse of Modernity: The Historical Thinking of Liang Qichao*, Stanford, Stanford University Press.

Tai, H. (1989) 'The oriental alternative: an hypothesis on culture and economy', in H. Tai (ed.) *Confucianism and Economic Development*, Washington, Washington Institute Press.

Tamaki, N. (2001) *Yukichi Fukuzawa 1835–1901: The Spirit of Enterprise in Modern Japan*, London, Palgrave.

Tanaka, S. (1993) *Japan's Orient: Rendering Pasts into History*, Berkeley, University of California Press.

Taussig, M. (1997) *The Magic of the State*, New York, Routledge.

Tavakoli-Targhi, M. (1990) 'Imagining Western women: occidentalism and Euro-eroticism', *Radical America*, 24, 3, pp. 73–87.

—— (2001) *Refashioning Iran: Orientalism, Occidentalism and Historiography*, Basingstoke, Palgrave.

Taylor, A. (1972) *Laissez-faire and State Intervention in Nineteenth-century Britain*, Macmillan, London.

Teng, S. and Fairbank, J. (1979) *China's Response to the West: A Documentary Survey 1839–1923*, Cambridge, Harvard University Press.

Thompson, E. (1991) 'Introduction', in R. Tagore *Nationalism*, London, Macmillan.

Tishkov, V. (1992) 'Inventions and manifestations of ethno-nationalism in and after the Soviet Union', in K. Rupesinghe and P. King (eds) *Ethnicity and Conflict in a Post-Communist World: The Soviet Union, Eastern Europe and China*, Basingstoke, Macmillan.

Tong, Q. (2000) Inventing China: the use of orientalist views on the Chinese language', *Interventions*, 2, 1, pp. 6–20.

Townsend, M. (1905) *Asia and Europe*, London, Archibald Constable.

Toynbee, A. (1923) *The Western Question in Greece and Turkey: A Study in the Contact of Civilisations: Second Edition*, London, Constable and Company.

—— (1931) 'World sovereignty and world culture: the trend of international affairs since the war', *Pacific Affairs*, 4, 9, pp. 753–778.

—— (1934) *A Study of History: Volume I*, Oxford, Oxford University Press.

—— (1939) *A Study of History: Volume VI*, Oxford, Oxford University Press.

—— (1948) *Civilization on Trial*, London, Oxford University Press.

—— (1953) *The World and the West*, Oxford, Oxford University Press.

—— (1954) *A Study of History: Volume VIII*, London, Oxford University Press.

Traynor, I. (2001) 'Putin shuns the US in favour of Europe', *The Guardian*, 4 April.

Trewarthara, G. (1926) 'Recent thoughts on the problem of White acclimatisation in the wet tropics', *Geographical Review*, 16, pp. 467–478.

Tripp, C. (1994) 'Sayyid Qutb: the political vision', in A. Rahnema (ed.) *Pioneers of Islamic Revival*, London, Zed.

Trotsky, L. (1962) *The Permanent Revolution: Results and Prospects (1906)* London, New Park Publications.

—— (1980) *The History of the Russian Revolution*, New York, Pathfinder.

Tucker, R. (1990) *Stalin in Power: The Revolution from Above 1928–1941*, New York, Norton.

Vasconcelos, J. (1997) *The Cosmic Race: A Bilingual Edition*, Baltimore, John Hopkins University Press.

Veer, P. van der (2001) *Imperial Encounters: Religion and Modernity in India and Britain*, Princeton, Princeton University Press.

Venn, C. (2000) *Occidentalism: Modernity and Subjectivity*, London, Sage.

Vivekananada, S. (n.d.) *A Collection of his Speeches and Writings*, Madras, G.A. Natesan.

Vivekananada, S. (1966) 'Indian thought to conquer the world', in W. de Bary (ed.) *Sources of Indian Tradition: Voume II*, New York, Columbia University Press.

Warburg, J. (1959) *The West in Crisis*, New York, Doubleday.

Ward, R. and Rustow, D. (eds) (1964) *Political Modernization in Japan and Turkey*, Princeton, Princeton University Press.

Webb, S. (1907) *The Decline in the Birth Rate*, London, Fabian Society.

Whetham, W. and Whetham, C. (1911) 'Decadence and civilisation', *The Hibbert Journal*, 10, 1, pp. 179–200.

White, A. (1899) 'The cult of infirmity', *National Review*, 34, pp. 239–241.

—— (1901) *Efficiency and Empire*, London, Methuen.

Wilkinson, E. (1990) *Japan versus the West: Image and Reality*, London, Penguin.

Winter, J. (1974) 'The Webbs and the non-white world: a case of socialist racialism', *Journal of Contemporary History*, 9, 1, pp. 181–192.

Wittfogel, K. (1957) *Oriental Despotism: A Comparative Study of Total Power*, New Haven, Yale University Press.

Woodruff, C. (1905) *The Effects of Tropical Light on White Men*, New York, Rebman, Co.

World Bank (1993) *The East Asian Miracle: Economic Growth and Public Policy*, Oxford, Oxford University Press.

Worsley, P. (1984) *The Three Worlds: Culture and World Development*, London, Weidenfeld and Nicolson.

Woolf, L. (1939) *Barbarians at the Gate*, London, Victor Gollancz.

World Export Processing Zone Association (1999) http://www.wepza.org/world.epzs.htm.

Wright, A. (1979) *G.D.H. Cole and Socialist Democracy*, Oxford, Clarendon Press.

Yabe, T. (1975) 'Greater East Asia Co-existence Sphere', J. in Lebra (ed.) *Japan's Greater East Asia Co-Prosperity Sphere in World War II: Selected Readings and Documents*, Oxford University Press, Kuala Lumpur.

Yarshater, E. (1982) 'Foreword' in J. Al-e Ahmad *Plagued by the West (Gharbzadegi)*, Delmar, Caravan Books.

Yeats, W. (1913) 'Introduction' in R. Tagore *Gitanjali (Song Offerings)*, London, Macmillan.

Young, R. (1990) *White Mythologies*, London, Routledge.

—— (1995) *Colonial Desire: Hybridity in Theory, Culture and Race*, London, Routledge.

Index